A Practical Guide to Testing Object-Oriented Software

The Addison-Wesley Object Technology Series

Grady Booch, Ivar Jacobson, and James Rumbaugh, Series Editors
For more information check out the series web site [http://www.awl.com/cseng/otseries/].

The Component Software Series

Clemens Szyperski, Series Editor
For more information check out the series web site [http://www.awl.com/cseng/csseries/].

A Practical Guide to Testing Object-Oriented Software

John D. McGregor
David A. Sykes

Addison-Wesley

Boston • San Francisco • New York • Toronto • Montreal
London • Munich • Paris • Madrid
Capetown • Sydney • Tokyo • Singapore • Mexico City

The publisher offers discounts on this book when ordered in quantity for special sales. For more information, please contact:

Pearson Education Corporate Sales Division
One Lake Street
Upper Saddle River, NJ 07458
(800) 382-3419
corpsales@pearsontechgroup.com

Visit us on the Web at www.awl.com/cseng/

Library of Congress Cataloging-in-Publication Data
McGregor, John D.
    A practical guide to testing object-oriented software / John D. McGregor, David A. Sykes.
      p. cm. – (Addison-Wesley object technology series)
    Includes bibliographical references and index.
    ISBN 0-201-32564-0
    1. Computer software–Testing. 2. Object-oriented programming (Computer science) I. Sykes, David A. II. Series.

QA76.T48 M47 2001
005.1'17–dc21   00-066513

ISBN 0-201-32564-0

Text printed on recycled paper.
1 2 3 4 5 6 7 8 9 10—CRS—05 04 03 02 01
First printing, March 2001

Contents

Chapter 4 Testing Analysis and Design Models   109

Chapter 9   Testing Systems   309

Chapter 10 Components, Frameworks, and Product Lines   343

Preface

Testing software is a very important and challenging activity. This is a book for people who test software during its development. Our focus is on object-oriented and component-based software, but you can apply many of the techniques discussed in this book regardless of the development paradigm. We assume our reader is familiar with testing procedural software—that is, software written in the procedural paradigm using languages such as C, Ada, Fortran, or COBOL. We also assume our reader is familiar and somewhat experienced in developing software using object-oriented and component-based technologies. Our focus is on describing *what* to test in object-oriented development efforts as well as on describing techniques for *how* to test object-oriented software, and how testing software built with these newer technologies differs from testing procedural software.

What is software testing? To us, testing is the evaluation of the work products created during a software development effort. This is more general than just checking part or all of a software system to see if it meets its specifications. Testing software is a difficult process, in general, and sufficient resources are seldom available for testing. From our standpoint, testing is done throughout a development effort and is not just an activity tacked on at the end of a development phase to see how well the developers did. We see testing as part of the process that puts quality into a software system. As a result, we address the testing of all development products (models) even before any code is written.

We do not necessarily believe that you will apply everything we describe in this book. There are seldom enough resources available to a development effort to do all the levels and kinds of testing we would like. We hope you will find a number of approaches and techniques that will prove useful to and affordable for your project.

In this book we describe a set of testing techniques. All of the techniques we describe have been applied in practice. Many of these techniques have been used in a wide variety of industries and on projects of vastly different sizes. In Chapter 3, we will consider the impact of some of these variables on the types of testing that are routinely performed.

To describe these techniques, we rely in many cases on one or more examples to illustrate their application. We hope from these examples and from our explanations that you can apply the same techniques to your project software in a straightforward manner. The complete code for these examples, test code, and other resources can be obtained from *http://cseng.aw.com/book/ 0.3828.0201325640.00.html*.

In order to make this book as useful as possible, we will provide two major organizational threads. The physical layout of the book will follow the usual sequence of events as they happen on a project. Model testing will be addressed earlier than component or code testing, for example. We will also include a set of questions that a tester might ask when he or she is faced with specific testing tasks on a project. This testing FAQ will be tied into the main body of the text with citations.

We have included alternative techniques and ways of adapting techniques for varying the amount of testing. Testing life-critical or mission-critical software requires more effort than testing an arcade game. The summary sections of each chapter should make these choices clear.

This book is the result of many years of research, teaching, and consulting both in the university and in companies. We would like to thank the sponsors of our research, including COMSOFT, IBM, and AT&T for their support of our academic research. Thanks to the students who assisted in the research and those who sat through many hours of class and provided valuable feedback on early versions of the text. The consultants working for Korson-McGregor, formerly Software Architects, made many suggestions and worked with early versions of the techniques while still satisfying client needs. The employees of numerous consulting clients helped us perfect the techniques by providing real problems to be solved and valuable feedback. A special thanks to Melissa L. Russ (formerly Major) who helped teach several tutorials and made her usual insightful comments to improve the material.

Most of all, we wish to thank our families for enduring our mental and physical absences and for the necessary time to produce this work: Gayle and Mary Frances McGregor; Susan, Aaron, Perry, and Nolan Sykes.

JDM
DAS

Introduction

Testing software well has always been challenging, but the process is fairly well understood. Some combination of unit testing, integration testing, system testing, regression testing, and acceptance testing will help to deliver usable systems.

We wanted to write this book because most people seem to believe that testing *object-oriented* software is not much different from testing procedural software. While many of the general approaches and techniques for testing are the same or can be adapted from traditional testing approaches and techniques, our experience and our research has demonstrated that some things are different and present new challenges. At the same time, well-designed object-oriented soft-

ware developed as part of an incremental process provides opportunities for improvements over traditional testing processes.

Object-oriented programming language features of inheritance and polymorphism present new technical challenges to testers. We describe solutions for many of these challenges. In this book, we describe processes and techniques for testing object-oriented software effectively during all phases of a development effort. Our approach to testing software is quite comprehensive and one that we believe software development organizations should undertake. At the same time, we realize that resources available for testing are limited and that there are many effective ways to develop software, so we think it is reasonable to pick and choose among the techniques we present in this book.

The adoption of object-oriented technologies brings changes not only in the programming languages we use but in most aspects of software development.

We use incremental development processes, refocus and use new notations for analysis and design, and utilize new programming language features. The changes promise to make software more maintainable, reusable, flexible, and so on. We have written this book because changes in the way we *develop* software produces changes in the way we *test* software, from both managerial and technical perspectives. The following changes provide opportunities for improving the testing process:

■ We have an opportunity to change attitudes toward testing. In many environments, managers and developers view testing as a necessary evil. Testing that needs to be done by the developers themselves interrupts code production. Reviews, code inspections, and writing unit test drivers take time and money. Testing processes imposed on the developers for the most part just get in the way of coding. However, if we can make everyone appreciate that testing contributes to developing the right software from the start, and that it can actually be used to measure progress and keep development on track, then we can build even better software.

■ We have an opportunity to change where testing fits into a development process. Almost everyone recognizes that the sooner problems are found, the cheaper they are to fix. Unit testing and integration testing uncover problems, but don't usually start until coding has started. System testing is typically done near the end of a development effort or perhaps at certain planned milestones. System testing is treated as a way to see how well the developers did in meeting requirements. Of course, this is a wrong approach. Decisions about how much testing is adequate, when it should be performed, and who should do it should be made only in the context of a well-considered testing strategy that works with the project's software development process. We will show how testing activities can begin early. We will show how testing and development activities can be intertwined and how each can contribute to a successful outcome of the other.

■ We have an opportunity to use new technology to do the testing. Just as object-oriented technologies have benefits for production software, they also can realize benefits in test software. We will show how you can test object-oriented analysis and design models, and how you can use object-oriented programming techniques to develop unit test drivers and reduce the coding necessary to test software components.

Who Should Read This Book?

We have written this book for

■ *Programmers* who already work in testing software, but want to know more about testing object-oriented software.

- *Managers* who are responsible for software development and who would like to know how and where testing fits into a plan.

- *Developers* who are responsible for testing the software they produce and who should take testing issues into consideration during the analysis, design, and coding activities.

With such a wide audience, we struggled with the level of detail we needed to include about object-oriented development and testing—the basic concepts associated with software testing, object-oriented programming, and the Unified Modeling Language (UML) to express analysis and design results. We decided to provide brief overviews of these topic areas—what we consider the minimum a reader needs to know to make sense of what we have to say. When we need to resort to code, we use C++ and Java. The approaches and techniques we present apply to all object-oriented programs, not just to those written in C++ and Java.

We have assumed the following software-development scenario, which we consider to be ideal:

- The process must be incremental, with iterations that occur within each increment.

- The models expressed in UML must be available.

- The software design must be in accordance with good design principles with respect to the use of inheritance, data hiding, abstraction, low coupling, and high cohesion.

However, we realize that most organizations have their own processes and notations. Consequently, our focus is primarily on principles and techniques.

What Software Testing Is—and Isn't

Informally, software testing (or just "testing" in the context of this book) is the process of uncovering evidence of defects in software systems. A defect can be introduced during any phase of development or maintenance and results from one or more "bugs"—mistakes, misunderstandings, omissions, or even misguided intent on the part of the developers. Testing comprises the efforts to find defects. Testing does *not* include efforts associated with tracking down bugs and fixing them. In other words, testing does *not* include the debugging or repair of bugs.[1]

---

1. We recognize that some people who test software are also responsible for debugging that software. This is particularly true during unit testing and integration testing. However, we distinguish between the two activities. Testing is the process of finding failures. Debugging is the process of tracking down the source of failures—bugs—and making repairs. There can be overlap in the sense that testing can sometimes be structured to help locate bugs. However, testing and debugging are two separate activities.

Testing is important because it substantially contributes to ensuring that a software application does everything it is supposed to do. Some testing efforts extend the focus to ensure an application does *nothing more than* it is supposed to do.[2] In any case, testing makes a significant contribution to guarding users against software failures that can result in a loss of time, property, customers, or life.

What is **software**? We define software as the instruction codes and data necessary to accomplish some task on a computer. We also include *all representations* of those instructions and data. In particular, representations include not only program source code and data files, but models created during analysis and design activities. Software can and should be tested in all its representations. Just as architects and builders can examine blueprints for a new building to spot problems even before ground is broken, so we can examine analysis and design models for software before the first line of program source code is written. We will show how you can test these models using a form of "execution."

Testing helps ensure that a product meets requirements, but *testing is not quality assurance*. Some people mistakenly equate testing and quality assurance. In many organizations, QA is typically responsible for developing test plans and performing system testing. QA might monitor testing during development and keep statistics. Testing is a necessary but insufficient part of any quality assurance process. Quality assurance addresses activities designed to *prevent* defects as well as to *remove* those defects that do creep into the product. A project's quality assurance group sets standards that project members should follow in order to build better software. This includes defining the types of documents that should be created to capture design decisions, the processes that guide project activities, and the measures that quantify the results of decisions.

No amount of testing will improve the quality of a computer program. Testing helps in identifying failures so that developers can find bugs and remove them. The more testing we do of a system, the more convinced we might be of its correctness. Yet testing cannot in general prove a system works 100% correctly. Thus, testing's primary contribution to quality is to identify problems that we wish we could have prevented in the first place. The mission of QA is to prevent problems in the first place. That requires processes beyond testing.

Testing can contribute to improved quality by helping to identify problems early in the development process. Fortunately, you can do some testing quite early in the development process—even before code is written. We describe useful techniques in this book, but these techniques require that testers work more closely with developers and that developers work more closely with testers.

---

2. Certainly this is important in systems in which "enhancements" threaten life or property. However, testing for additional functionality is hard to do without reading code, which few testers ever do. Without reading code, a tester has to anticipate mistakes and enhancements that a developer might make and then develop tests to detect them. Consider, for example, the challenge of detecting *Easter eggs* hidden in software.

What Is Different about Testing Object-Oriented Software?

Object-oriented programming features in programming languages obviously impact some aspects of testing. Features such as class inheritance and interfaces support polymorphism in which code manipulates objects without their exact class being known. Testers must ensure the code works no matter what the exact class of such objects might be. Language features that support and enforce data hiding can complicate testing because operations must sometimes be added to a class interface just to support testing. On the other hand, the availability of these features can contribute to better and reusable testing software.

Not only do changes in programming languages affect testing, but so do changes in the development process and changes in the focus of analysis and design. Many object-oriented software-testing activities have counterparts in traditional processes. We still have a use for unit testing although the meaning of *unit* has changed. We still do integration testing to make sure various subsystems can work correctly in concert. We still need system testing to verify that software meets requirements. We still do regression testing to make sure the latest round of changes to the software hasn't adversely affected what it could do before.

The differences between "old" and "new" ways of developing and testing software are much deeper than a focus on objects instead of on functions that transform inputs to outputs. The most significant difference is in the way object-oriented software is designed as a set of objects that essentially model a problem and then collaborate to effect a solution. Underlying this approach is the concept that while a solution to a problem might need to change over time, the structure and components of the problem itself do not change as much or as frequently. Consequently, a program whose design is structured from the problem (and not on an immediately required solution) will be more adaptable to changes later. A programmer familiar with the problem and its components can recognize them in the software, thereby making the program more maintainable. Furthermore, because components are derived from the problem, they can often be reused in the development of other programs to solve similar or related problems, thereby improving the reusability of software components.

A big benefit of this approach to design is that analysis models map straightforwardly to design models that, in turn, map to code. Thus, we can start testing during analysis and refine the tests done in analysis to tests for design. Tests for design, in turn, can be refined to tests of implementation. This means that a testing process can be interwoven with the development process. We see three significant advantages to testing analysis and design models:

1. Test cases can be identified earlier in the process, even as requirements are being determined. Early testing helps analysts and designers to better understand and express requirements and to ensure that specified requirements are "testable."

2. Bugs can be detected early in the development process, saving time, money, and effort. It is widely acknowledged that the sooner problems are detected, the easier and cheaper they are to fix.

3. Test cases can be reviewed for correctness early in a project. The correctness of test cases—in particular, system test cases—is always an issue. If test cases are identified early and applied to models early in a project, then any misunderstandings of requirements on the part of the testers can be corrected early. In other words, model testing helps to ensure that testers and developers have a consistent understanding of system requirements.

Although testing models is very beneficial, it is important to not let testing them become the sole focus of testing efforts. Code testing is still an important part of the process.

Another difference between traditional projects and projects using object-oriented technologies concerns objectives for software. Consider, for example, that an important new goal in many companies is to produce reusable software, extensible designs, or even object-oriented frameworks that represent reusable designs. Testing can (and should) be done to uncover failures in meeting these objectives. Traditional testing approaches and techniques do not address such objectives.

Overview of Our Testing Approach

Our goal is to test software as thoroughly as possible, while recognizing that time and money constraints are real concerns. Our approach to testing object-oriented software is based on academic research as well as experience we have gained in working with clients in a variety of industries, such as telecommunications and finance.

Under our approach, testing is not an afterthought. Testing is a process separate from the development process, but intimately related to it. We have a motto: *Test early. Test often. Test enough.* We favor the following iterative development process:

- Analyze a little.
- Design a little.
- Code a little.
- *Test what you can.*

Testing what you can includes both what you can do technically and what you can do under time and resource constraints. A surprising amount of beneficial testing can be done within an iteration. Regular testing can detect failures early and save reworking in subsequent iterations. System testing and acceptance testing follow the last iteration. However, if you can develop a software system incrementally, then you can perform system testing at the end of each increment.

What kinds of testing do we promote for object-oriented software?

- Model testing
- Class testing, which replaces unit testing
- Interaction testing, which replaces integration testing
- System (and subsystem) testing
- Acceptance testing
- Deployment/self-testing

Each of these is covered in this book. Our testing process will define testing activities for every development activity.

We do not believe that you will—or even should—apply everything we describe in this book. There are seldom enough resources available to a development effort to do all the levels and kinds of testing we describe. We hope you will find a number of approaches and techniques that will prove applicable, useful, and affordable for your project.

We now provide a rationale for our motto of, "*Test early. Test often. Test enough.*"

Test Early

Instead of engaging system testers toward the end of a project, start them testing at reasonable points during the analysis and design phases of a project. Testing analysis and design models not only can help to uncover problems early in the development process (where they are fixed more easily and more cheaply), but it can also help to scope the size of the effort needed to perform adequate system testing by determining what needs to be tested.

Testing early and often implies that the representations of the software are abstract or incomplete.

Test Often

We firmly believe that an iterative, incremental—sometimes also referred to as **iterative enhancement**—development process is best suited to the vast majority of projects. As iterations are completed on analysis, design, and implementation phases, the products should be tested. After completion of the first increment, some testing takes the form of regression testing.

Test Enough

Complete testing of every aspect of a software system is infeasible. Resources spent on testing should be directed where they provide the best payback. We favor techniques that are based on risk analysis, the reuse of test cases, and the statistical sampling of inputs for test cases.

The Testing Perspective

Good testers—people who are responsible for testing software—need a special set of skills. In many ways, being a good tester is harder than being a good developer because testing requires not only a very good understanding of the development process and its products, but it also demands an ability to anticipate likely faults and errors. As a simple example, consider how a developer might need to find an algorithm to bounce an image around in a rectangular area of a computer screen. A tester must be able to anticipate likely errors and faults a developer might make and then develop effective ways to detect failures resulting from likely bugs. For example, a tester might want to test that the image hitting exactly in the corner of the rectangle doesn't move completely out of it. The tester has a tough job.

A tester must approach software with an attitude that questions everything about that software. We refer to that approach as *the testing perspective*. It is the subject of Chapter 2. To be effective, a tester must adopt that perspective. The techniques and processes described in this book have been developed and are presented from the testing perspective.

Organization of This Book

This book contains eleven chapters. The first three chapters are concerned primarily with testing concepts and the testing process. Chapters 4 through 10 detail techniques for various kinds of testing that can be done. Chapter 11 is a summary. Each chapter ends with a summary and a set of exercises. You are encouraged to read through the exercises and work on the ones that interest you or are relevant to your job as a tester. For most of the exercises, there are no correct answers, although for most of them some answers are better than others. We hope the exercises will be useful in helping you apply our techniques to your own project.

Chapter 1 (this chapter) provides an introduction to this book. We have presented an overview of testing concepts, a synopsis of how testing object-oriented software is different from testing other kinds of software, and a brief overview of our approach.

Chapter 2 describes the testing perspective. We adopt that perspective to address various aspects of the testing process, to review various products of the development process, and to examine the basic concepts of object-orientation.

and in this book, is solely to illustrate concepts about the design and testing of object-oriented programs.

Basic *Brickles* Components

Brickles is an arcade game whose starting configuration is shown in Figure 1.1. The play field is rectangular, bounded by two walls, a ceiling, and a floor. The play field contains an array of bricks referred to as the "brick pile." A player's objective is to break all the bricks in the brick pile by hitting each brick with a puck that can be struck by a paddle under the player's control. When the puck hits a brick, the brick breaks. A puck bounces off walls, the ceiling, bricks (as they break), and the paddle. At the start of play, a player is given three pucks with which to destroy the bricks. A player wins a game when all bricks have been broken. A player loses if the supply of pucks is exhausted before all of the bricks are broken.

When play starts, a puck placed in the center of the play field begins to move in a downward direction. The paddle is controlled by the player with a mouse attached to the computer. The player must move the paddle so that the puck hits the paddle and not the floor. When the puck hits the paddle, it bounces upward. Whenever the puck hits a brick, the brick is destroyed. If the puck misses the paddle and hits the floor, it is removed from play and one of the remaining pucks is put into play. If all pucks are lost to the floor, play ends and the player loses.

Brickles Physics

As the puck moves through the play field, it encounters various components of the play field. The interactions between them are as follows (see also Figure 1.2, Figure 1.3, and Figure 1.4).

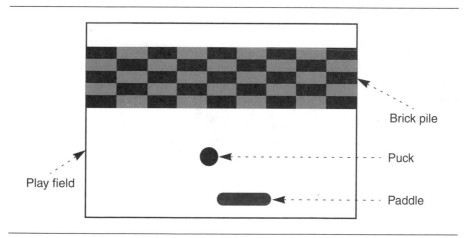

Figure 1.1 The *Brickles* start-up configuration

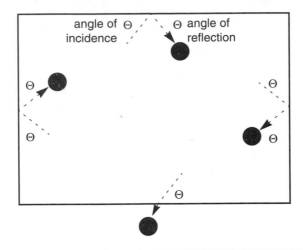

Figure 1.2 Interactions between puck and boundaries

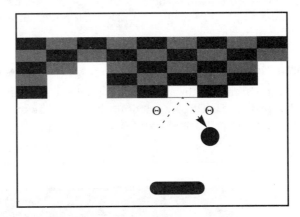

Figure 1.3 Puck interactions with bricks

Ceiling and walls The puck bounces off the ceiling and walls in accordance with the laws of physics, neglecting friction and gravity—that is, the angle of reflection equals the angle of incidence.

Floor The floor absorbs pucks. A puck that hits the floor does not rebound, but is removed from play.

Bricks The puck bounces off a brick such that the angle of reflection equals the angle of incidence. Upon being struck, a brick is destroyed. Note that

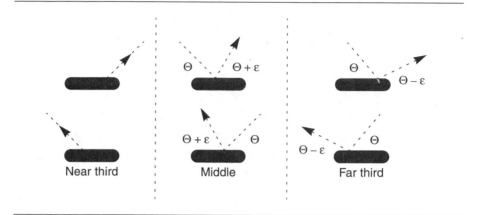

Figure 1.4 Puck interactions with the paddle

bricks can be hit by a puck from above as well as from below. They also have sufficient thickness that they can be hit from the side. For the sake of simplicity, it is acceptable to assume that bricks are treated as though they have no thickness. Thus, it is only the vertical component of the puck's direction that is changed when the puck hits the brick.

Paddle The player uses a paddle to control the direction of the puck. The puck bounces off the paddle based on both the direction of the puck as it hits the paddle and the part of the paddle that's hit. Divide the paddle into thirds and define the *near third* as being the left third of the paddle if the puck is coming in from the left, and the right third if the puck is coming in from the right. Define the *far third* similarly, and the *middle third* as the remaining third. The rules of reflection are as follows:

- If the puck hits the paddle on its near third, then the puck returns in the exact opposite direction from which it came.

- If the puck hits the paddle on the middle third, then the angle of reflection is a little steeper than the angle of incidence. The puck's movement is constrained such that it must never be completely vertical.

- If the puck hits the paddle on the far third, then the angle of reflection is a little shallower than the angle of incidence. The puck's movement is constrained such that it must never be completely horizontal.

Puck The player is given a fixed number of pucks at the beginning of the game, but only one is in play at any given time. Once one puck hits the floor, the next is brought into play (assuming another is available). The puck has a current direction and speed and moves according to an automatic timer. Collisions may change the direction of the puck, but not the speed.

Game Environment

The first implementation of *Brickles* runs as an application within a Microsoft Windows environment and behaves as follows:

- The game shall start when the program is launched.
- A player can "exit" the game at any time before it is won or lost.
- A player can "pause" the game at any time until play ends.
- A player can "resume" a paused game.
- A congratulatory message shall be displayed in the case of a player winning the game. Similarly, a consolation message shall be displayed in the case of a player losing the game.

Exercises

1-1. Consider an application that will be used to schedule conference rooms in an office. The application has a graphical user interface that allows a user to indicate a date, a time of day, and a duration (in fifteen-minute increments). It then shows a list of conference rooms available at that time and allows a room to be reserved. The system also allows a user to cancel a room reservation. The project is to be developed incrementally—that is, in increasing amounts of functionality. Consider the following two plans. Which is more likely to succeed? What testing can be done at the end of each increment?

Plan A	Plan B
Increment 1: Develop user interface	Increment 1: Develop capability to enter date, time, and duration, and show room availability
Increment 2: Develop data storage subsystem	
	Increment 2: Develop capability to reserve a room
Increment 3: Develop application subsystem (reservation handling)	
	Increment 3: Develop capability to cancel a reservation

1-2. Make a list of the features in the object-oriented programming language(s) your company is using that have no counterparts in a language used previously. Next to each feature, jot down how you might approach testing software that's using your specific language.

1-3. If you are currently working on a project, identify increments or major milestones. Some of them might be informal. Think about the testing activities that you can do during each increment and what you can test at the end of each.

The Testing Perspective

☞ **Want to explore the testing role? See Testing Perspective on page 15**

☞ **Don't understand object concepts? See Object-Oriented Concepts on page 17**

☞ **Need an overview of UML models? See Development Products on page 39**

Chapter 2

Testing Perspective

The **testing perspective** is a way of looking at any development product and questioning its validity. The person examining work products from this perspective utilizes a thorough investigation of the software and all its representations to identify faults. The search for faults is guided by both systematic thinking and intuitive insights. It is a perspective that makes reviews and inspections just as powerful a tool as execution-based testing. A review will almost never find something that is missing—that is, a review typically only seeks to validate what exists and does not systematically search to determine if all things that *should be* in the software actually *are* in it. The testing perspective requires that a piece of software demonstrate that it not only performs according to its specification, but performs *only* to that specification. Thus, a product is tested to determine that it will do what it is supposed to do, and it is also tested to ensure that it does not do what it is not supposed to do.

Inspections, Reviews, and Test Executions

Software testing is typically accomplished by a combination of inspections, reviews, and test executions. The purpose of these activities is to observe failures.

An **inspection** is an examination of software based on a checklist of typical problems. Most items on a checklist are based on programming language semantics and/or coding conventions—for example, ensuring that each program variable is initialized before its first use and that pointers or references have been set to reasonable values before they are used. Modern compilers for object-oriented programming languages can detect many of the problems called out on traditional inspection checklists.

A **review** is an examination of software with the purpose of finding errors and faults even before the software is executed. Reviews are made in the context of the system being developed and have a deeper interest in the software than do inspections. A review delves into the meaning of each part of a program and whether it is appropriate for meeting some or all of the application's requirements. A review is intended to uncover errors such as missed or misunderstood requirements or faults in a program's logic. Some reviews examine programming details such as whether variable names are well chosen and whether algorithms are as efficient as they could be.

Test execution is testing software in the context of a running program. Through executing the software, a tester tries to determine whether it has the required behavior by giving the program some input and verifying that the resulting output is correct. Among the challenges to testers are identifying suitable inputs, determining correct outputs, and determining how to observe the outputs.

Testing using program execution (versus inspection and review) is the primary focus of this book, although we extend the idea of execution to include not only execution of the software under testing, but a special kind of review that uses the symbolic execution of nonexecutable representations of the system. Recall how we defined *software* as code and all its representations.

The testing perspective may be adopted by the same person who developed a product undergoing testing or by another person who brings an independent view of the specification and the product. Anyone assigned to test specific work products and every person assigned to a project at one time or another should adopt the testing perspective. We will refer to anyone who adopts this perspective by the title **tester**. A developer testing his or her own work is a tester, and so is the person who applies the testing perspective full time.

The testing perspective is as follows:

Skeptical: Wants proof of quality.

Objective: Makes no assumptions.

Thorough: Doesn't miss important areas.

Systematic: Searches are reproducible.

In this chapter we discuss aspects of object-oriented technologies using this testing perspective. First, we will review central concepts of object-oriented programming. What features of these concepts affect the testing of software that was developed using them? We will also delineate some assumptions we make in regard to using object-oriented technologies properly. Then we will look at various products of the development process and discuss the potential causes of failures in the software they represent.

Object-Oriented Concepts

Object-oriented programming is centered around six basic concepts:

1. object
2. message
3. interface
4. class
5. inheritance
6. polymorphism

People seem to have attached a wide range of meanings to these concepts, most of which are quite serviceable. We define some of these concepts perhaps a little more tightly than most people do because precision facilitates a better understanding of testing the concepts and eliminates some potential confusion about what needs to be tested. For example, while a distinction between *operations* and *methods* (or member functions) is not significant for most programmers, the distinction is significant to testers because the approach to testing an operation, which is part of a class specification and a way to manipulate an object, is somewhat different from testing a method, which is a piece of code that implements an operation. The distinction helps to differentiate the concerns of specification-based testing from the concerns of implementation-based testing.

We will review each of the basic object-oriented programming concepts and offer observations about them from a testing perspective. While we know that object-oriented programming languages support a variety of object-oriented programming models, we use the concepts as they are formulated for languages such as C++ and Java. Some of the variations between languages will affect the types of faults that are possible and the kinds of testing that are required. We try to note such differences throughout this book.

Object

An **object** is an operational entity that encapsulates both specific data values and the code that manipulates those values. For example, the data about a specific bank account and the operations needed to manipulate that data form an object. Objects are the basic computational entities in an object-oriented program, which we characterize as a community of objects that collaborate to solve some problem. As a program executes, objects are created, modified, accessed, and/or destroyed as a result of collaborations. Within the context of a good object-oriented design, an object in a program is a representation of some specific entity in the problem or in its solution. The objects within the program have relationships that reflect the relationships of their counterparts in the problem domain. Within the context of *Brickles*, many objects can be identified, including a paddle, pucks, a brick pile containing bricks, the play field, the play field boundaries (walls, ceiling, and floor), and even a player. A puck object will encapsulate a variety of attributes, such as its size, shape, location on a play field (if it is in play), and current velocity. It also supports operations for movement and for the puck's disappearance after it hits the floor. In the program that implements *Brickles*, we would expect to find an object for each of the pucks—for example, at the start of a *Brickles* match, we see the puck in play and any that are in reserve. When in play, a puck object will collaborate with other objects—the play field, paddle, and brick pile—to implement *Brickles* physics, which are described in the game description (see page 11).

Objects are the direct target of the testing process during software development. Whether an object behaves according to its specification and whether it interacts appropriately with collaborating objects in an executing program are the two major focuses of testing object-oriented software.

An object can be characterized by its **life cycle**. The life cycle for an object begins when it is created, proceeds through a series of states, and ends when the object is destroyed.

Definitional versus Operational Semantics of Objects

There is a bit of confusion among many of our clients and students with respect to the distinction between those aspects of object-oriented programming that are concerned with the definition of classes and interface and those that are concerned with the use of objects. We refer to these as the **definitional** and **operational** aspects of object-oriented programming.

Definitional: The class definition provides what might, at first glance appear to be the extreme point on the definitional end of the continuum; however, in some languages such as CLOS, the structure and content of this definition is defined by a metaclass. The metaclass approach may theoretically extend the continuum indefinitely in the definitional direction since it is possible to have a metaclass for any class, including metaclasses. The dynamic dimension represents the possibility in some languages, such as Java, to define classes during program execution.

Operational: The operational end of this continuum corresponds to the concept that an object is the basis of the actions taken in the system. An object provides the mechanisms needed to receive messages, dispatch methods, and return results. It also associates instance attributes with methods. This information may be on the static end of that dimension (as in a C++ object), or it may be more dynamic in the case of a CLOS object that contains arbitrary slots.

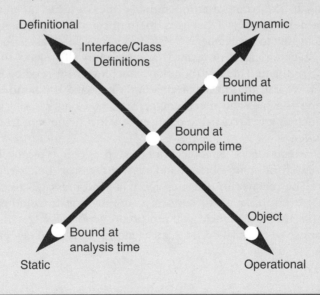

We make the following observations about objects from a testing perspective.

- An object encapsulates. This makes the complete definition of the object easy to identify, easy to pass around in the system, and easy to manipulate.

- An object hides information. This sometimes makes changes to the object hard to observe, thereby making the checking of test results difficult.

- An object has a state that persists for the life of the object. This state can become inconsistent and can be the source of incorrect behavior.

- An object has a lifetime. The object can be examined at various points in that lifetime to determine whether it is in the appropriate state based on its lifetime. Construction of an object too late or destruction of it too early is a common source of failures.

In Chapter 6 we will describe a variety of techniques for testing the interactions among objects. We will address other aspects of testing objects in Chapter 5 and Chapter 7.

Message

A **message**[1] is a request that an operation be performed by some object. In addition to the name of an operation, a message can include values—**actual parameters**—that will be used to perform that operation. A receiver can return a value to the sender.

An object-oriented program is a community of objects that collaborate to solve a problem. This collaboration is achieved by sending messages to one another. We call the object originating a message the **sender** and the object receiving the message the **receiver**. Some messages result in some form of reply such as a **return value** or an **exception** being sent from the receiver to the sender.

The execution of an object-oriented program typically begins with the instantiation of some objects, and then a message being sent to one of the objects. The receiver of that message will send messages to other objects—or possibly even to itself—to perform computations. In some event-driven environments, the environment will repeatedly send messages and wait for replies in response to external events such as mouse clicks and key presses.

---

1. In C++ terminology, a message is referred to as a **member function call**. Java programmers and Smalltalk programmers refer to messages as **method invocations**. We will use these terms in discussions of C++ and Java code, but we will use the more generic term *message* in language-independent discussions. Keep in mind that a member function *call* is distinct from a member function. A method *invocation* is distinct from a method.

We make the following observations about messages from a testing perspective.

- A message has a sender. The sender determines when to send the message and may make an incorrect decision.

- A message has a receiver. The receiver may not be ready for the specific message that it receives. The receiver may not take the correct action when receiving an unexpected message.

- A message may include actual parameters. These parameters will be used and/or updated by the receiver while processing the message. Objects passed as parameters must be in correct states before (and after) the message is processed, and they must implement the interfaces expected by the receiver.

These issues are the primary focus of interaction testing in Chapter 6.

Interface

An **interface** is an aggregation of behavioral declarations. Behaviors are grouped together because they define actions related by a single concept. For example, an interface might describe a set of behaviors related to being a moving object (see Figure 2.1).

An interface is a building block for specifications. A specification defines the total set of public behaviors for a class (we will define this next). Java contains a syntactic construct interface that provides this capability and does not allow the declaration of any state variables. You can produce the same result in C++ by declaring an abstract base class with only public, pure virtual methods.

```java
public interface Movable{
  public Point getPosition();
  public Velocity getVelocity();
  public void setVelocity(Velocity newVelocity);
  public void tick();
  public void move();
  public void collideWith(ArcadeGamePiece aPiece,Point aPoint);
  public void collideWithPaddle(Paddle aPaddle,Point aPoint);
  public void collideWithPuck(Puck aPuck,Point aPoint);
  public void reverseY();
  public void reverseX();
}
```

Figure 2.1 A Java declaration for a Movable interface

We make the following observations about interfaces from a testing perspective.

■ An interface encapsulates operation specifications. These specifications incrementally build the specifications of larger groupings such as classes. If the interface contains behaviors that do not belong with the other behaviors, then implementations of the interface will have unsatisfactory designs.

■ An interface has relationships with other interfaces and classes. An interface may be specified as the parameter type for a behavior to allow any implementer of that interface to be passed as a parameter.

We will use the term **interface** to describe a set of behavior declarations whether or not you use the interface syntax.

Class

A **class** is a set of objects that share a common conceptual basis. Many people characterize a class as a template—a "cookie cutter"—for creating objects. While we understand that characterization makes apparent the role of classes in writing object-oriented programs, we prefer to think of a class as a set. The class definition then is actually a definition of what members of the set look like. This is also better than definitions that define a class as a *type* since some object-oriented languages don't use the concept of a type.

Objects form the basic elements for *executing* object-oriented programs, while classes are the basic elements for *defining* object-oriented programs. Any concept to be represented in a program must be done by first defining a class and then creating objects defined by that class. The process of creating the objects is referred to as **instantiation** and the result is referred to as an **instance**. We will use *instance* and *object* interchangeably.

The conceptual basis common to all the objects in a class is expressed in terms of two parts:

■ A **class specification** is the declaration of *what* each of the objects in the class can do.

■ A **class implementation** is the definition of *how* each of the objects in the class do what they can do.

Consider a C++ definition for a class PuckSupply from *Brickles*. Figure 2.2 shows a C++ header file and Figure 2.3 shows a source file for such a class. The use of a header file and one or more source files is a typical way to structure a C++ class definition.[2] In the context of C++, a header file contains the class specification as a set of operations declared in the public area of a class declaration.

---

2. Java prescribes that specification and implementation physically be in the same file. Nonetheless, there is a logical separation between *what* an object does and *how* it does it.

```
#ifndef PUCKSUPPLY_H
#define PUCKSUPPLY_H
class PuckSupply {
public:
  PuckSupply();
  ~PuckSupply();

  Puck* get();
  int size() const;

private:
  static const int N = 3;
  int _count;
  Puck* _store[N];
};
#endif
```

Figure 2.2 A C++ header file for the class PuckSupply

```
#include "PuckSupply.h"
PuckSupply::PuckSupply() : _count(N) {
  int i;
  for ( i = 0 ; i < N ; ++i ) {
    _store[i] = new Puck;
  };
}

PuckSupply::~PuckSupply() {
  int i;
  for ( i = 0 ; i < _count ; ++i ) {
    delete _store[i];
  };
}

Puck* PuckSupply::get() {
  return ( _count > 0 ? _store[--_count] : 0 );
}

int PuckSupply::size() const {
  return _count;
}
```

Figure 2.3 A C++ source file for the class PuckSupply

Unfortunately, as part of the implementation, the private (and protected) data attributes, must also be defined in the header file.

To create or manipulate an object from another class, a segment of code only needs access to the specification for the class of that object. In C++, this is typically accomplished by using an `include` directive naming the header file for the object's class:

```
#include "PuckSupply.h"
```

This, of course, gives access to all the information needed to compile the code, but it provides more information than is necessary to design the interactions between classes. In Chapter 4 we will discuss problems that can arise from designers having a view into possible implementations of a class and how to detect these problems during reviews.

Classes as Objects

Object-oriented programming languages typically support, either explicitly or implicitly within the semantics of the language, the notion that a class is itself an object, and as such can have operations and attributes defined for it. In both C++ and Java, operations and data values associated with a class are identified syntactically by the keyword *static*. We will refer to such operations as **static operations**. The presence of public static operations in a class specification implies that the class itself is an object that can be messaged. From a testing perspective, we must treat such a class as an object and create a test suite for the class as well as its instances. From a testing perspective, we should always be skeptical of nonconstant, static data associated with a class because such data can affect the behavior of instances.

Class Specification

A specification for a class describes what the class represents and what an instance of the class can do. A class specification includes a specification for each of the operations that can be performed by each of its instances. An **operation** is an action that can be applied to an object to obtain a certain effect. Operations fall into two categories:

■ **Accessor** (or **inspector**) **operations** provide information about an object—for example, the value of some attribute or general state information. This kind of operation does not change the object on which the operation is being requested. In C++, accessor operations can and *should* be declared as const.

■ **Modifier** (or **mutator**) **operations** change the state of an object by setting one or more attributes to have new values.

We make this classification because testing accessors is different from testing modifiers. Within a class specification, some operations might both provide information and change it.[3] Some modifier operations might not make changes under all circumstances. In either case, we classify these operations as modifier operations.

There are two kinds of operations that deserve special attention:

■ A **constructor** is a class object operation used to create a new object, including the initialization of the new instance when it comes into existence.

■ A **destructor** is an instance object operation used to perform any processing needed just prior to the end of an object's lifetime.

Constructors and destructors are different from accessors and modifiers in that they are invoked implicitly as a result of the birth and death of objects. Some of these objects are visible in the program and some are not. The statement

x = a + b + c;

in which a, b, c, and x are all objects from the same class, invokes the constructor of that class at least twice to create objects that hold intermediate results and die by the end of the statement, as follows:

$tmp_1 = a + b$;
$tmp_2 = tmp_1 + c$;
$x = tmp_2$;

A class represents a concept, either in the problem being solved by a software application or in the solution to that problem. We expect a description of what a class represents to be a part of a class specification. Consider, for example, that the class PuckSupply declared in Figure 2.2 probably does not have much meaning without an explanation that it represents the collection of pucks that a player has at the start of a *Brickles* match. As the player loses pucks to the floor during play, the program will replace it with another puck from a puck supply until that supply is exhausted, at which time the match ends with a loss for the player.

We also expect some meaning and constraints to be associated with each of the operations defined in a class specification—for example, do the operations size() and get() for the class PuckSupply have any inherent meaning to you? Consequently, each operation should have a specification that describes what it does. A specification for PuckSupply is given in Figure 2.4.

■ The size() operation can be applied at any time (no preconditions) and returns the number of pucks in the receiver.

■ The get() operation can only be applied if at least one puck is left in the receiver—that is, size() > 0. The result of the operation is to return a puck and to reduce the number of pucks by one.

---

3. It is good object-oriented design practice for an operation to be one or the other, but not both.

A puck supply is a set of pucks not in play that can be retrieved one at a time. The pucks are created by a puck supply when it is created.

- Class invariant: The count associated with a puck supply is always an integer in the range zero through three, inclusive.

- The `size()` operation can be applied at any time. It returns (replies with) the number of pucks left in the receiver and has no effect on the receiver.

- The `get()` operation can only be applied if the receiver has at least one puck—that is, its size attribute is greater than zero. The result of the operation is to return a puck and to reduce the number of pucks by one.

- The constructor has no preconditions. The result of the constructor is a puck supply containing three pucks—that is, the size attribute has a value of three.

- The destructor has no preconditions. The destructor deletes any pucks that remain in the object being deleted.

Figure 2.4 A specification for the PuckSupply class based on contracts

Well-specified operation semantics are critical to both development and testing efforts and definitely worth the time and effort needed to express them well. You can use any form of notation to specify the semantics provided it is well-understood by all who must use it. We will specify semantics at several different points:

- ■ **Preconditions** for an operation prescribe conditions that must hold before the operation can be performed. Preconditions are usually stated in terms of attributes of the object containing the operation and/or attributes of any actual parameters included in the message requesting that the operation be performed.

- ■ **Postconditions** for an operation prescribe conditions that must hold after the operation is performed. Postconditions are usually stated in terms of (1) the attributes of the object containing the operation; (2) the attributes of any actual parameters included in the message that is requesting that the operation be performed; (3) in terms of the value of any reply; and/or (4) in terms of the exceptions that might be raised.

- ■ **Invariants** prescribe conditions that must always hold within the lifetime of the object. A **class invariant** describes a set of operating boundaries for an instance of a class. It is also possible to define interface invariants as well as operational invariants for segments of code. A class invariant can be treated as an implied postcondition for each operation.

They must hold whenever an operation completes, although a method for an operation is allowed to violate invariants during its execution. Invariants are usually stated in terms of the attributes or states of an object.

The aggregate of the specifications of all of the operations in a class provides part of the description of the *behavior of its instances*. Behavior can be difficult to infer from operation specifications alone, so behavior is typically designed and represented at a higher form of abstraction using states and transitions (See State Diagrams on page 49). Behavior is characterized by defining a set of states for an instance and then describing how various operations effect transitions from state to state. The states associated with a puck supply in *Brickles* define whether it is empty or not empty. Being empty is determined by the size attribute of a puck supply. If the size is zero, then it is empty, otherwise it is not empty. You can remove a puck from a supply only if that supply is not empty—that is, if its size is not zero.

When you write a specification for an operation, you can use one of two basic approaches to define the interface between the receiver and the sender. Each approach has a set of rules about how to define the constraints and responsibilities of the sender and the receiver when an operation is to be performed. A **contract** approach is embedded in the specification in Figure 2.4. A **defensive programming** approach underlies the specification in Figure 2.5. The contract approach emphasizes preconditions, but has simpler postconditions, while the defensive programming approach is just the reverse.

Under the contract approach, which is a design technique developed by Bertrand Meyer [Meye94], an interface is defined in terms of the obligations of the sender and the receiver involved in an interaction. An operation is defined in terms of the obligations of each party. Typically, these are set forth in preconditions and postconditions for an operation and a set of invariant conditions that must hold across all operations, thereby acting as postconditions required of all operations. The preconditions prescribe the obligation of the sender—that is, before the sender can make a request for a receiver to perform an operation, the sender must ensure that all preconditions are met. If preconditions have been met, then the receiver is obligated to meet the requirements set forth in the postconditions as well as those in any class invariant. Under the contract approach, care must be taken in the design of a class interface to ensure that preconditions are sufficient to allow a receiver to meet postconditions (if not, you should add additional preconditions) and to ensure that a sender can determine whether all preconditions are met before sending a message. Typically, a set of accessor methods allow for checking specified conditions. Furthermore, care must be taken to ensure that postconditions address all possible outcomes of an operation, assuming preconditions are met.

Under the defensive programming approach, an interface is defined primarily in terms of the receiver, and any assumptions it makes on its own state and the values of any inputs (arguments or global data values) at the time of the request. Under this approach, an operation typically returns some indication concerning the status of the result of the request—success or failure for a particular reason, such as a bad input value. This indication is traditionally in the form of a **return code** that associates a value with each possible outcome. However, a receiver can provide to a sender an object that encapsulates the status of the request. Furthermore, exceptions are being used more frequently because many object-oriented programming languages now support them. Some operations are defined so that no status is returned in case of failure, but instead, execution is terminated when a request cannot be met. Certainly this action cannot be tolerated in most software systems.

The primary goal of defensive programming is to identify "garbage in" and hence eliminate "garbage out." A member function checks for improper values coming in and then reports the status of processing the request to a sender. The approach tends to increase the complexity of software because each sender must follow a request for an operation with code to check the processing status and then, for each possible outcome, provide code to take an appropriate recovery action. The approach tends to increase both the size of code

---

A puck supply is a set of pucks not in play that can be retrieved one at a time. The pucks are created by a puck supply when it is created. Note: Eventually a way to increase the number of pucks in a supply might be added.

- Class invariant: The count associated with a puck supply is always an integer in the range zero through three, inclusive.
- The size() operation can be applied at any time.

  It returns (replies with) the number of pucks left in the receiver and has no effect on the receiver.
- The get() operation can be applied at any time.

  If the receiver has at least one puck—that is, if its count attribute is greater than zero, then the result of the operation is a pointer's return to a puck, which reduces the number of pucks by one. Otherwise, a null pointer value is returned and the count attribute remains at zero.
- The constructor has no preconditions.

  The result of the constructor is a puck supply containing three pucks—that is, the count attribute has a value of three.
- The destructor has no preconditions.

  The destructor deletes any pucks that remain.

Figure 2.5 A specification for the class PuckSupply based on defensive programming

and to increase execution time because inputs are checked on every call, even though the sender may have already checked them.[4]

The contract and defensive programming approaches represent two opposite views of software specification. As the name implies, defensive programming reflects a lack of trust of a sender on the part of a receiver. By contrast, a contract reflects a mutual responsibility shared by both a sender and a receiver. A receiver processes a request based on inputs believed to meet stated preconditions. A sender assumes that conditions have been met after the request has been processed. It is not uncommon for the approaches to be mixed in specifying the operations within a single class because they each have advantages and disadvantages.

Interface design based on contracts eliminates the need for a receiver to verify preconditions on each call.[5] It makes for better software engineering and better program (and programmer) efficiency. However, it introduces one important question: "In the context of an executing program, how are contracts enforced?" Clearly, the contract places obligations on both sender and receiver. Nonetheless, can a receiver truly trust every sender to meet preconditions? The consequences of "garbage in" can be disastrous. A program's execution in the presence of a sender's failure to meet a precondition would most likely result in data corruption that would in turn have serious consequences! It is critical that all interactions under contracts be tested to ensure compliance with a contract.

From a testing perspective, the approach used in an interface determines the types of testing that need to be done. The contract approach simplifies class testing, but complicates interaction testing because we must ensure that any sender meets preconditions. The defensive programming approach complicates class testing (because test cases must address all possible outcomes) and interaction testing (because we must ensure all possible outcomes are produced and that they are properly handled by a sender).

Tip

Review pre- and postconditions and invariants for testability during design. Are the constraints clearly stated? Does the specification include means by which to check preconditions?

---

4. It is curious that code we have seen that was written using a defensive programming approach rarely checks to ensure the receiver actually performed the requested operation—that is, the mistrust is only on the part of a receiver. Perhaps this practice arises from the fact that the code for the receiver has usually been tested and is considered trustworthy enough to work correctly. Misuse can come only on the sender's side; we'll address this in Chapter 5.

5. It is still useful for debugging to include code to check preconditions. This code can be "removed" from the executable after a system is debugged, but before the final testing. Eiffel [Meye00] has language-level support for contract checking and compiler switches to enable and disable the checking.

Class Implementation

A class implementation describes how an object represents its attributes and carries out operations. It comprises several components:

■ A set of data values stored in **data members**, which are sometimes referred to as **instance variables** or **variables**. The data values store some or all of the values associated with the attributes of an object. There is not necessarily a one-to-one mapping of attributes to data values. Some attributes can be derived from others—for example, the direction a puck is moving in the horizontal direction can be deduced from its velocity. Some redundant representation of derivable attributes is sometimes desirable in order to improve the performance of member functions with respect to time. In some cases, an attribute identified for an object might not be represented at all because the attribute is not needed in an application. By removing the attribute, we can reduce the memory space needed to hold such an object.

■ A set of methods, referred to as member functions in C++ or methods in Java, constitutes code that will be used to implement an algorithm that accomplishes one operation declared in the public or private class specification. The code typically uses or sets an object's variables. It processes any actual parameter values, checks for exceptional conditions, and computes a return value if one is specified for the operation.

■ A set of constructors to initialize a new instance (at the start of its lifetime). A constructor is really an operation on a *class* object.

■ A destructor that handles any processing associated with the destruction of an instance (when it reaches the end of its lifetime).

■ A set of private operations in a private interface.[6] Private operations provide support for the implementation of public operations.

Class testing is an important aspect of the total testing process because classes define the building blocks for object-oriented programs. Since a class is an abstraction of the commonalities among its instances, the class testing process must ensure that a representative sample of members of the class are selected for testing.

By viewing classes from a testing perspective, we can identify the following potential causes of failures within their design and implementation.

■ A class specification contains operations to construct instances. These operations may not properly initialize the attributes of new instances.

■ A class relies on collaboration with other classes to define its behaviors and attributes. For example, an instance variable might be an instance of

---

6. For simplicity, we will generally use the term *private* to refer to any aspect of a class that is not public. C++ supports *private* and *protected* components of a class and Java supports even more levels of access to components.

Subsystems and Classes

A class is a very interesting concept in terms of systems and subsystems. In many ways, a system or a subsystem can be specified as a class—one associated with a complex behavior, but a class nonetheless—that has states and transitions and an interface. Much of the focus of this book is on class testing. Many of the techniques we discuss could be scaled up to system and subsystem testing if the system is indeed specified as a class. Note, however, that the complexity of such a class far exceeds that of a class such as Point. This is an indication of some of the issues we must address with respect to class testing.

another class or a method might send a message to a parameter (which is an instance of another class), to do some part of its computation. These other classes may be implemented incorrectly and contribute to the failure of the class using them in a definition.

■ A class's implementation "satisfies" its specification, but that is no guarantee that the specification is correct. The implementation may violate a higher requirement, such as accepted design criteria, or it may simply incorrectly model the underlying concept.

■ The implementation might not support all required operations or may incorrectly perform operations.

■ A class specifies preconditions to each operation. The class might not provide a way for that precondition to be checked by a sender before sending a message.

The design approach used, contract or defensive, gives rise to different sets of potential problems. Under a contract approach, we only need to test situations in which the preconditions are satisfied. Under a defensive programming approach, we must test every possible input to determine that the outcome is handled properly.

Inheritance

Inheritance is a relationship between classes that allows the definition of a new class based on the definition of an existing class.[7] This dependency of one class on another allows the reuse of both the specification and the implementa-

---

7. In a programming language that supports **multiple inheritance,** a new class can be defined in terms of one or more existing classes. C++ supports multiple inheritance, but most other object-oriented programming languages do not. Most designers tend to avoid the use of multiple inheritance because of its complexity. Sometimes multiple inheritance is very useful, especially in modeling similarities between two subclasses at the same level in an inheritance hierarchy. We will focus primarily on single inheritance, but we will address multiple inheritance in important areas of testing.

tion of the preexisting class. An important advantage of this approach is that the preexisting class does not have to be modified or made aware in any way of the new class. The new class is referred to as a **subclass** or (in C++) a **derived class**. If a class inherits from another, the other class is referred to as its **superclass** or (in C++) **base class**. The set of classes that inherit either directly or indirectly from a given class form an **inheritance hierarchy**. Within that hierarchy, we can refer to the **root**, which is the class from which all others inherit directly or indirectly. Each class in a hierarchy, except the root, has one or more **ancestors**, the class(es) from which it inherits directly or indirectly. Each class in a hierarchy has zero or more **descendents**, which are the classes that inherit from it directly or indirectly.

Good object-oriented design requires that inheritance be used only to implement an *is a* (or *is a kind of*) relationship. The best use of inheritance is with respect to specifications and not implementation. This requirement becomes evident in the context of *inclusion polymorphism* (see page 34).

Viewed from the testing perspective, inheritance does the following:

- Provides a mechanism by which bugs can be propagated from a class to its descendents. Testing a class as it is developed eliminates faults early before they are passed on to other classes.

- Provides a mechanism by which we can reuse test cases. Because a subclass inherits part of its specification and implementation from its superclass, we can potentially reuse test cases for the superclass in testing the subclass.

- Models an *is a kind of* relationship. Use of inheritance solely for code reuse will probably lead to maintenance difficulties. This is chiefly a design quality issue, but we argue that it is such a common mistake in object-oriented development that testers can make a significant contribution to a project's success by checking that inheritance is used properly. Besides, proper use of inheritance in design leads to benefits in execution testing of classes (see Chapter 7).

Polymorphism

Polymorphism is the ability to treat an object as belonging to more than one type. The typing system in a programming language can be defined to support a number of different type-conformance policies. An exact match policy may be the safest policy, but a polymorphic typing system supports designs that are flexible and easy to maintain.

Substitution Principle

Inheritance should be used only to model the *is a* (or *is a kind of*) relationship. That is, if D *is a* subclass of C, then it should be understood that D *is a kind of* C. Based on the substitution principle [LiWi94], an instance of a subclass D can be used whenever an instance of the class C is expected. In other words, if a program is designed to work with an instance of the class C in some context, then an instance of the class D could be substituted in that same context and the program still could work. In order for that to happen, the behavior associated with D must somehow conform to that which is associated with C.

One way to enforce "substitutability" is to constrain behavior changes from class to subclass. The behavior associated with a class can be defined in terms of the observable states of an instance and the semantics associated with the various operations defined for an instance of that class. The behavior associated with a subclass can be defined in terms of incremental changes to the observable states and operations defined by its base class.

Under the substitution principle, only the following changes are allowed in defining the behavior associated with a new subclass:

- The preconditions for each operation must be the same or weaker—that is, less constraining from the perspective of a client.
- The postconditions for each operation must be the same or stronger—that is, must do at least as much as defined by the superclass.
- The class invariant must be the same or stronger—that is, add more constraints.

These constraints on behavior changes must be enforced by the developers. Viewed from the perspective of observable states, we can show that

- The observable states and all transitions between them associated with the base class must be preserved by the subclass.
- The subclass may add transitions between these states.
- The subclass may add observable states as long as each is either concurrent or a substate of an existing state.

Inclusion Polymorphism

Inclusion polymorphism is the occurrence of different forms in the same class. Object-oriented programming language support for inclusion polymorphism[8] gives programmers the ability to substitute an object whose specification matches another object's specification for the latter object in a request for an operation. In other words, a sender in an object-oriented program can use an object as a parameter based on its implementation of an interface rather than its full class.

In C++, inclusion polymorphism arises from the inheritance relationship. A derived class inherits the public interface of its base class[9] and thus instances of the derived class can respond to the same messages as the base class.[10] A sender can manipulate an instance of either class with a value that is either a reference or a pointer whose target type is the base class. A member function call can be made through that value.

In Java, inclusion polymorphism is supported both through inheritance between classes and an implementation relationship between interfaces and classes. A sender can manipulate objects with a reference declared for either a class or an interface. If a reference is associated with a class, then the reference can be bound to an instance of that class or any of its descendents. If a reference is associated with an interface, then the reference can be bound to an instance of any class that is declared to implement that interface.

Our definition of a class as a set of objects that share a common conceptual basis (see page 22) is influenced primarily by the association of inheritance and inclusion polymorphism. The class at the root of a hierarchy establishes a common conceptual basis for all objects in the set. A descendent of that root class refines the behavior established by that root class and any of its other ancestors. The objects in the descendent class are still contained in the set that is the root class. Thus, a descendent class defines a subset of each of the sets that are its ancestors. Suppose that the *Brickles* specification is extended to incorporate additional kinds of bricks—say, some that are hard and have to be hit twice with a puck before they disappear, and some that break with a considerable force that increases the speed of any puck that hits it. The HardBrick and Power-Brick classes could each be defined as a subclass of Brick. The relationship

---

8. Some people refer to this support as **dynamic binding**. Dynamic binding is an association at runtime between the operation specified in a message and a method to process the requested operation. However, dynamic binding is the *mechanism* by which inclusion polymorphism is implemented by runtime environments. In C++, dynamic binding must be requested by the keyword `virtual` in a member function declaration.

9. We assume **public** inheritance is used. We believe **protected** and **private** inheritance should be used only under rare circumstances.

10. Instances of the derived class can potentially respond to additional messages because the derived class defines additional operations in its public interface.

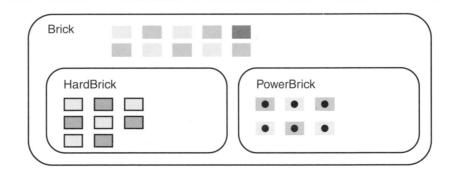

Figure 2.6 A set diagram for a Brick inheritance hierarchy

between the sets are illustrated in Figure 2.6. Note how in a polymorphic sense, the class Brick contains 24 elements—10 "plain" bricks, 8 hard bricks, and 6 power bricks. Hard bricks and power bricks have special properties, but they also respond to the same messages as "plain" bricks, although probably in different ways.

Sets representing classes can be considered from two perspectives:

1. From a *class's* perspective, each set contains all instances. Conceptually, the size of the set could be infinite, as is the case with bricks since, in theory, we can create bricks for any number of *Brickles* matches or even for any other arcade games because the Brick class is not necessarily tied to *Brickles*. Infinite sets are most easily represented using Venn diagrams.

2. From an *executing program's* perspective, each set is drawn with one element per instance in existence. The sets in Figure 2.6 are drawn from this perspective.

Both perspectives are useful during testing. When a class is to be tested outside the context of any application program (see Chapter 5 and Chapter 6), we will test it by selecting arbitrary instances using the first perspective. When the use of a class is to be tested in the context of an executing application program or in the context of object persistence, then we can utilize the second perspective to ensure that the size of the set is correct and that elements correspond to appropriate objects in the problem or in its solution.

Inclusion polymorphism provides a powerful capability. You can perform all design and programming to interfaces, without regard to the exact class of the object that is sent a message to perform an operation. Inclusion polymorphism takes design and programming to a higher level of abstraction. In fact, it is useful to define classes for which no instances exist, but for which its subclasses do have instances. An **abstract class** is a class whose purpose is primarily to

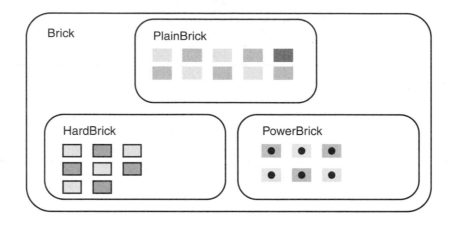

Figure 2.7 A set diagram for a Brick class inheritance hierarchy

define an interface that is supported by all of its descendents.[11] In terms of the example extending the kinds of bricks in *Brickles*, an alternate formulation is to define an abstract class called Brick and define three subclasses for it: Plain-Brick, HardBrick, and PowerBrick (see Figure 2.7).

Among the abstract classes that we used in the design of *Brickles* are the following:

- Sprite to represent the things that can appear on a play field.

- MovableSprite, which is a subclass of Sprite, to represent sprites that can move in a play field.

- StationarySprite, which is a subclass of Sprite, to represent sprites that cannot move in a play field.

Puck and Paddle are **concrete subclasses** of MovableSprite, while Brick is a subclass of StationarySprite. The use of abstractions allows polymorphism to be exploited during design. For example, we can design at the level of a play field containing sprites without detailed knowledge of all the various kinds of sprites. We can design at the level of movable sprites moving in a play field and colliding with other sprites—both movable and stationary. If the game specification were extended to incorporate hard bricks and power bricks, most parts of the program would not need to be changed because, after all, hard bricks and power bricks are just stationary sprites. The parts of the program that are affected should be limited to those that construct the actual instances of the classes.

---

11. An abstract class might also define portions of the implementation for its descendents. Both C++ and Java provide syntax for the definition of abstract classes and ensure that instances of them cannot be created in a running program.

Subclassing and Subtyping

Consider a design solution that involves inclusion polymorphism. In the diagram below, classes C and D inherit from class B. Instances of class A think they are sending messages to an instance of class B (the type of formal parameter B). The polymorphic attribute of the typing system allows instances of C and D in place of the instance of B. Each class has a different implementation of the doIt() method.

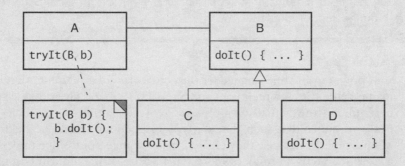

Designing software well, within the context of inheritance and inclusion polymorphism, requires a disciplined use of inheritance (and interfaces in Java). It is important that *behavior* is preserved as classes are added to extend a class hierarchy. If, for example, bricks can move, then they are not really classifiable as stationary sprites. Good design requires that each subclass be a **subtype**—that is, the specification for the subclass must fully meet all specifications of its direct ancestor. This is an enforceable design requirement when the following rules are applied with respect to pre- and postconditions for each inherited operation:

- The tryIt() method of A is written to satisfy the preconditions of the doIt() operation of B before it calls doIt(). If an instance of C or D is to be substituted, the preconditions for C::doIt() or D::doIt() must not add any new conditions to those for B::doIt() or we would have to modify A to accommodate C and D.

- The tryIt() method of A is written to satisfy the preconditions of the doIt() operation of B before it calls doIt(). If an instance of C or D is to be substituted, the preconditions for C::doIt() or D::doIt() must not add any new conditions to those for B::doIt() or we would have to modify A to accommodate C and D.

- The invariant defined for B must still be true in instances of C and D. Additional invariants may be added.

Continued

These requirements are easy to understand in the context of a software contract (see page 27). Preconditions set forth the obligations of any sender and the postconditions and class invariants set forth the obligations of a receiver in any interaction. The requirement for same or weaker (less strict) preconditions means that in meeting its obligations in terms of the contract for A, a sender still meets its obligations for B, which is not as constraining. The requirement for the same or stronger (more strict) postconditions and invariants means that a receiver still can meet a sender's expectations in terms of the contract for A, even though that receiver might do more than the sender expects.

A polymorphic reference hides the actual class of a referent. All referents are manipulated through their common interface. C++ and Java provide support for determining the actual class of a referent at runtime. Good object-oriented design requires that such runtime type inspections should be held to a minimum, primarily because they create a maintenance point since the extension of a class hierarchy introduces more types to be inspected. However, situations arise in which such inspections can be justified.

The following are the functions of inclusion polymorphism viewed from a testing perspective:

■ Inclusion polymorphism allows systems to be extended incrementally by adding classes rather than modifying existing ones. Unanticipated interactions can occur in the extensions.

■ Inclusion polymorphism allows any operation to have one or more parameters of a polymorphic reference. This increases the number of possible kinds of actual parameters that should be tested.

■ Inclusion polymorphism allows an operation to specify replies that are polymorphic references. The actual class of the referent could be incorrect or unanticipated by the sender.

This dynamic nature of object-oriented languages places more importance on testing a representative sample of runtime configurations. Static analyses can provide the potential interactions that might occur, but only the runtime configuration can illustrate what actually happens. In Chapter 6 we consider a statistical technique that assists in determining which configurations will expose the most faults for the least cost of resources.

Parametric Polymorphism

Parametric polymorphism is the capability to define a type in terms of one or more parameters.

Templates in C++ provide a compile-time ability to instantiate a "new" class. It is new in the sense that an actual parameter is provided for the formal param-

```
template<class ItemType, class Key>
class List{
public:
    void add(ItemType* item);
    ItemType* retrieve(Key searchValue);
}
```

Figure 2.8 A C++ List class template

eter in the definition. Instances of the new class can then also be created. This capability has been used extensively in the C++ Standard Template Library. The interface of a simple list class template is shown in Figure 2.8.

From a testing perspective, parametric polymorphism supports a different type of relationship from inheritance. If the template works for one instantiation, there is no guarantee it will work for another because the template code might assume the correct implementations of operations such as making (deep) copies and destructors. This should be checked during inspection. It is possible to write templated drivers for testing many parts of templates.

Abstraction

We have referred to the concept of abstraction throughout this chapter. **Abstraction** is the process of removing detail from a representation. Abstraction allows us to look at a problem or its solution in various levels of detail, thereby letting us leave out any considerations that are irrelevant to the current level of interest. Object-oriented technologies make extensive use of abstraction—for example, the root class in an inheritance hierarchy models a concept more abstract than its descendents. In the next section we will see a number of system models that are developed in order of increasing detail.

Viewed from the testing perspective, layers of abstraction in the development products are paralleled by layers of test analysis. That is, by beginning with the highest levels of abstraction, we can provide a more thorough examination of the development product and, therefore, a more effective and accurate set of tests.

Development Products

Good documentation is critical for successful development and successful testing.

A development process will generate a collection of work products that represent the system under development and/or the requirements for it. The form and content of those products will be determined by many factors, including the corporate policies, the skills and expertise of developers, and the schedule constraints. These products are written in a variety of notations. In this book we use the **Unified Modeling Language** (UML) [RJB98] as the conceptual modeling language and C++ as the programming language.

The end products of any software development effort are code and the documentation for that code, including user manuals and maintenance documentation. Other development work products are typically produced, including analysis and design models, architectural models, and requirements that influence the quality of the system being produced. These products have a lifetime longer than the current project and may be reused on other development efforts.

In this section, we describe a set of products that we think are essential to the successful development of object-oriented software. We use the UML in our examples.[12] Your products might be written in another notation, but the models should in some way capture the same information that we describe in this section. Since these products are models that represent the software, we will discuss them from a testing perspective.

In UML, a model is a collection of diagrams. Each model captures the system at a specific level of abstraction. We present these models because in Chapter 4, we will talk about how to conduct a "system" test with models rather than code. The kinds of UML diagrams we use for system modeling are listed in Figure 2.9.

Analysis Models

Analysis comprises the activities in a software development process whose purpose is to define the problem to be solved and to determine requirements for a solution to that problem. In our development process, two levels of analysis—domain and application—are performed:

■ **Domain analysis** focuses on an understanding of the problem domain—that is, the general area of interest (or universe of discourse) in which the problem of immediate interest lies. With respect to *Brickles*, domain analysis might focus on the domain of arcade games, which would include games that have similar components such as *Asteroids* or *PacMan*, or of computer games, which would include card games or board games such as *Solitaire* or *Monopoly*. Domain analysis is concerned primarily with abstract concepts. In the domain of arcade games, abstractions include players, sprites, and play fields.

Domain analysis is particularly useful if similar problems in the same domain are to be solved in the future or if the requirements are not well

---

12. *UML Distilled: A Brief Guide to the Standard Object Modeling Language* [FoSb99] provides a good, concise overview of UML.

Use case diagram	Represents the actors and uses of the system and relationships between the uses.
Class diagram	Represents the individual class definitions and the relationships between classes.
Package diagram	Presents conceptual groupings of classes with dependencies between groups.
Sequence diagram	Records the sequences of messages that represent an algorithm.
State diagram	Presents different configurations of data-attribute values and the messages that transform the data from one configuration to another.
Activity diagram	Aggregates all possible paths through the logic of a method.

Figure 2.9 UML diagrams used in this book

defined. The products of the one domain analysis provide a starting point for the analysis of each particular application.

■ **Application analysis** focuses on a specific problem and the requirements for a solution. With respect to *Brickles*, application analysis focuses on the game itself. Application analysis is concerned primarily with concrete concepts. In *Brickles*, these include pucks, a paddle, and bricks.

Commonalities among concrete classes might be reflected by the use of interfaces or abstract classes, such as Brick in Figure 2.7. These commonalities might be identified as abstractions during domain analysis or might be synthesized based on the features common to two or more concrete classes identified during application analysis.

In terms of testing the representations of software generated during analysis, we do not need to distinguish between the products of domain analysis and application analysis. The difference will be reflected by the scope of the model (domain models are very broad) and by the level of completeness at which testing is performed (domain analysis models contain less detail).

Object-oriented analysis centers on what the system does from the perspective of the kinds of objects involved and how the objects are related to one another. Analysis encompasses classifying objects in the problem, including the identification of relevant attributes and operations, the identification of

Do products of analysis represent software if the focus of analysis is the problem (or problem domain) and requirements for a solution, but not an actual solution?

Yes. The design of an object-oriented program should construct a representation of the problem by creating appropriate objects to represent entities in the problem, and then establishing appropriate relationships among those objects to reflect the relationships between objects in the problem. A solution is effected by empowering the software objects to collaborate toward a solution. Since a good solution is based on problem structure and that structure is reflected in analysis models, then analysis models are representations of the software.

relationships between classes and instances of various classes, and the characterization of the behavior of the various kinds of objects. These are represented in a model comprising different kinds of diagrams.

An **analysis model** represents a system from the perspective of *what* it is supposed to do. The purpose of an analysis model is to provide developers, their clients, and other stakeholders with an understanding of the problem and the requirements for a solution. Typically, analysis efforts will produce a restatement of the requirements specification written first, from a development perspective as opposed to a marketing perspective and second, from a model of the problem to be solved described in terms of objects. A variety of diagrams is used to present the system from different views. Viewed from the testing perspective, the various diagrams that comprise the representation might contain incorrect information or might not represent the same information consistently in all diagrams; or, the model might not completely capture all of the necessary information. In Chapter 4 we will address testing these representations. We now describe some of these diagrams, which will serve as the basis for both development and testing.

Use Case Diagram

In object-oriented development, requirements are captured quite effectively by a collection of use cases and supporting diagrams. The description of *Brickles* in Chapter 1 expresses the components and rules of the game in natural language and pictures. This description is a reasonably good definition of the required software, although it leaves some requirements open for interpretation such as the size of the play field, the tone of a consolation message, whether a player can "exit" if the game is paused, the size and speed of a puck, and how sensitive paddle movement is to mouse movement.

A **use case** describes a **use** of the system by an **actor** to perform some task. Actors really represent the various *roles* users[13] play with respect to the system—that is, one person can use a system in several different roles. There is one actor in *Brickles* as it was described in Chapter 1—namely, the player, who is involved in the actual play of the game. We could postulate another actor for *Brickles* who is responsible for establishing some parameters for the game as it is installed on different computers—for example, the speed of the puck; the size of the initial puck supply; and the colors of the bricks, puck, paddle, and play field. The specification does not identify such an actor, but a good analyst would consider the need for an administrative user of the system. Of course, the person who installs *Brickles* on a system can also be a player. (See [FoSb99] or [JCJO92] for a discussion of use cases.)

Use cases can be expressed in various levels of abstraction. Consider, for example, some high-level uses of *Brickles* by a player shown in Figure 2.10.

None of these use cases states *how* a player starts, pauses, resumes, or stops a match. In fact, none of them even mention *Brickles* explicitly. They can apply to many arcade games. They all have the same actor (a player) and are concerned with manipulating a match, which is an object (or class) we identified to represent an arcade game for which play is in progress.[14] As such, we might consider them **domain-level use cases**. These domain-level use cases can be refined for *Brickles* as shown in Figure 2.11.

Use cases do not necessarily capture *every* requirement. The use cases are usually accompanied by additional text or diagrams that capture details (such as performance requirements) that are not immediately obvious to users and interfacing requirements for subsystems that are hidden from the user.

Use cases are organized hierarchically using two relationships: **uses** and **extends**. You can refine some use cases into a set of more specific use cases.

Name	Description
Start	A player starts a match.
Pause	A player pauses a match.
Resume	A player resumes playing a match.
Stop	A player stops a match.

Figure 2.10 Domain-level use cases for arcade games

13. An actor does not have to be a person. It could be, for example, another software system.

14. In common usage, the term *game* is used both to denote an activity governed by certain rules, such as football, and a single instance of such activity as in, "We won the first game of the new season." In our analysis, we make a distinction between these two ideas and represent the former concept by a class Game and the latter by a class Match. One could argue against this by treating the class Game itself as an object and letting each instance be what we have termed a *match*.

Name	Description
Start Brickles	A player starts playing *Brickles* by starting the application program under *Windows*.
Pause Brickles	A player pauses a *Brickles* match by pressing the mouse button.
Resume Brickles	A player resumes a *Brickles* match by releasing the mouse button.
Stop Brickles	A player stops a *Brickles* match by selecting *Quit* from the *File* menu.
Move Paddle	A player moves the mouse left or right to move the paddle left or right.

Figure 2.11 Application-level use cases for *Brickles*

The first four use cases in Figure 2.11 are **extended** from the use cases in Figure 2.10. This structure helps to organize what can be a large number of cases. Locating a specific use case is accomplished by finding the high-level use case that covers the conceptual area of the specific case. The high-level use case then points to successively more specialized cases.

Behavior common between two use cases can be grouped into a single "functional" use case. Each of the original use cases now has a *uses* relation with the common use case. In *Brickles*, the use cases of *Breaking a Brick* and *Hitting a Wall* would each have a *uses* relation with the *Move Paddle* use case. This simplifies maintenance by encapsulating details of common behavior.

Use cases do not represent software. They represent *requirements* that software must meet. Consequently, you cannot test use cases; however, you can review them. Requirements play an important role in testing because they serve as the source of test cases—in particular, system requirements give rise to test cases for system testing. In Chapter 4 we will show how to start with use cases to test the analysis and design models that represent the system. The test cases identified for testing models can be refined for execution-based testing of a running system, as we describe in Chapter 8.

You can define one or more scenarios within the context of a use case. A **scenario** shows a particular application or instantiation of a use case. For example, the *Move Paddle* use case can give rise to scenarios:

■ Move the paddle left so that a collision with the puck, which is moving from left to right, involves the middle third of the paddle.

- Move the paddle left so that a collision with the puck, which is moving from left to right, involves the far third of the paddle.

- Move the paddle left so that a collision with the puck, which is moving from left to right, involves the near third of the paddle.

These scenarios involve objects that have values for relevant attributes, such as defining which third of the paddle hits a puck [see *Brickles* Physics on page 11] and which general direction the puck is moving. By contrast, use cases involve objects without regard for values of attributes.

Use cases are typically expressed using natural language, but use case diagrams can be used to depict all of a system's uses graphically. The diagram for the use cases in Figure 2.11 is shown in Figure 2.12.

Class Diagrams

A class diagram presents a static view of a set of classes and the relationships between the classes. The diagram can show operations and attributes for each class as well as constraints on relationships between objects. Figure 2.13 illustrates an analysis model for *Brickles* using UML.

You might expect to see a Mouse class in the diagram. We chose to omit it because the mouse is the mechanism by which a paddle can be moved. However, you could use any input pointing device, or even the arrow keys on a keyboard. We chose to make those considerations in design.

Within this design, Sprite, MovableSprite, and StationarySprite are abstract classes indicated in the diagram by italicized names. A sprite is a graphical

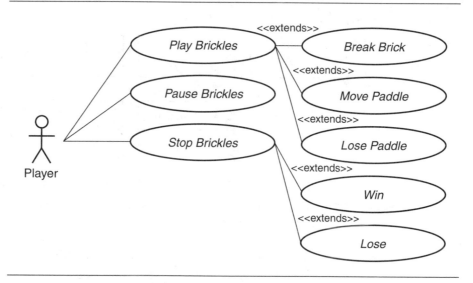

Figure 2.12 Use cases for *Brickles*

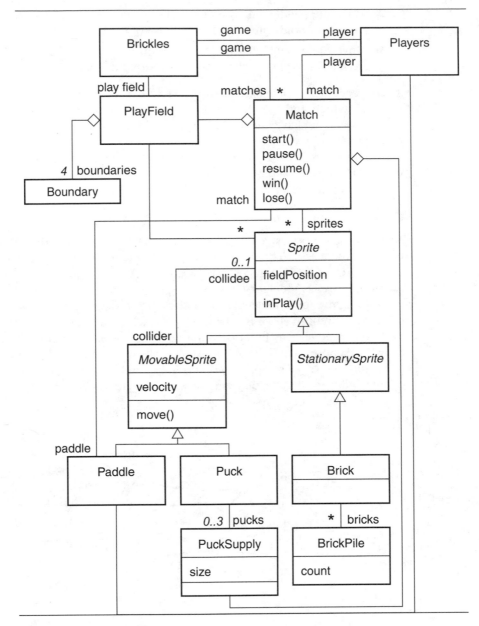

Figure 2.13 An application analysis class diagram for *Brickles*

component of an arcade game.[15] A movable sprite is a sprite that can move around in a play field while a stationary sprite cannot move. A movable sprite can interact with other sprites—for example, in *Brickles* a paddle hits a puck or a puck hits some bricks. These abstract classes originated from a domain analysis of arcade games and were incorporated into this model. When we started, we considered a possibility of implementing similar arcade games, so we took the time to identify abstractions. Even if we had not started with domain analysis, we likely would have noticed similar operations and attributes associated with pucks and paddles and bricks and ended up introducing these abstract classes anyway, even though we may not have used the term *sprite*, which is widely used by game implementers.

In practice, class diagrams can become quite large. Groups of classes can be represented as packages. Java has a direct package syntax while C++ uses a namespace syntax. Some people use UML package diagrams to identify packages and the dependencies among them. In Figure 2.14, the *Brickles* package diagram contains three packages. The domain classes are in the game.domain package so that they can easily be reused with another game in the future. The dashed arrow indicates that the *Brickles* specific-classes are dependent on the domain classes. The domain classes are also dependent on the container classes grouped into game.containers.

Diagrams such as class diagrams that describe classes, their features, and relationships play a central role in modeling. They reflect the structure of software and are a central focus of model testing (see Chapter 4). Testing associations can be challenging, especially in the presence of polymorphism, as in the association in Figure 2.13 between PlayField and Sprite or MovableSprite and Sprite. The most challenging aspects of associations are the topic of Chapter 6.

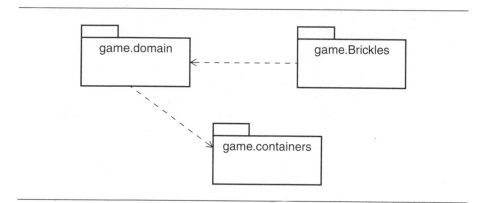

Figure 2.14 *Brickles* package diagram

---

15. The name dates to the Atari era of video games.

UML Class Diagrams—Elementary Components

A class box has three divisions. A specific diagram may not use all three if the resulting diagram is more clear. Abstract classes and operations are denoted by italics.

ClassName
data attributes
operation signatures

The connections between class boxes are relationships. There are three basic relationships, each represented by a different end on the line.

Concept	Symbol
Association—peer-to-peer visibility	1..n 1
Aggregation—one is a part of the other	◇
Inheritance—one definition used as the basis for the other.	▷

Numbers, letters, and symbols indicate the number of instances of each class that will be involved in the relationship. The previous association states that one instance of the class on the left end is related to one or more instances of the class on the right end. The visibility of attributes is indicated by a prefix:

Prefix	Visibility
+	*public*—Visible to all associated objects
#	*protected*—visible only to methods in classes related by inheritance
-	*private*—Visible only within the current class

State Diagrams

A **state diagram** describes the behavior of the objects in a class in terms of its observable states and how an object changes states as a result of events that affect the object. Two sample diagrams are shown in Figure 2.19. A **state** is a particular configuration of the values of data attributes. What is observable about the state is a difference in behavior from one state to another. That is, if the same message is sent to the object twice, it may behave differently depending on the state of the object when the message is received. A **transition**, or change, from one state to another is triggered by an **event,** which is typically a message arrival. A **guard** is a condition that must hold before the transition can be made. Guards are useful for representing transitions to various states based on a single event. An **action** specifies processing to be done while a transition is in progress. Each state may specify an **activity** to perform while an object is in that state.

A Puck instance is either *in play* or *not in play.* If an instance is in play, then it is either *moving* or *not moving.* The observable state In Play of a puck has substates of Moving and Not Moving. In Play is a **superstate**; Moving and Not Moving are its **substates.** A substate inherits all the transitions entering and leaving its superstate.

A **concurrent state diagram** can show groups of states that reflect the behavior of an object from the perspective of two or more independent ways. We will discuss the concurrent states in the Java implementation of *Brickles* later. Such diagrams can be treated from a testing perspective as a nonconcurrent state diagram by first defining states that are defined from all the combinations of the states from the various concurrent parts, and then defining the appropriate transitions.

Class Specifications

Class diagrams define classes and show attributes and operations associated with their instances. State diagrams illustrate the behavior of an instance of a class. However, neither diagram details the semantics associated with each operation. We use the Object Constraint Language (OCL) [WK99] for such specifications. OCL constraints are expressed in the context of a class diagram. Constraints involve attributes, operations, and associations that are defined in the diagram.

As illustrated in the example shown in Figure 2.15, OCL expresses semantics of operations in terms of preconditions and post conditions. Invariant conditions can be prescribed for a class or interface and must hold at the time any operation is requested both in a message and upon the completion of the processing of the requested operation. (A method for an operation is allowed to temporarily violate an invariant during execution.) OCL conditions are Boolean-valued expressions and are tied to a class diagram. The constraints in Figure 2.15 use the size attribute of a puck supply and the zero-to-three navigable association of pucks shown in the design class diagram (see Figure 2.18). The pucks-> symbol in the constraint for the get() operation means to follow the pucks link to the set of associated objects. The use of the size attribute in a

State Diagrams—A UML Summary

In a state diagram, a state is represented by an oval and a transition as an arc from one state to another. Each arc has a label with three parts, each of which is optional:

event [guard] / action

Concept	Symbol
State—configuration of data values	
Transition—permitted next state	
Substate/superstate	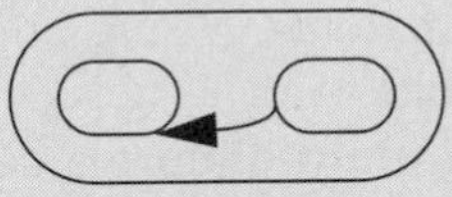
Concurrent states	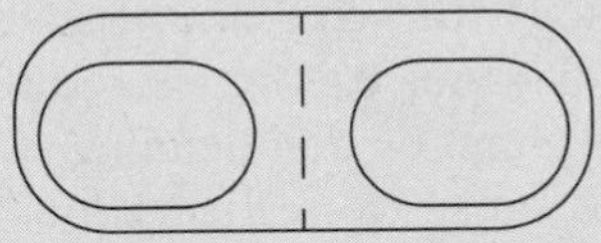

```
PuckSupply
      size >= 0 AND size <= 3

PuckSupply::PuckSupply()
pre:      - none
post:     size = 3 AND pucks->forAll( puck: Puck | not puck.inPlay() )

PuckSupply::~PuckSupply()
pre:      - none
post:     Puck->size() = Puck@pre->size() - size@pre

void PuckSupply::size() const
pre:      - none
post:     result = size

Puck * PuckSupply::get()
pre:      count > 0
post:     result = pucks->asSequence->first AND size = size@pre - 1
```

Figure 2.15 OCL for the operations of PuckSupply

constraint in no way requires the implementation of the class to use a variable named size. It just means that the implementation will in some way need to represent that attribute, either as a variable or as an algorithm that computes the value based on other attributes. Specifications for operations should rarely ever prescribe an implementation. The syntax of OCL is too detailed for a summary box (see [WK99] for the language details).

You might prefer a more informal notation, such as the one in Figure 2.5. Some sort of good specification for each operation is needed for testing. If the developers have not generated such specifications, then we think testers should take the task upon themselves. It is virtually impossible to test code whose purpose is vague or ambiguous. It is virtually impossible to use code whose purpose is vague or ambiguous. Thus, not only will the existence of such specifications make testing easier, but their existence will improve the quality of the software and perhaps even promote the subsequent reuse of classes.

Sequence Diagrams

An algorithm can be described as an interaction among objects. A **sequence diagram** captures the messaging between objects, object creation, and replies from messages.[16] In analysis, sequence diagrams illustrate process in the domain—how common tasks are usually carried out through the interaction of various objects in a scenario. A sample sequence diagram is shown in Figure 2.16. Within a sequence diagram, an object is represented by a box and its lifeline is represented by a dashed line that extends downward. The passing of time is reflected down the page. Objects drawn at the top of the diagram exist at the start of processing. Objects drawn farther down are created at that point. A message is represented by an arrow with a filled-in arrowhead. A reply value is represented by an arrow with an open arrowhead. A widening of a lifeline reflects an activation in which one of the object's operations is involved in the current sequence.

A sequence diagram may be created at any level of abstraction. A scenario for a use case can be represented by a sequence diagram. The algorithm for a single method in a class may also be represented using this notation. Figure 2.16 shows a sequence diagram for winning a match in *Brickles*.

Sequence diagrams can also represent concurrency. An asynchronous message is indicated by a half arrowhead (→). Asynchronous messages can be used to create a new object, create a new thread, or communicate with a running thread.

---

16. UML defines collaboration diagrams, which convey similar information but emphasize structure of associations over sequence. We use sequence diagrams in this book, but collaboration diagrams are useful, especially when you want to show the relationships among objects explicitly.

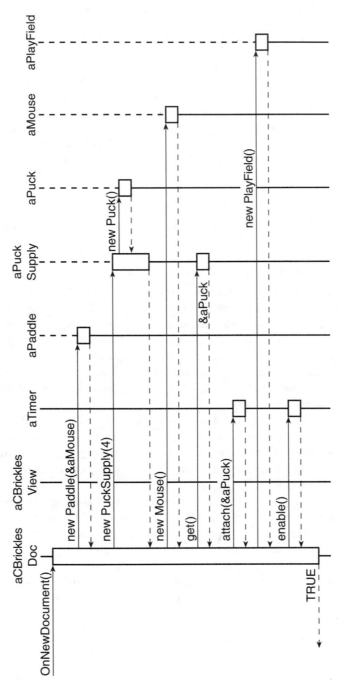

Figure 2.16 A sequence diagram for *Brickles*

Tip

Define accessor operations that provide the observable state of a receiver.

The OCL specification in Figure 2.15 conveys the same state information as the diagram for PuckSupply below. The OCL specification is more complete, but the state diagram is easier to understand for most people.

Some of the preconditions for operators are implicit in the state diagram, while state definitions are implicit in the OCL specification. For example, within the context of the state diagram, the get() operation is permitted only when a puck supply object is in a Not Empty state since no transition from the Empty state is labeled with a get() event. This precondition is expressed in the OCL specification as a constraint on the count attribute associated with a Puck-Supply, with no mention of a Not Empty state.

We prefer to design classes so that states are represented explicitly in a class's interface. This makes the specification more intuitive, thereby making the checking of preconditions by senders a little easier and more reliable, thus making testing a little easier. For PuckSupply, we would add the Boolean-valued query operation isEmpty() to the interface and express preconditions in terms of this state-querying operation. A revised OCL specification for PuckSupply is

```
PuckSupply
-    count >= 0

PuckSupply::PuckSupply();
pre:    -- none
post:   count = 3 AND pucks->asSet->size = 3 AND
            pucks->forAll( puck: Puck |not puck.inPlay()

PuckSupply::~PuckSupply();
pre:    -- none
post:   pucks@pre->isEmpty

void PuckSupply::size() const;
pre:    --none
post:   result = count

bool PuckSupply::isEmpty() const;
pre:    -- none
post:   result = ( count = 0 )

Puck * PuckSupply::get();
pre:    not self.isEmpty()
post:   result = pucks->asSequence->first AND
            count = count@pre - 1
```

Of course, the state diagram must be updated to reflect the new operation.

Accessor operations that return state information make testing a little easier (see Chapter 5) and can also make checking preconditions possible. The inclusion of such operations in a class interface is an example of *designing for testing*.

Sequence Diagrams in Testing

Sequence diagrams and collaboration diagrams are useful in analysis and especially in design. We use them quite extensively in testing models to capture results of test case "execution." The diagram reflects the objects and their states for a test case input and shows the sequence of messages that produce a correct output.

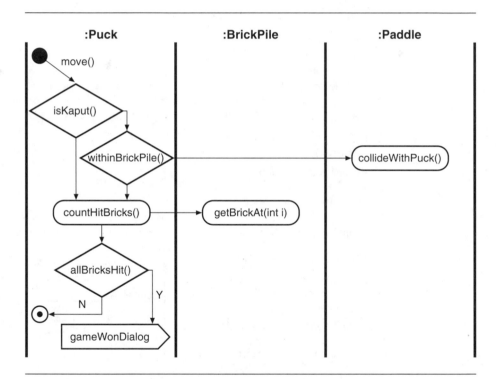

Figure 2.17 Activity diagram for the move() method in Puck

Activity Diagrams

Sequence diagrams capture single traces through a set of object interactions. It is difficult if not impossible to represent iteration and concurrency. The activity diagram provides a more comprehensive representation that uses a combination of flowchart and petri net notations. The activity diagram in Figure 2.17 is from the move() method in Puck.

Activity Diagrams—A UML Summary

In an activity diagram, the vertical lines form **swim lanes**. Each lane is the space for the object named at the top of the lane. In this case, each object is anonymous as indicated by the colon in front of the class name. The horizontal bar is a synchronization point at which two threads must meet. The signal throw and catch boxes show `try` and `catch` exceptions. The diamond box is a decision in the code.

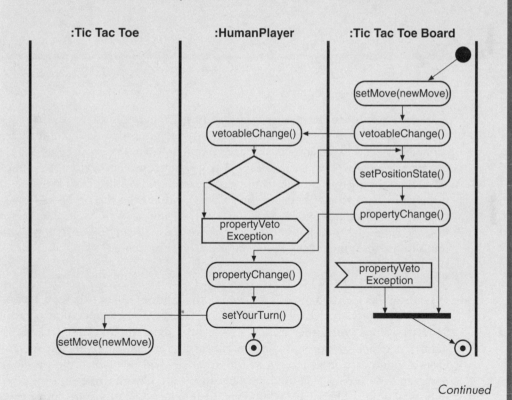

Continued

Concept	Symbol	Concept	Symbol
Decision box	◇ Condition	Signal throw	propertyVeto Exception
Processing	(propertyChange())	Signal catch	propertyVeto Exception
Synchroniza-tion point	▬▬▬	Initiation of thread	●
Termination of thread	⊙		

Design Models

A **design model** represents *how* the software meets requirements. A major strength of the object-oriented development paradigm is that design models are refinements and extensions of the analysis models. That is good news from a testing perspective because it means that we can reuse and extend test cases developed for analysis models. Many of the same kinds of diagrams are used in design, but with an emphasis on the *solution* rather than the *problem*. Consequently, the diagrams reflect solution-level objects as well as problem-level objects. Since the notation is the same as we have already described, we will focus on the meaning of the design information represented.

Class Diagrams

Class diagrams are used in design to depict the kinds of objects that will be created by the software. Each class has a name, attributes, and operations as well as relationships with other classes shown on a diagram. In a design-class diagram, we expect to see most of the classes and relationships in the analysis class diagram as well as classes whose instances will help solve the problem. Some analysis classes will disappear because they have no role in a solution. Others will most likely have additional attributes and relationships introduced for them with solution-level classes and objects. The crux of good object-oriented design is reflected in a class diagram that maintains most of the structure of the problem (as reflected in the analysis class diagram), and then augments the software versions of the objects in the problem to collaborate to bring about a solution.

A class diagram for the design of *Brickles* is shown in Figure 2.18. Note the introduction of implementation-level classes such as Mouse, which represents a mouse attached to the computer, and Hint, which represents an object needed to track events during an execution that results in a need to repair the contents of the screen. This diagram also shows some of the classes in the Microsoft Foundation Classes (MFC) [MFC], such as CMainFrame, CView, and CDocument, which invoke *Brickles* in a *Windows* environment as set forth in the requirements. The open arrowheads on some of the associations indicate **navigability**—that is, the directions in which associations are actually to be implemented. An association can be bidirectional or unidirectional. Arrows indicate which objects know about a certain relationship. We seldom indicate navigability in an analysis class diagram, but find them most useful in design class diagrams. In sequence diagrams, messaging between objects can occur only in the direction of a navigable association.

State Diagrams

The state diagrams used in design are the same as those in analysis. The major difference would be state diagrams for new classes in the design class diagram and, potentially, new substates that might aid implementation. Design diagrams might also incorporate more actions associated with transitions and more activities associated with states. In *Brickles*, some mechanism is needed to control the movement of the puck and the paddle. We chose to use timer events provided by *Windows* with MFC to make the execution independent of the processor speed. Consequently, we introduced a design class, Timer (see Figure 2.18), which processes timer events and manipulates appropriate sprites in a match. A state diagram for the class Timer is shown in Figure 2.19. A timer maintains a list of observers—that is, the objects interested in being notified each time a timer event arrives. When a timer is enabled, it notifies each of its attached observers that a timer event has occurred with a notify() message. TimerObserver is an abstract class (see Figure 2.18) that represents observers. Inclusion polymorphism allows an instance of any subclass of TimerObserver to be attached and, hence, notified. This part of the implementation is based on the *Observer* design pattern [GHJV94].

From a testing perspective, we will want to ensure the test cases for a class that adequately tests transitions between states and provides for the proper processing of messages within each state. We might also want to check that the *Observer* pattern is correctly incorporated into the design of Timer and TimerObserver. It might even be possible to reuse some test cases and test drivers that were developed for testing other classes whose design is based on the same pattern.

Sequence Diagrams

Sequence diagrams are used in design to describe algorithms—that is, what objects are involved in the processing of some aspect of the solution and how those objects interact to affect that processing. The main distinction from their use in analysis is the presence of solution-level objects in the design diagrams. A sequence diagram for the start-up processing associated with *Brickles* is shown in Figure 2.20. This represents an algorithm for creating the objects needed to

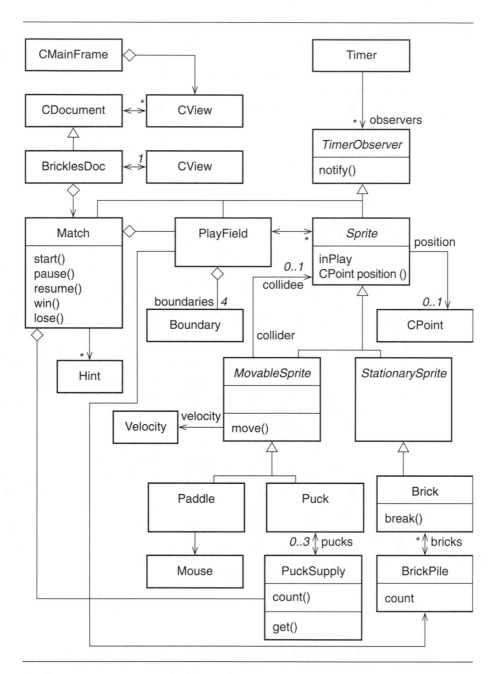

Figure 2.18 A design class diagram for *Brickles*

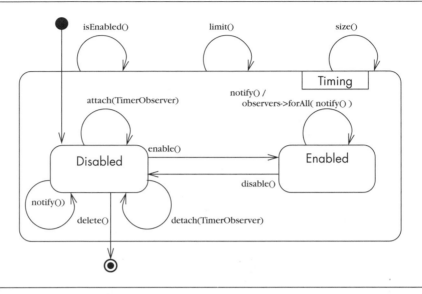

Figure 2.19 A state diagram for the class Timer

get a match underway. From a testing perspective, possible errors include violation of contracts, failure to create objects of the correct class, and sending of messages for which no navigability is indicated between sender and receiver on the class diagram.

Source Code

Source code and source code documentation are the final representations of the software. A translator (a compiler or interpreter) makes source code executable.

The source code is expected to be an accurate translation of the detailed design models into a programming language, although we certainly must test for that. For object-oriented systems, the code contains class definitions and a segment that creates instances of some class(es) and gets processing started—for example, the main() function in C++ or a static method main() in Java. Each class uses instances of other classes to provide parts of its implementation. These instances, along with the parameters to messages, make up most of the relationships among objects.

Testing actual code has been the principal concern of most traditional testing efforts and is the focus of most chapters in this book. Source code can be

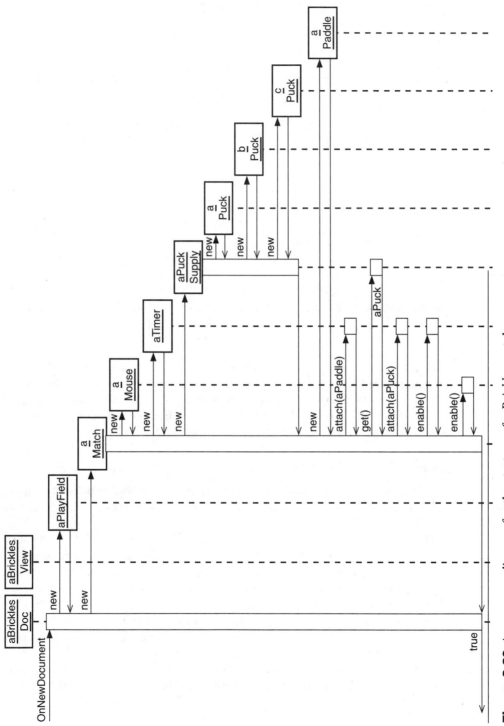

Figure 2.20 A sequence diagram for the start-up of a *Brickles* match

Does programming language affect testing?

The programming language used for implementation will impact testing. Some languages will enable certain kinds of errors and eliminate other kinds. For example, C++ is strongly typed and can reduce the number of interface errors that might occur since a C++ compiler will ensure type conformity between actual and formal parameters. Java has strong typing, but is more dynamic than C++ so compilers are less effective at catching problems involving reflective code, for example. Smalltalk is not strongly typed, so more effort will be needed to ensure that a design and an implementation do not harbor interface errors—namely, the wrong types of actual parameters. On the other hand, C++—in the tradition of C—harbors the potential for a program to contain errors involving pointers—for example, dangling references and garbage. Languages such as Smalltalk and Java, which use garbage collection, eliminate these pointer errors.

C++ supports *friends* that allow data hiding to be circumvented by certain parts of a program. Executable test code could be declared a friend of a class under test, thereby allowing the test code to access the implementation and potentially make the test code shorter, although this can create a problem because testing becomes tightly coupled with the implementation.

Java supports interfaces. Do they need to be tested? Assuming a class implements an interface, then testing should be done to adequately ensure that the full semantics of each of the interface's operations are supported by the class. Testers will have to know whether the interface requires exact semantics or whether a class can meet its obligations if it weakens preconditions and/or strengthens postconditions. Remember, class invariants are implied pre- and postconditions (see Subclassing and Subtyping, on page 37).

tested as it is developed, component by component, or as a completed product at the end of development. The major issues to be addressed are:

■ Who tests. Testing can be done by developers, who adopt a testing perspective toward their own code. Each test suite must be reviewed by someone for completeness and adequacy.

■ What is tested. Each class can be tested separately before it is used in parts of a system. However, some classes are so complex in their implementations that constructing test drivers for testing them outside the system context is very expensive.

- When testing is done. Testing can be done at many times during development. Earlier is usually better, but testing in the presence of changing specifications could prove inefficient and even demoralizing. Early testing could increase the amount of regression testing needed, which consumes resources. In Chapter 4 we consider how to test analysis and design models before code is available.

- How testing is done. In Chapter 1, we reviewed function-based and specification-based testing. Both approaches need to be applied to test well.

- How much testing is done. Exhaustive testing of each software component and of a whole system is seldom practical or possible. Conditions of adequate testing must be determined and then applied. Adequacy is often based on code coverage or specification coverage.

These will be addressed in detail in association with planning for testing in Chapter 3.

We note that some CASE tools—for example, Rational Rose—can generate code from design models. What is the impact on testing?

Assuming the code-generation facilities of the tool work correctly, we see two major impacts:

1. Most testing is required within the context of the design model.

2. Applying an implementation-based approach, perhaps in connection with determining the adequacy of testing, requires that a tester understand the structure of the code produced. Code-profiling tools can help, but someone still must be able to read the generated code.

If programmers are allowed to manually change generated source code, then testing—and maintenance—becomes harder.

Summary

We have reviewed the basic concepts of object-oriented programming. We have examined some of the kinds of documentation that is produced during development and that plays a role in testing. We have considered these things from a testing perspective—that is, in terms of what failures would likely result from the use of various object-oriented programming concepts.

In the next chapter we will examine the testing process.

Exercises

2-1. Identify some object-oriented software that you can use to try the various techniques and issues we have discussed. Ideally the software will comprise a complete application, but you could select a few classes that work together. Collect analysis and design documents that relate to the software. If specifications exist for each class, then make sure they are well written—that is, that they contain complete and unambiguous descriptions of every operation. If specifications do not already exist, create them. We recommend using OCL (see [WK99] for a description).

2-2. Review the various diagrams in this chapter for *Brickles* and make sure you understand them.

2-3. Think about how you would approach testing the class PuckSupply as specified in this chapter. Does testing this class depend on the correctness of the class Puck? Would Puck have to be tested first?

Planning for Testing

☞ Want to plan a test process that complements your development process? See A Testing Process on page 78.

☞ Want to analyze the risks associated with verifying the required functionality? See Risk Analysis—A Tool for Testing on page 74.

☞ Need to develop test plans for the different levels and types of testing required for the comprehensive test process? See Planning Activities on page 91.

Chapter **3**

Testing requires considerable resources. Effective utilization of those resources requires good planning and good management. In this chapter we will focus on the technical aspects of planning and scheduling testing activities. We will look at determining what must be done on a technical level, who can do it, and when it should be done. We will suggest ways of constructing estimates, but we will not consider scheduling details.

Planning at the technical level is guided by templates that are "instantiated" as needed by developers. We will describe a hierarchy of test plans and relate them to standard templates using the IEEE test plan standard as an example. We will also discuss the incorporation of risk analysis into the test planning process.

Our basic testing process can be summed up as follows: *Test early, test often, test enough.* We will define a more detailed process in which there is a testing step for each development step. (*Analyze. Test. Design. Test. Code. Test.*) We will also explain a generic set of steps in which we define the basic tasks that are carried out at each of these development steps. We will also discuss testing from a management/allocation of resources perspective, describe the different dimensions of testing, and relate how we balance the trade-offs along these dimensions.

A Development Process Overview

A **process** is a continuous series of activities that convey you to an end. Most software engineering textbooks and software developers list four main activities in a software development process (subsequent to the completion of systems engineering and prior to the first deployment):

- **analysis**—which focuses on understanding the problem and defining the requirements for the software portions of a system
- **design**—which focuses on solving the problem in software
- **implementation**—which focuses on translating the design into executable code
- **testing**—which focuses on ensuring that inputs produce the desired results as specified by the requirements

Maintenance begins after deployment with a focus on bug repairs and enhancements. Maintenance usually involves further analysis, design, implementation, and testing. Among the testing activities during maintenance is regression testing, which ensures that successful test results after changes are the same as those before changes.

These activities can be refined into more specific tasks. Analysis sometimes is decomposed into **domain analysis**, whose focus is in understanding the problem in a more general context, and **application analysis**, whose focus is in understanding the specific problem to be solved in design. Design encompasses architectural design, subsystem and package design, class design, and algorithm design. Implementation includes class implementation and integration. Testing includes checking the basic units, integrated units, subsystems, and systems.

Many software development projects follow an evolutionary process model—an incremental model, a spiral model, or concurrent engineering. We will focus on an incremental process model.

Under an incremental development process, a system is developed as a sequence of increments. An **increment** is a deliverable, including models, documentation, and code, which provides some of the functionality required for the system. The products developed in one increment feed into the development of the next increment. Successive increments add (and sometimes change) system functionality. The final increment delivers a deployable system that meets all requirements. Increments can be developed in sequence or one or more can be developed concurrently.

To build each increment, developers analyze, design, code, and test as needed. They typically have to perform these activities repeatedly in building an increment because they find errors in previous work. As development progresses, they gain new insights into the problem and the solution. We prefer to acknowledge this iterative aspect of incremental development and make it part of the process. We refer to this as an **incremental, iterative process**. In planning each increment, we include explicit steps for repeating various activities. Among these are steps for systematically reviewing current models, identifying errors based on experiences in later tasks, and modifying the models (or code) that have already been produced—not just those that will be produced in the future. Figure 3.1 illustrates the process when the increments are planned sequentially.

Object-oriented development is particularly well suited to evolutionary development because object-oriented analysis, design, and implementation entail the successive refinement of a single model. This is the case both within an increment and among increments. In object-oriented analysis, we understand a problem by modeling it in terms of objects and classes of objects, their relationships and responsibilities. In object-oriented design, we solve the problem by manipulating those same objects and relationships identified in analysis and introducing solution-specific classes, objects, relationships, and responsibilities. Implementation is straightforward from a well-specified set of design

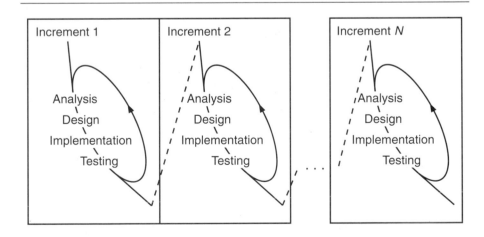

Figure 3.1 A simplified sequential, incremental, iterative development process

products. Thus, the entire development process involves a refinement of a model. Design products are primarily an extension of analysis products and implementation products are coded expressions of design products. The products of one increment are extended and refined in the next increment. This is also a strength of the paradigm with respect to testing because we can utilize refinements of the same test cases in testing refined models.

The incremental development of products requires the incremental testing of those products. Products can change from increment to increment in both planned and unplanned ways. Test suites must change in concert. Regression tests must be run between increments and within iterations to ensure that changes do not adversely affect correctly working code. A process in which work on one increment overlaps work on another adds to the complexity of development and testing. Coordination is required to sequence the development of interacting increments so that objects that are associated with, but assigned to different increments, can be tested in a timely fashion.

The development of *Brickles* followed a plan based on an incremental, iterative development process. Our initial plan is outlined in Figure 3.2. When we started, we understood the requirements quite well, but we had no experience developing applications with the Microsoft Foundation Classes (MFC), nor did we have any experience developing arcade games. We recognized those as the biggest risks to success and planned to address those issues first. We also planned to test as much as we could as work progressed, which means we tested products within and/or at the end of each iteration. This is not shown in the figure.

There were significantly more informal iterations than those listed in Figure 3.2. This was particularly true during design, where we found that a number of decisions about scope and behavior had not been made during analysis.

A Testing Process Overview

Testing is usually listed last as an activity in virtually every software development process after *implementation*. This activity refers to the type of testing that attempts to determine whether the product as a whole functions as it should. From our view, testing is a type of activity that is applied at various

Increment	Iteration
1. Present user interface showing puck bouncing in window.	1.A. Domain Analysis: Construct class diagram.
	1.B. Application Analysis: Construct class diagram and state diagrams.
	1.C. Design: Study MFC and animation.
	1.D. Implement: Code Hello World using MFC. Include Quit on File menu.
	2.A. Design: Complete class diagram for puck bouncing in window.
	2.B. Implementation: Code puck bouncing in window.
2. Move paddle in window and detect collisions.	1.A. Application Analysis: Add details of paddle control and collisions to class diagram, other diagrams.
	1.B. Design: Design Paddle and Collision classes.
	1.C. Implementation: Code paddle class incrementally from MovableSprite and collision class from Exception.
3. Display brick pile and detect collisions.	1.A. Application Analysis: Add collections of sprites to class diagram.
	1.B. Design: Design collision detection algorithm.
	1.C Implementation: Code Brickpile class by aggregating collection class.
4. Add supply of pucks and detect end of match.	1.A. Design: End of match algorithm to use exceptions to detect endOfMatch.
	1.B. Implementation: PuckSupply class.

Figure 3.2 Outline of our incremental, iterative development plan for *Brickles*.

points during development, not just at the end and not just to code. We define a process separate from, but intimately related to, the development process because the goal of testing is really different from the goal of development. Consequently, we prefer to consider development and testing as two separate, but intimately connected, processes.

Development and testing processes are distinct primarily because they have different goals and different measures of success. Development strives to build a product that meets a need. Testing strives to answer questions about the product, including whether the product meets the need that it is intended to meet. Consider, for example, the number of defects identified after testing some developed software. The lower the defect rate (ratio of test cases that fail to the total number used), the more successful the development is considered to be. On the other hand, the higher the defect rate, the more successful the testing is considered to be.

The roles of developing and testing functionality are assigned to different people, thereby reinforcing the idea that the processes are distinct. Using different people for development and testing activities is particularly productive from a system test perspective. The testers write test cases independently from those who will develop the code to ensure that the resulting system does what the requirements actually intend rather than what the developers interpreted the requirements to mean.

The same is true at all levels of testing. In most shops developers are responsible for some testing—such as, what has been traditionally called *unit and integration testing*. However, to be successful, any person who takes on the role of both developer and tester must ensure that the proper goal is pursued with equal vigor. To achieve this, we use buddy testing in which one developer is assigned to unit test the code of another developer. In this way, at least a developer is responsible for one goal and one set of functionality, and the other is responsible for another goal and another set of functionality.

Even though the two processes are distinct, they are intimately related. Their activities even overlap when test cases have to be designed, coded, and executed. Together they encompass the activities necessary to produce a useful product. Defects can be introduced during each phase of the development process. Consequently, each development activity has an associated testing activity. The relationship between the two processes is such that when something is developed, it is tested using products of the testing process to determine that it appropriately meets a set of requirements.

The testing and development processes are in a feedback loop (see Figure 3.3). The testing process feeds identified failures back into the development process.[1] Failure reports provide a set of symptoms that a developer uses to identify the exact location of a fault or error. The development process feeds new and revised designs and implementations into the testing process. Testing of development products will help identify defective test cases when testers determine that "failures" result from problems with test cases themselves or the drivers that execute them, and not the software under test.[2]

---

1. The purpose of testing is to identify failures and not to identify the error or the fault that gave rise to a failure. The developers are responsible for finding the source of a failure.

2. An interesting aspect of test case development is determining who checks the test cases. Most cases are reviewed, but most processes involve very little formal testing of test cases.

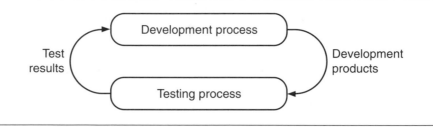

Figure 3.3 The testing and development processes form a feedback loop

In the context of this feedback loop, the form and content of development products affect the testing process. When developers select methods and tools, they establish constraints on the testing process. Consider, for example, how the degree of formality of class specifications affects the ease with which test cases can be identified for testing a class. The testing perspective must be considered, preferably by the presence of professional testers, when development methods and tools are selected.

Testability

One of the pieces of information that is fed back to the developers is an evaluation of how amenable the software is to being tested. Testability is related to how easily you can evaluate the results of the tests. In Chapter 7 we will show how our testing architecture, PACT, improves testability by overcoming information hiding. Testability is also an appropriate context to examine the question about when to test. As layers of software are added on top of layers, the visibility to the stored values becomes more cloudy. The lower the level at which a piece is tested, the more easily visible are its internals for the verification of test results and, by definition, the more testable it is.

The form and quality of a requirements specification also affects the process. Product requirements comprise the source of test cases in system and acceptance testing. System testers should participate in the gathering and validation of the requirements in order to have a sufficient understanding of them to assess risks and testability.

Test Cases and Test Suites

The basic component of testing is a test case. In its most general form, a **test case** is a pair *(input, expected result)*, in which *input* is a description of an input to the software under test and *expected result* is a description of the output that the software should exhibit for the associated input. Inputs and expected results are not necessarily simple data values, such as strings or integer values, but they can be arbitrarily complex. Inputs often incorporate system state information as well as user commands and data values to be processed. *Expected result* includes not only perceivable things, such as printed reports, audible sounds, or changes in a display screen, but changes to the software system itself—for example, an update to a database or a change in a system state that affects processing of subsequent inputs. A **test case execution** is a running of the software that provides the inputs specified in the test case and observes the results and compares them to those specified by the test case. If the actual result varies from the expected result, then a failure has been detected and we say the software under test "fails the test case." If the actual result is the expected result for a test case, then we say the software "passes the test case."

Test cases are organized into a **test suite**. Most test suites have some sort of organization based on the kinds of test cases. For example, a test suite might have one part containing test cases that are concerned with testing system capacities and another part containing test cases concerned with testing typical uses of the system well within any specified capacities. If software passes all the test cases in a test suite, then we say that the software "passes the test suite."

One of the greatest challenges in testing is developing and organizing a test suite. The main issues in test suite development are correctness, observability of results, and adequacy.

The STEP testing technique developed by William Hetzel [Hetz84] provides a three-step approach for each type of testing performed on a project.

1. *Analysis*—The product to be tested is examined to identify any special features that must receive particular attention and to determine the test cases that should be constructed. We will present a number of analysis techniques. Some can be automated, such as branch testing, but many require the tester to manually determine what to test.

2. *Construction*—In this phase the artifacts that are needed for testing are created. The test cases identified during analysis are translated into programming languages and scripting languages, or they are entered in a tool-specific language. There is also often the need for data sets, which may require an extensive effort to build a sufficiently large set.

3. *Execution and Evaluation*—This is the most visible and often the only recognized part of the test effort; however, it is also typically the quickest part of the test effort. The test cases that were identified during analysis and then constructed are executed. The results are examined to determine whether the software passed the test suite or failed it. Often many of these activities can be automated. This is particularly useful in an iterative environment since the same tests will be applied repeatedly over time.

Test suites are maintained. As requirements change, so must the test suite. You must correct test cases that are found to be in error. As problems are found by users, test cases will be added to catch those problems in future releases before deployment.

A testing process is iterative and incremental and must be planned in connection with the planning of its associated development.

What do testers want developers to specify about the system?

The template for the use case that we have presented provides most of the information that a person needs to develop system-level tests. In particular the pre- and postconditions are important in terms of sequencing tests and communicating information about hidden dependencies. A structured use case model can assist the person writing the tests with information about the possible reuse of test scripts and data. A series of state models related to subsystems and the system itself also helps communicate information about sequencing of actions and expected responses.

When are testers needed on a project?

The culture in some companies specifies that testing personnel are not assigned to a project until it is well underway. The linkages described here between the development and testing processes are evidence that early project decisions require input from personnel who are knowledgeable about testing. This may be one of the testers who is assigned to the project very early, or a developer with testing experience.

Risk Analysis—A Tool for Testing

Risk analysis is a part of planning any development effort. It also can be critical in determining what to test in development and how much. In this section we will describe some basic concepts in risk analysis. Then we will apply those concepts to testing. We will also compare using risk-based testing to basing test case selection on the functionality's frequency of use.

Risks

In general, a *risk* is anything that threatens the successful achievement of a project's goals. Specifically, a risk is an event that has some probability of happening and, if it occurs, there will be some loss. The loss may be down time, financial loss, or even injury depending on the type of system. Every project has a set of risks; some risks are rated "higher" than others. This ordering takes into account both the likelihood the loss will occur and how serious the loss will be in terms of its impact. In the context of risk-based testing, a fundamental principle is to *test most heavily those portions of the system that pose the highest risk to the project to ensure that the most harmful faults are identified.*

Risks are divided into three general types: *project, business,* and *technical* risks.

Project risks include managerial and environmental risks (such as an insufficient supply of qualified personnel) that cannot directly be affected by the testing process.

Business risks are associated with domain-related concepts. For example, changes in IRS reporting regulations would be a risk to the stability of the requirements for an accounting system because the system's functionality must be altered to comply with new regulations. This type of risk is related to the functionality of the program and therefore to system-level testing. When a system under test addresses a volatile domain, the system test suite should investigate the extensibility and modifiability attributes of the system's architecture.

Technical risks include some implementation concepts. For example, the quality of code generated by the compiler or the stability of software components is a technical risk. This type of risk is related to the implementation of the program and hence is associated primarily with testing at the code level.

Risk Analysis

Risk analysis is a procedure for identifying risks and for identifying ways to prevent potential problems from becoming real. The output of risk analysis is a list of identified risks in the order of the level of risk that can be used to allocate limited resources and to prioritize decisions. The definition of risk varies from one project to another and even over time within the same project because priorities and development strategies change. Typical risks on object-oriented projects are specific and unique to the architectural features, the areas of complex interactions among objects, the complex behaviors associated with a class specification, and the changing or evolving project requirements. A class being developed for inclusion in a library needs much more testing than one that's being developed for use in a prototype. Other definitions of risk might be the complexity of the class as measured by the size of its specification, or the number of relationships it has with other classes.

Sources of Risk

For system testing, the various uses of the system are prioritized based on the importance to the user and the proper operation of the system. Risk may also be evaluated based on the complexities of the concepts that must be implemented in different subsystems, the volatility of the requirements in a particular subsystem, or the maturity of domain knowledge within a particular subsystem.

Risks are also associated with the programming language and development tools that are being used to implement the software. Programming languages permit certain classes of errors and inhibit others—for example, the strong typing in C++ and Java ensures that every message sent (member function called) in a program execution can be understood by its receiver. By contrast, the lack of strong typing in Smalltalk means "message not understood" exceptions can occur during program execution. Strong typing can make identifying test cases much easier because some kinds of inputs are eliminated as possibilities by the programming language itself.

Conducting the Analysis

Our approach to risk analysis identifies the risk that each use case poses to the successful completion of the project. Other definitions are possible for risk, but this definition fits our purpose of planning a testing effort.

The risk analysis technique includes three tasks:

1. Identify the risk(s) each use case poses to the development effort.
2. Quantify the risk.
3. Produce a ranked list of use cases.

The use case writer can assign a risk rating to an individual use case by considering how the risks identified at the project level apply to the specific use case. For example, those requirements that are rated most likely to change are high risks; those requirements that are outside the expertise of the development team are even higher risks; and those requirements that rely on new technology such as hardware being developed in parallel to the software are high risks as well. In fact it is usually harder to find low-risk use cases than high-risk ones.

The exact set of values used in the ranking scale can vary from one project to another. It should have sufficient levels to separate the use cases into reasonably sized groupings, but it should not have so many categories so that some categories have no members. We usually start with three rankings: *low*, *medium*, *high*. In a project with 100 use cases, this might result in approximately 40 in the *high* category. This is probably more than we have time to give special attention. Adding a *very high* category and reclassifying the uses might result in 25 *high* and 15 *very high* cases. Those fifteen will receive the most intense examination.

The assigned risks result in an ordering of the use cases. The ordering is used for a couple of project activities. First, managers can use it to assign use cases to increments (not our problem!). Second, the ordering can be used to determine the amount of testing applied to each item. Risk-based testing is used when the risks are very high, such as in life-critical systems. In our examples in the text, we will consider both risk-based and use profile approaches to test case selection.

Let us consider a couple of examples. First, we will apply risk analysis to the *Brickles* game. Since this is a very simple system, we will then present a more illustrative example.

For a game such as *Brickles*, the biggest risks are things that affect the player's satisfaction. In Figure 3.4, the analysis information for the two basic use cases is summarized. The "winning the game" use case is rated as more critical than the "losing the game" use case. Imagine winning the game but the software refuses to acknowledge it! The frequency of winning is rated as lower than the frequency of losing. There are $n!$ sequences in which the bricks can be broken, in which n is the number of bricks in the pile. There are many more sequences when the variability of wall and ceiling bounces are included. There are $(n-1)+(n-2)+...+2+1$ ways to lose the game with a given puck, but there are many more possibilities when misses are considered. There are many more ways to lose than ways to win. Since winning and losing are accomplished by the same code, there is the same amount of risk in implementing each use case so the risk is rated the same. If we combine the frequency and criticality values using the scheme shown in Technique Summary—Creating Test Cases from Use Cases, on page 127, the two uses are both rated as *medium*. The program should be tested with roughly the same number of winning results as losing.

Consider another example for an application in which personnel records are being modified, saved, and possibly deleted. The use cases are summarized in

Use	Risk Level	Frequency	Criticality	Scenario
Wins	Medium	Low	High	Player wins game
Loses	Medium	High	Low	Player loses game

Figure 3.4 Two *Brickles* use cases

Figure 3.5. The use cases address a record update that changes an employee's name, thereby committing that update and deleting a record. An analysis of the use cases identifies domain objects of name, personnel, and security.

The risk information indicates that deleting a record is a high risk. Being able to save is highly critical. The usual approach is to schedule high-risk uses for early delivery because then those uses can take longer than estimated without delaying the completion of the project. The criticality and frequency of uses are combined to determine which should be tested more heavily. Obviously we would want to test most of the uses that are the most critical and frequent. But sometimes a critical operation is not very frequent in comparison to other uses. For example, logging on to your Internet Service Provider is critical, but it is only done once per session whereas you might check e-mail many times during a single login. So the values of the frequency and criticality attributes are combined to determine the relative amount of testing.

The technique for combining these values varies from one project to another, but there are a couple of general strategies. A conservative strategy combines the two values by selecting the higher of the two values. For example, the "Modify name" use case would have a combined value of *medium* using a conservative strategy. Likewise, an averaging strategy would choose a value between the two values. In this case there is none unless we invent a new category such as *medium high*. This should only be done if there is a large number of cases being categorized in one cell and there is a need for better discrimination.

By applying the selected strategy, you can make an ordered list of uses. For the three uses noted, using a conservative strategy, the list in order of increasing rank is *Edit name*, *Delete record*, and *Save record*. Thus, *Save record*

Use	Risk	Frequency	Criticality	Scenario
Modify Name	Low	Medium	Low	The user modifies the name field of an existing personnel record to which they have the appropriate security authorization.
Save Record	Medium	High	High	The user saves a record that has been newly created or modified.
Delete Record	High	Medium	Medium	The user deletes an existing record for which they have the appropriate authorization.

Figure 3.5 Three use cases for a personnel management system

would be tested more heavily than *Delete record,* which in turn would be tested more heavily than *Edit name.* Exactly how many test cases would be used will be discussed later as we consider techniques for selecting test cases.

A Testing Process

Given an incremental, iterative development process model, we can now sketch out a process for testing. We will defer many of the details to later chapters because basically all the information in this book belongs in the process. First, we will outline a series of issues that must be addressed to give a basic shape to the test process. Then we will consider how each development product is tested.

Planning Issues

Testing is traditionally incorporated into a development process at the point where executable code is available. Common practice is to perform a unit test on individual modules as they are developed, an integration test on subsystems as they are assembled from units and/or other subsystems, and a system test as the system becomes available. If an iterative, incremental process is used, then, at a minimum, system testing is performed after each increment is completed. Class testing and interaction testing are performed during or after each iteration for an increment. Regression testing is performed on any software whose implementation changed but whose specification did not. If both have changed, the test suites are revised and then reapplied.

In our approach, testing is conducted even before code is written. Models, being representations of the system just as code is a representation of the system, can be tested. In particular, design models lend themselves to testing by a form of execution that we describe in Chapter 4. Using analysis models, we can test a system in the sense of validation testing, thus ensuring that the right system is being specified. This last type of testing does not change much from traditional approaches, and so it is only a peripheral focus to this book.

Dimensions of Software Testing

Testing embraces many activities that must be performed. All these activities comprise *testing.* With respect to these activities, we identify five **dimensions** of testing that describe the answers to the following five questions[3]:

---

3. A sixth dimension concerning *where* testing will be performed is important from an organizational perspective, but it is not of concern to us in the context of this book.

1. *Who performs the testing?* Will the software's developers test it, will there be an independent group of people to test the software, or will there be some combination of the two?

2. *Which pieces will be tested?* Will every component of the software be tested or just the ones associated with higher risks?

3. *When will testing be performed?* Will testing be an ongoing process, an activity done at special milestones, or an activity performed at the end of development?

4. *How will testing be performed?* Will the testing be based solely on *what* the software is supposed to do or based also on *how* it is implemented?

5. *How much testing is adequate?* How will it be decided that *enough* testing has been done or where limited resources are best allocated for testing?

These are *dimensions* in the sense that each one represents an important consideration over a continuum of possible levels of effort or approaches, but each is independent of all the others. Each dimension must be considered when designing a testing effort, and a decision must be made about where on a continuum the project wishes to place itself. A decision made for one dimension will have no impact on decisions made for any of the other dimensions. All decisions together will determine the resources needed, the methods used, and the quality of the results of the total testing effort.

We will now take a look at each of these dimensions in more detail. These dimensions will also be considered in various discussions throughout the book. We represent each dimension with a continuum. A **continuum** is a sequence of possible levels for which it is difficult to delineate where one level ends and a subsequent one begins. In the physical world, the visible spectrum of light is a continuum, ranging from red to indigo. Orange is in the spectrum, but there is no widespread agreement exactly where orange begins and ends. That does not, however, prevent us from using orange or discussing its merits for athletic-team colors.

Just as there is no color that is better than another, so there is no "best" choice on each dimension. However, certain colors are more appropriate in certain situations and certain choices on a testing dimension are better than others in a given situation. In this chapter, our focus is on describing the five dimensions. We will address implications of each dimension on total testing efforts in the next chapters when we discuss individual techniques. Along the way, we hope to give you some view of how various combinations of positions relate to levels of quality in the software product.

Who Performs Testing?

A project includes both developer and tester roles. **Developer** is a role characterized by performing activities that generate a product—for example, analysis, design, programming, debugging, or documenting. **Tester** is a role characterized by performing activities to detect failures in a product. This includes selecting tests for a specific purpose, constructing the tests, and executing and evaluating the results. A given project member could assume both roles of developer and tester. Giving programmers responsibility for unit testing their own code is a common practice, although we strongly recommend a buddy testing scheme. System testing is commonly assigned to **independent testers**—people assuming the role of tester, but not of developer.

Figure 3.6 illustrates a continuum ranging from the situation in which the developers are responsible for all testing to the situation in which the independent tester is responsible for all testing. In the latter case, each end of the continuum is not encountered in practice as often as the middle. In particular, it is typical only in small projects for developers to have responsibility for the final system testing of the implementation against the system requirements. Projects that involve life-critical functionality are typically the ones in which each component is unit tested by an independent tester. Some government regulations make this the expected choice. In between these two extremes are two popular choices. In one case, developers are totally responsible for class testing, but pairs of developers exchange code and test each other's code, hence the previously mentioned buddy testing. In the other case, an independent tester is given responsibility for specifying test cases while the developer is responsible for the construction and execution of the tests.

In this book, we discuss testing processes and techniques and usually do not identify just who is performing them. That decision must be based on the effective use of resources at various points along the whole effort. The decision also is influenced by government and industry regulations. Actual test plans for a project should call out who is responsible for various testing activities to be performed. There are many ways to assign roles to project team members, and we have not yet discovered a "best" way.

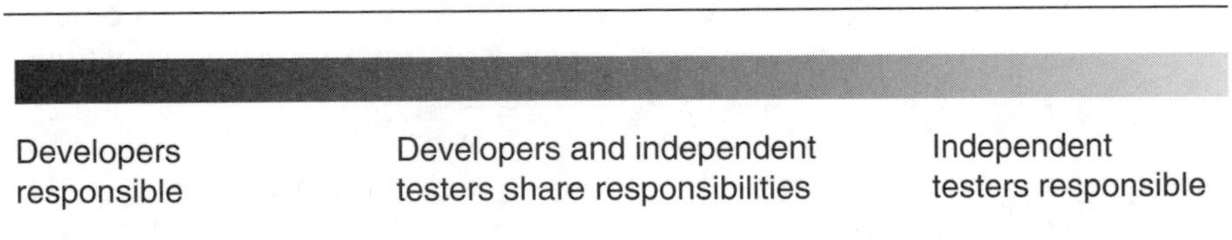

Developers responsible	Developers and independent testers share responsibilities	Independent testers responsible

Figure 3.6 Continuum for assignments of roles in class testing

Which Pieces Are Tested?

Which parts of a system should be tested? Options vary from testing nothing to testing every single component (or line of code) that goes into the final software product. The continuum is represented in Figure 3.7.

A software system comprises many components. In object-oriented programming, the most basic component is a class. At one end of this continuum is the position "we will test every class that is included in this system." At the other end is the position "we will not test any piece." Faults are found as a result of random operation of the system or through providing "evaluation copies" on the Web and letting users report errors.

The middle ground is to have a systematic approach, perhaps statistical methods, for selecting a subset of the total set of components to be tested. The classes being reused from other projects or taken from class libraries may not need to be tested. Some of the classes will not be easy to test individually because testing them requires complex drivers to provide input or examine output. The drivers themselves will require considerable effort to write and might need considerable testing and debugging. Part of choosing where to be on this continuum is based on balancing the yield (defects found per hour of effort) of testing with the effort needed to build the test infrastructure.

If testing all classes is not feasible, what strategy can you use to select the test cases to develop? One strategy is to generate test cases at random. Of course, this is not a very good strategy since it might not test commonly used functions of the software. Another strategy might focus on probable uses of the system, thereby putting primary emphasis on tests that use the more common inputs to the software. Still another strategy might emphasize pathological cases—obscure uses of the system—under the (probably incorrect) assumption that if the developers paid attention to more obscure or obtuse requirements, then they must have understood all the requirements.[4]

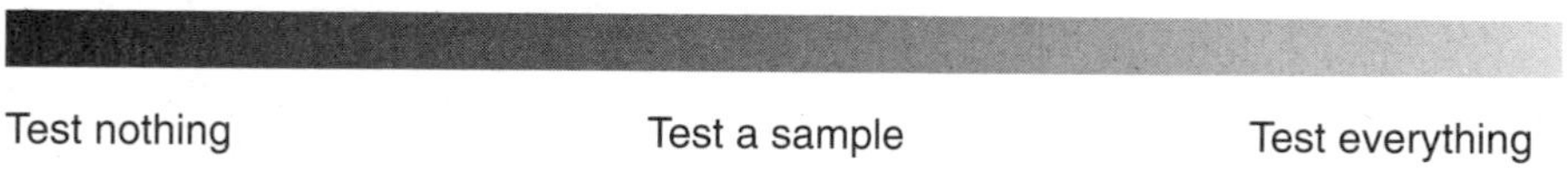

| Test nothing | Test a sample | Test everything |

Figure 3.7 Continuum for which parts of the software to test

4. Testing solely using pathological cases is not a good strategy.

When Is Testing Performed?

Components can be tested as they are developed, or testing can be delayed until all components are integrated into a single executable, as shown in Figure 3.8. The further into development we wait, the more disruptive it will be to make changes based on test results.

When should testing be done? Sometimes testing is done only at the end of the development process—that is, system testing and/or acceptance testing is the only formal testing done on software. This approach might work well when there are relatively few developers working from a well-understood set of requirements, but it is wishful thinking for most development efforts. It is widely recognized that the sooner a problem can be identified, the easier and cheaper it is to fix. Therefore, at the other end of the continuum is the decision to test every day. Between the extremes is testing each software component as it is produced. This will slow down the early progress of a development effort; however, it can pay off by greatly reducing the problems encountered later in a project as these pieces are composed into the larger system.

Also between the extremes is testing at the end of each increment. Rather than assembling individually tested pieces into the deliverable for the increment, this approach takes untested pieces, integrates them, and then tests the complete set of code as a monolithic whole. This is intended to reduce the cost of testing each individual piece as it is written. Success depends upon how complex each piece is and how experienced the development staff is. In very simple functionality, there may be sufficiently few defects that can be found by testing from the "outside." For more complex functionality, the defects may be buried so deeply in the code that it may be difficult to validate specific attribute values from outside the assembled increment. This approach is useful for components for which implementing a test driver is a significant effort.

One important issue in testing development products is the level of detail each represents. Consider, for example, an analysis model that is under refinement. What are the inputs to such a model? In other words, how detailed can we be in defining a test case for something that itself is not very well defined? We will address this issue in Chapter 4. The goal of this process is to provide feedback that can assist developers in making correct decisions.

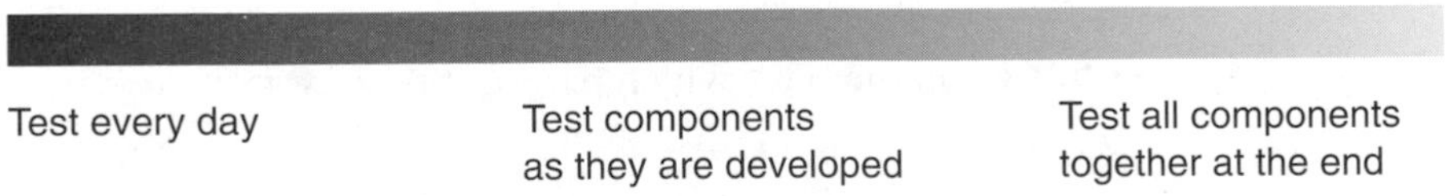

Test every day	Test components as they are developed	Test all components together at the end

Figure 3.8 Continuum for when software can be tested

How Is Testing Performed?

How will testing be performed? The basic approaches to testing software are based on the specification and the implementation, Figure 3.9.

The **specification** for a software entity states what that entity is supposed to do—that is, it describes the valid set of inputs to the entities, including the constraints on how multiple inputs might be related to one another, and what outputs correspond to the various inputs. The **implementation** for a software entity is an expression of an algorithm that produces the outputs for various inputs so that the specifications are obeyed. In short, a specification tells *what* a software entity does and an implementation tells *how* that software entity does what it does. Exhaustively covering specification information assures us that the software does what it is supposed to do. Exhaustively covering implementation information assures us that the software does not do anything that it is not supposed to do.

Specifications play a significant role in testing. We will need to have a specification written for many components of the software to be developed and tested, including specifications for systems, subsystems, and classes. It seems reasonable that we can generate test cases for a component based solely on its specification. However, for some components, implementation-based testing will be important to make certain the test suite is as thorough as it can be. For high-risk components, for example, we will want to make certain every bit of the code has been executed.

Besides testing individual components, we will also want to test the interactions between various components. This is traditionally referred to as **integration testing**, which occurs when components are integrated to create larger systems. The purpose of integration testing is to detect faults that arise because of interface errors or invalid assumptions about interfaces. Integration testing is particularly important in object-oriented systems because of the presence of inclusion polymorphism (see page 32), which is implemented using dynamic binding.

In an iterative, incremental process, integration testing will occur on a continuing basis. It will start with primitive objects being aggregated into more complex objects and move to complex objects that represent subsystems that are being integrated. In Chapter 6 we will provide some techniques for building effective test cases for interactions.

Knowledge of specification only	Knowledge of specification and implementation

Figure 3.9 Continuum for how software is tested

Adequacy of Test Cases

From practical and economic perspectives, testing software *completely* is usually just not possible. A reasonable goal for testing is to develop enough test cases to ensure that the software exhibits no failures in typical uses or in life-critical situations. This captures the idea of **adequacy** of testing a software product. Test it enough to be reasonably sure the software works as it is supposed to.

Adequacy can be measured based on the concept of **coverage**. Coverage can be measured in at least two ways. One way is in terms of how many of the requirements called out in the specification are tested. Of course, some requirements will require many test cases. Another way is in terms of how much of the software itself was executed as a result of running the test suite. A test suite might be adequate if some proportion of the lines of source code—or possible execution paths through the source code—was executed at least one time during test suite execution. These measures reflect two basic approaches to testing. One is based on what the software is supposed to do. The other is based on how the software actually works. Both approaches must be adopted to perform adequate testing.

In **functional testing**, which is also referred to as **specification-based** or **black box testing**, test cases are constructed based solely on the software's specification and not on how the software is implemented. This approach is useful for all levels of testing because it has the advantage that test cases can be developed even before coding begins. However, the effectiveness of functional testing depends greatly on the quality of the specification and the ability of the test suite developers to interpret it correctly.

In **structural testing**, which is also referred to as **implementation-based** or **white box testing**, test cases are constructed based on the code that implements the software. The output of each test case must be determined by the software's specification, but the inputs can be determined from analyzing the code itself to determine various values that cause various execution paths to be taken. The main advantage of this approach is improved coverage. The main disadvantage is that if the programmer did not implement the full specification, then that part of the functionality will not be tested.

To adequately test software, some combination of both approaches is usually most effective. Function-based is the stronger approach, but structural testing improves confidence in case the software does not do something it should not do.

How Much Testing Is Adequate?

This question is impossible to answer in general and it is not an easy question to answer even for a specific piece of software.[5] There are many aspects to consider when addressing this question. The expected lifetime of the software is

---

5. Do not confuse this with the earlier continuum in which we considered which pieces to test.

one consideration. Applications that will transform data from an old application to a new one seldom require extensive testing. Another consideration is whether the application containing the software is life-critical, which obviously requires very extensive testing. Note this is a decision about how thoroughly to test an individual piece chosen for testing.

One ad hoc view of adequacy is that testing continues as long as the costs of uncovering faults are balanced by the increased quality of the product. Another view considers the prevailing standards within the domain in which the software application is situated. Testing is designed to conform to those standards—for example, there are obvious differences in quality standards between drug manufacturing and furniture manufacturing.

The differing levels of adequate testing can be viewed on a continuum, shown in Figure 3.10, from no testing at all, to minimal coverage in which we select a few tests to perform, and on to exhaustive testing in which every possible test case is run. Companies—and sometimes even individual projects—set testing policies based on a position along the continuum where they are comfortable.

The amount of testing required should be determined relative to the long-term and short-term goals of the project, and relative to the software being developed. We frequently speak of "coverage" with respect to adequacy. **Coverage** is a measure of how completely a test suite exercises the capabilities of a piece of software. Different measures are used by different people—for example, one measure might be based on whether every line of code is executed at least once when a test suite is run while another measure might be based on the number of requirements that are checked by the test suite. Consequently, coverage is expressed in phrases such as "75% of the code was executed by this test suite," or "One test case was constructed from each specified requirement."

We believe test coverage measures should be formulated primarily in terms of requirements and can vary depending on the priorities and objectives of the project. If, for example, requirements are specified by use cases, coverage will be measured by how many of the use cases are used and how many scenarios are created for each use case. Coverage measured in terms of implementation is useful in measuring the completeness of the specification-based test suite. If some code is not executed, then testers should work with developers to determine what test cases are missing or whether the software implements unspecified functionality.

No testing   Exhaustive testing

Figure 3.10 Continuum for how much testing can be done

We apply risk analysis in the testing process to determine the level of detail and amount of time to dedicate to testing a component—for example, more time will be spent testing classes that are identified as reusable assets than those that are intended for use in a prototype. A reasonable scale of increasing risk for components is as follows:

- Prototype components
- Production components
- Library components
- Framework components

The result of recognizing differing levels of risk is the acceptance of differing levels of adequate test coverage. We will present testing algorithms that guide the testing of specific products. These algorithms will include what we term a **rheostat effect,** which produces differing levels of test coverage from the same algorithm. For example, in Orthogonal Array Testing on page 228 we will talk about testing different numbers of combinations of attribute values.

Roles in the Testing Process

We have identified several important roles related to testing in a project. Each role is essential to the success of the testing aspect of the project. The test plan should schedule the testing responsibilities of each of these roles.

The people in each of these roles must plan the amount of time and effort that they will expend in testing. They must schedule their time relative to testing and any other obligations they must meet. The development schedule will drive much of the test scheduling. In this environment, testing will often be shortchanged if there is not a clear specification of levels of adequate test coverage and a commitment to quality. Our experience shows that the more active the integration test and system test people are in the total project the more likely it is that testing will be given appropriate resources.

We now describe each of the roles. One or more people can assume each role. One person can assume multiple roles, but you must be careful to keep the roles separate.

Class Tester

A **class tester** has the responsibility to test individual classes as they are produced. Part of the planning process is to coordinate the efforts of all of these individuals. The development community, through the project test plan, must agree on who will assume this role, the levels of coverage that will be considered adequate, and how these tests will be scheduled. Scheduling is particularly important given the relatively large number of artifacts to be tested and the need for a quick turnaround. If this role is taken by developers, as is often the case, then specific amounts of time must be allocated to the activity. This seems like an obvious statement, but many managers simply ignore this step when scheduling.

Integration Tester

An **integration tester** is responsible for testing a set of objects that are being brought together from different development sources, such as two development teams. They have the responsibility to test sufficient functionality to be certain that the various components from different development teams and/or outside vendors will work together correctly. This role is particularly important in a project that is using large frameworks that are still immature. People in this role should have both developer and testing skills.

System Tester

A **system tester** has domain knowledge and is responsible for independently verifying that the completed application satisfies the system requirements. System testers represent a user's perspective on the project. This is a valuable perspective to have even in the early planning phases of the project. One or more system testers should participate in use case modeling efforts and begin test case identification and construction during requirements definition.

Test Manager

A **test manager** is responsible for managing the test process. This may be a part-time role for one manager, or a role for a number of people who are dedicated to managing just the testing portion of the process. The role of the test manager is similar to that of any manager. The person is responsible for requesting, coordinating, and making effective use of the resources allocated to testing. Often this person will be assigned "matrix" authority over a set of developers. That is, the developers will report to the development manager and to the test manager as well. Developers in this role will assist in the construction of a test infrastructure.

A Detailed Set of Test Activities

Figure 3.11 provides a synopsis of the test activities for each of the phases we have defined for our development process. These will be elaborated as we discuss the techniques in later chapters.

Product	Components		(Sub)Systems	
	Model-based	Implementation-based	Model-based	Implementation-based
Domain Analysis — Domain class model	Check that objects can be created from the classes in the model and that relationships can be established.		Check that all objects required to define the subsystem are available and correct.	
Domain dynamic model	Check that all states of the object can be reached and that preconditions can be checked.		Check that all states of the subsystem can be reached and that preconditions can be checked.	
Domain requirements specification—for example, use cases	Check that an expert user cannot find any uses not present in the model.		Check for consistency across the complete set of use cases; check for completeness against the expert user.	
Application Analysis — Application class model	Check that objects can be created from the classes in the model and that relationships can be established.		Check that all objects required to define the subsystem are available and correct.	
Application dynamic model	Check that all states can be reached and that preconditions can be checked.		Check that all states of the subsystem can be reached and that preconditions can be checked.	
Application requirements specification—for example, use cases	Check that an expert user cannot find any uses not present in the model.		Check for consistency across the complete set of use cases; check for completeness against the expert user.	

Figure 3.11 Synopsis of testing activities

Product	Components		(Sub)Systems	
	Model-based	Implementation-based	Model-based	Implementation-based
Architectural Design	Check that objects can be created from the new classes in the model and that relationships can be established. Check the correct application of design patterns.			
	Check that all states can be reached and that preconditions can be checked.			
	Check that each message received by a component requests an operation in its interface and that each component is in the proper state to receive that message. Check that the sender of each message has an acquaintance with the receiver.			
	Check that each component has relationships necessary for communication.		Check that requirements can be met for capturing the results in interaction diagrams.	
	Check that the components of a subsystem have established necessary acquaintances, within and without.		Check that the subsystem can support its specification.	

Figure 3.11 Synopsis of testing activities *(Continued)*

Product	Components		(Sub)Systems	
	Model-based	Implementation-based	Model-based	Implementation-based
Detailed Design	Check independent of the application.		Check independent of the application. Check structure against architecture. Check operation against interaction diagrams.	
Class Implementation / Completed classes		Check implementation against the class's specification.		Check the interactions between classes using test cases based on relationships from a class diagram.
Application Implementation / Completed application				Check implementation using test cases developed from use cases.

Figure 3.11 Synopsis of testing activities *(Continued)*

Planning Activities

Now we want to discuss the process of planning for testing. We will present a set of planning documents that are useful in organizing information such as specific test cases. We will relate these documents to how and when testing activities are scheduled.

These planning documents are working documents. After each increment, and sometimes after a specific iteration, these documents are reviewed and revised. Risks are updated as are priorities and schedules.

Scheduling Testing Activities

Class tests are scheduled at the discretion of a developer as they become useful or necessary. A class test is useful during coding when the developer wishes to identify missing features or verify the correctness of part of an implementation. A class test becomes necessary when a component is to be added to the code base. The class may not be completely developed, but the behaviors that it does provide should be complete and correct.

Integration tests are typically scheduled at specific intervals, usually at the end of major iterations that signal the completion of an increment and/or just prior to releases. Alternatively, integration may be an ongoing, highly iterative process that occurs each evening. Integration test cycles can also be scheduled to coincide with deliveries from major outside vendors, such as a new version of a base framework.

System tests will be performed on major deliverables at specified intervals throughout the project. This schedule is usually specified in the project plan since there is often a need to coordinate with a separate organization that may be providing testing services to numerous projects simultaneously.

Estimation

Part of scheduling is estimating the resources—cost, time, and personnel—that will be needed to support the plans being made. This is not easy and we have no magic formulas. In this section we will discuss the factors—levels of coverage, domain type, equipment required, organization model, and testing effort—that should be considered.

Levels of Coverage

The more comprehensive the level of coverage, the more resources that will be required. Estimates of the amount of code written to support testing vary. Beizer estimates from 2% to 80% of the application size [Beiz90]. Other estimates are even higher. We have had success in considering each system use case as a unit measure. By estimating the amount of effort for one use case (perhaps through a prototyping effort), you can construct the estimate for the complete system. Some use cases are much broader in scope or more abstract in level. Choose a set of use cases that are at approximately the same level of detail in the model and use those for estimating. If two use cases extend another more general case, then use either the two specific or the one more general use case, but not both.

Domain Type

Often more technically oriented software embodies much of its complexity in the programming logic, while the program inputs are fairly simple. On the other hand, systems that are data intensive often have relatively simple logic, but the test cases require large amounts of effort to construct. The amount of effort required to construct a complete test case including complete inputs and correct outputs can vary considerably. A simple program that queries a large database requires much time to build the data set and much time to verify that the answer produced is correct.

Equipment Required

System testing should be conducted in an environment as close as possible to the deployment environment. Even some aspects of class testing may require either special hardware environments or a hardware simulator. The cost of installing and maintaining the equipment or constructing the simulator must be included in any estimate.

Organization Model

We have discussed a couple of schemes that are commonly used to staff the testing process. Our experience has shown that the more independent the testers are from the development organization, the more thorough the tests are. However, this independence requires a longer learning curve and thus more expense. Common estimates are that one independent tester can only handle the output of two to three developers.

Conversely, tying the testers to the development organization (or using personnel from the development team to test) reduces the time required to learn the system. Specifications are seldom completely written down or up-to-date. If a tester is a person who also participates in discussions about the solution, then that tester can understand the implicit assumptions in a specification more completely. However, it may be more difficult for testers to be as rigorous or objective if they become too closely tied to the development effort.

Consider using a **buddy approach** to class testing. It provides much of the objectivity that makes testing most effective. Rather than have developers test their own classes, form buddy groups. Two developers swap code with each other and test. The advantage is more thorough testing. Since the tester is another developer who is also developing closely related code, this person can be productive much more quickly than a person from the independent test team who must first learn about the context.

Testing Effort Estimation Form

Developer-level person-hours required for class test planning	_____
Developer-level person-hours required for PACT class construction	_____
Staff person-hours required for test environment	_____
Tester person-hours for system test planning	_____
Tester person-hours for PAST class construction	_____
Total Tester person-hours	_____

Figure 3.12 A testing effort estimation form

Testing Effort Estimate

Estimation techniques almost always rely on historical data to make projections. We will not take the space here to discuss these techniques. Figure 3.12 provides a very simple form to use in accounting for all of the hours required for the various testing activities. As we proceed through the book, we will provide more detailed guidance for completing the various sections of the form.

For now we can summarize much of this by using historical data to determine the cost of producing a single class. From the list in Figure 3.12 we can identify the classes that will have to be constructed:

- Construct one PACT[6] class per class in the application that will be tested in isolation.
- Construct one PAST[7] class per use case.
- Estimate the number of classes needed for the infrastructure.

The total number of classes times the effort per class gives the effort for all testing classes. Planning is addressed in Planning Effort on page 105.

A Process for Testing *Brickles*

In this section we will illustrate the following five dimensions by applying each of them to our case study.

1. *Who performs the testing?* The testing duties will be divided between the two authors. Sykes is doing most of the implementation, so he will do the class and integration testing. McGregor wrote the use cases and constructed much of the high-level design. He will create test cases

---

6. PACT is Parallel Architecture for Component Testing. We will discuss this in Chapter 7.

7. PAST is Parallel Architecture for System Testing. This will be discussed in Chapter 9.

from the use cases and execute these when the system's implementation is available. Sykes will moderate the model testing.

2. *Which pieces will be tested?* The basic primitive classes will be tested. Higher-level classes that are composed from the primitive ones have so many interrelationships that they will be tested as a cluster. The final system will be tested as a completed application.

3. *When will testing be performed?* The class testing will be performed repeatedly during the development iterations. The cluster tests of the high-level classes will also be repeated during iterations, but these tests will not start until the second increment after the primitive classes have been completed in the first increment. System testing will be initiated after an initial version of the system becomes available at the end of the first increment.

4. *How will testing be performed?* Test cases will be constructed as methods in a class. There will be one test class for each production class. Use case testing will be conducted by a person using the system rather than by using any automation. This will require the game to be played many times.

5. *How much testing is adequate for an individual piece?* The classes will be tested to the level that every public method has been invoked at least once. We will not attempt to test every possible combination of values for the parameters. The test cases derived from the use cases will cover all possible final results.

Document Templates

We will discuss a project test plan, a component test plan, an integration test plan, a use case test plan, and a system test plan. The relationships among these plans are illustrated in Figure 3.13. Each arrow in the figure indicates that the pointed-to document is included by the reference in the document that originates the arrow.

We will present these in template format. This is a useful approach for several reasons. Except for the system test plan, there will be multiple instances of these documents. A template ensures consistency of form and content among these independent, but related, documents. The more of the document that can be incorporated into the template, the less effort a developer will need to expend in producing the multiple instances. The template approach will also simplify the inspection process since each document will follow the same style, this specific content can be located quickly.

The IEEE test plan outline in Figure 3.14 lists the basic sections for a test plan regardless of level. We want to address those that are most important in an incremental, iterative object-oriented software development environment. In the following test plans we will not name the sections exactly according to the outline, but we will include the basic required information. The following test plan items are particularly important:

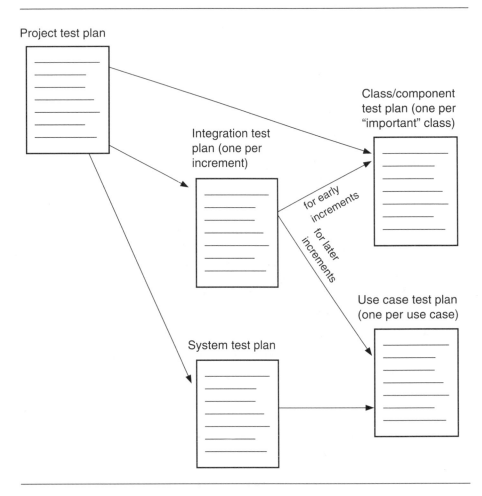

Project test plan

Integration test
plan (one per
increment)

Class/component
test plan (one per
"important" class)

for early
increments

for later
increments

Use case test plan
(one per use case)

System test plan

Figure 3.13 Relationships among test plans

■ *Features Not Tested*—For class-level testing. This section reports the results of the HIT analysis (see Chapter 7). This information includes features that have already been tested and that do not need to be retested, and features that are not scheduled for development until later iterations or a later increment.

■ *Test-Suspension Criteria and Resumption Requirements*—Testing is suspended when the yield reaches an unacceptable level, that is, when the number of faults being found per hour of effort drops below the criteria set in this section, and then no further testing is conducted. This section is particularly important for a project using iterative development. We usually define one set of criteria for early iterations and a

1.0   Introduction

2.0   Test Items

3.0   Tested Features

4.0   Features Not Tested (per cycle)

5.0   Testing Strategy and Approach

    5.1 Syntax

    5.2 Description of Functionality

    5.3 Arguments for Tests

    5.4 Expected Output

    5.5 Specific Exclusions

    5.6 Dependencies

    5.7 Test Case Success/Failure Criteria

6.0   Pass/Fail Criteria for the Complete Test Cycle

7.0   Entrance Criteria/Exit Criteria

8.0   Test-Suspension Criteria and Resumption Requirements

9.0   Test Deliverables/Status Communications Vehicles

10.0 Testing Tasks

11.0 Hardware and Software Requirements

12.0 Problem Determination and Correction Responsibilities

13.0 Staffing and Training Needs/Assignments

14.0 Test Schedules

15.0 Risks and Contingencies

16.0 Approvals

Figure 3.14 The IEEE 829 Standard Test Plan outline

second set for the later iterations. For an iterative project, the resumption criteria is simply the progression in the development cycle back to the test point.

■ *Risks and Contingencies*—A risk, in this context, identifies potential problems with conducting the tests. These include possible errors about correct answers in large data sets and the possibility that different platforms will produce different results, but that only some will be tested.

Project Test Plan

The purpose of this document is to summarize the testing strategy that is to be employed for the project. It should define the steps in the development process at which testing will occur, the frequency with which the testing should occur, and who is responsible for the activity.

The project test plan may be an independent document or it may be included in either the overall project plan or the project's quality assurance plan. Because its format is so variable and its content quite flexible, we will only provide a couple of tables below that summarize the information usually included.

The table in Figure 3.15 summarizes the activities that are required, the frequency with which each activity will be employed, and the entity that is responsible for this phase of testing. More specific information about each of these is included in the detailed plan for that level.

A second table, in Figure 3.16, associates each of the phases with a specific strategy for that phase. We will describe several testing strategies in the appropriate chapters and you can pick your favorite. This table also records project standards for adequate testing for each risk level within the three phases.

Project Test Plan Template—Part 1

Project:_____

Responsible Party: _____.

Level of Testing	Activities	Frequency of Testing	Responsible Party
Component	Select test cases	As components are ready	Component developer
	Write PACT classes		Component tester
Integration	Select test cases	Prior to release of an increment	Integration team
System	Select test cases from use cases	Prior to any release to an external client	Quality assurance department
	Construct PAST classes		

Figure 3.15 Project test plan template—Part 1

Project Test Plan Template—Part 2

Level of Testing	Test Strategy	Use Profile Level	Coverage Criteria
Component		high	
		medium	
		low	
Integration		high	
		medium	
		low	
System		high	
		medium	
		low	

Figure 3.16 Project test plan template—Part 2

Component Test Plan

The purpose of a component test plan is to define the overall strategy and specific test cases that will be used to test a certain component. One test plan will be completed on each component that is sufficiently significant to require isolated testing. We present here a template that we have used successfully. Two types of guiding information are included in the template: project criteria and project procedures. These are included to serve as handy reminders and to avoid the need to produce a component test plan that summarizes all of the component-testing information for the project. Project criteria are standards that have been agreed upon as to how thoroughly each component will be tested. For example, project criteria might call for 100% of the postconditions on modifier methods to be tested. These criteria should be providing more detail on the coverage criteria defined in the project test plan. Project procedures identify techniques that have been agreed upon as the best way to handle a particular task. For example, constructing a PACT class (see Chapter 7) for each component that will be tested is a project procedure. These procedures will provide the details of the test strategies that were identified in the project test plan.

We will give a brief comment on each section of the template. Figure 3.17 shows the template. We will not comment on sections that simply record information such as the name of the component. Italicized portions will represent actual entries in the template.

Objectives for the Class. The developer will replace this paragraph with a prioritized list of objectives for the component. For example, this component is an element of the basic framework for the application and is intended as a high-level abstraction from which the more specific variants are derived.

Guided Inspection Requirements. Project Criteria: *100% of the products associated with critical components will be inspected. 75% of the products associated with noncritical components will be inspected. Library components will be subject to additional quality checks.* Project Procedure: *Risk analysis is used to prioritize the portions of the class with respect to inspections and testing.*

Building and Retaining Test Suites. The developer will replace this paragraph with information about

- the results of applying HIT and details of the use of the PACT process for creating test driver classes (see Chapter 7).
- the scheduled deadline for the delivery of test cases.
- the specification of the test driver.
- the relative number of test cases in each category and the priorities among the three.

Functional Test Cases. The developer will replace this paragraph with information about

- the test cases developed from the specification.
- the class invariant method.
- how many different "types" of objects are being tested. The types are based on the initial state of the object.

Structural Test Cases. The developer will replace this paragraph with information about

- the test cases developed for code coverage and about the code-review process.
- how to use the required test-coverage tool.

State-Based Test Cases. The developer will replace this paragraph with information about the state representation for the class. Refer to the state diagram if available.

Interaction Test Cases. The developer will replace this paragraph with information about which messages will be tested based on the OATS selection process (see Chapter 6).

Component Test Plan Template

Component Name: _____

Responsible Party: _____

Developer Name: _____

Objectives for the Class

Project Procedure: Test cases are intended to test a component based on its stated objectives.

Guided Inspection Requirements

Project Criteria: 100% of the products associated with critical components will be inspected. 75% of the products associated with noncritical components will be inspected. Library components will be subject to additional quality checks. Check one of the following:

Critical application component   _____

Noncritical application component   _____

Library component   _____

Project Criteria: A risk analysis is to be used to prioritize the portions of the class with respect to inspections and testing.

Building and Retaining Test Suites

Project Procedure: The HIT algorithm will be used to determine which test cases actually need to be executed for a given component.

Project Procedure: It is a responsibility of the developer to prepare the test suites in the structure required by the project.

Project criteria: For each component there is a test driver class that contains the test cases for the component.

Project criteria: For each method there are test harness methods that represent functional, structural, and interaction test cases.

Functional Test Cases

Project criteria: Execute test cases for each postcondition of every method. Also check the class invariant as part of each test case.

Project criteria: Execute test cases based on possible significant values for each of the parameters.

Structural Test Cases

Project criteria: Execute test cases that cover every line of code in each method.

Criteria for risk analysis on the component: _____

State-based Test Cases

Project criteria: Execute test cases that cover every transition in the state representation.

Interaction Test Cases

Project Procedure: Execute test cases based on each contract between components. Use OATS to select the cases to be executed.

Figure 3.17 A component test plan template

Use Case Test Plan

The purpose of this plan is to describe the system-level tests to be derived from a single use case. These plans are incorporated by reference into both the integration and system test plans. Figures 3.18, 3.19, and 3.20 show portions of the use case test plan template. Other parts will be shown in Chapter 9.

The test plans can be constructed in a modular fashion following the same pattern as the dependencies between the "partial" use cases. Use case models can be structured in the same way class diagrams are. The **includes** and **extends** relations provide the means for decomposing the use cases into "partial" use cases as described in Chapter 2. The partial use cases are combined using the relationships to form what we refer to as "end-toed" use cases.

We identify three levels of use cases: high-level, end-to-end system, and functional sub-use cases. The high-level use cases are abstract use cases that are the basis for being extended to end-to-end use cases. The functional sub-use cases are aggregated into end-to-end system-level use cases. We have built actual test scripts, in the scripting language of test tools, that use the generalization/specialization relationship between the high-level and end-to-end use cases. These test scripts also aggregate fragments of test scripts from the functional sub-use cases. By having these three levels, our projects are more manageable and our test scripts are more modular.

The project for which this was the template also identified two different "types" of use cases: functionality and report use cases. Functionality use cases modified the data maintained by the system in some way. Report use cases accessed information in the system, summarized it, and formatted it for presentation to the user. These differences led to different numbers of tests for security and persistence. You may identify other groupings of the use cases that are useful to your project.

Integration Test Plan

The integration test plan is particularly important in an iterative development environment. Specific sets of functionality will be delivered before others. Out of these increments the full system slowly emerges. One implication from this style of development is that the integration test plan changes character over the life of the project more than the component or the system test plans. The components that are integrated in early increments may not directly support any end-user functionality and hence none of the use cases can be used to provide test cases. At this stage the best source is the component test plans for the aggregated components. These are used to complete the component test plan for the component that integrates these objects. After a number of increments have been delivered, the functionality of the integrated software begins to correspond to system-level behavior. At that time the best source of test cases is the use case test plans.

In both cases, the test cases are selected based on the degree to which the test case requires behavior across all of the parts that are being integrated. Small, localized behavior should have already been tested. This means that the

Use Case Test Plan Template—Part 1

Use Case Name:_____

Responsibility: The developer who *owns* the component is responsible for class testing.

Developer Name:_____

Part 1—Appearance and Layout (Repeat for each screen/report)

1.1 All required data fields are present.	Y	N
1.2 Items appear in the correct order.	Y	N
1.3 No unspecified fields are present.	Y	N
1.4 Initial system defaults are correct.	Y	N
1.5 (Screen only) Tab traversal is in correct order.	Y	N
1.6 (Screen only) Shortcuts work correctly.	Y	N
1.7 (Screen only) Fields may be accessed in random order.	Y	N
1.8 (Screen only) Menus are in the correct order.	Y	N
1.9 (Screen only) Appropriate menu choices are active.	Y	N
1.10 (Screen only) Objects acted appropriately (double-click events, etc.).	Y	N

Test Case Standards

1. For every "required" field there will be test cases in which the value for that field is missing.

2. For every boundary value there will be test cases that use that specific value. There should also be test cases that use values from each equivalence class between the boundaries.

3. For every field of an enumeration data type, unless a checkbox is used, there will be test cases for invalid and blank values.

4. For every field of a date data type there will be test cases for invalid and blank values. However, unless there is an explicit constraint in the use case, there will be no checks of boundary values. Dates may be invalid because of the format or because of the violation of business rules.

5. For any scenario in which there is to be a retrieval, there should be a test case in which all fields are blank except for one field in which an entry is made. There should be one such test case for every field that the user can edit. For fields that accept types input, such as a name field, there should be two test cases. For example, a full name and a partial name are both tested.

Part 3—Security/Integrity

The test script indicates the security level of the user and tests for each level.	Y	N
Each field accurately detects incorrect data types and their processing.	Y	N
The system presents the correct error and warning message in unusual situations.	Y	N
Output data are successfully replicated to all servers.	Y	N

1. Related tests that must be passed prior to executing these scripts:

2. Related tests that should be run if these scripts fail:

3. Related tests that should be run upon successful completion of these tests:

Figure 3.18 Use case test plan template—Part 1

Use Case Test Plan Template—Part 2

Use Case Name:_____

Responsibility: The developer who *owns* the component is responsible for the class testing.

Developer Name:_____

Part 4—Test Scripts

This section provides the tester with a detailed outline for performing each test. The outline comes from the "The system responds by. . ." section of each use case scenario and from the tables created in Section 2 of the use case template which is omitted from Figure 3.18 for reasons of space but is shown in Figure 9.7.

Script #

Establish preconditions for test

User type: Any

The user has the specified authority required to perform the operation.	Y	N
The system enforces the appropriate access control.	Y	N
The required error message appeared when unauthorized access was attempted.	Y	N
The system resisted repeated attempts at unauthorized access.	Y	N

Environmental needs

Needed test databases and tables are in place.	Y	N

Execute the following scenario:

Evaluate test results

General test results:

The expected output occurred.	Y	N
Any related fields were correctly computed.	Y	N
An out-of-synch set of related fields results in an error message.	Y	N
The required error message(s) appeared.	Y	N
The message accurately and clearly described the problem.	Y	N
The system recovered appropriately after the error message.	Y	N
It was not possible to save until any errors were corrected.	Y	N
The program met performance standards.	Y	N

Figure 3.19 Use case test plan template—Part 2

Use Case Test Plan Template—Part 3

Use Case Name:_____

Responsibility: The developer who *owns* the component is responsible for the class testing.

Developer Name:_____

Part 5—Use Case Test Summary

Summary of test activities (personnel responsible, location, etc.):

_____

_____

_____

Description of hardware used for test execution (printer model, network connection type, etc.): _____

_____

Unspecified behavior that occurred:_____

_____

Variances from specified test procedures:

_____

_____

_____

   Retesting is required.   Y   N

Approved: _____

Figure 3.20 Use case test plan template—Part 3

tests should be more complex and more comprehensive than the typical component tests. In a properly integrated object-oriented system, there will be certain objects that span a number of other objects in the build. Choosing tests from the test plans for those components will often be sufficient for good integration test cases.

Because of this dependence on other test cases, we do not provide a separate template for the integration test plan. Its format will follow that of the system test plan in that it will be a mapping of which individual test plans are combined to form the integration test plan for a specific increment.

System Test Plan

The system test plan is a document that summarizes the individual use case test plans and provides information on additional types of testing that will be conducted at the system level. In each of the techniques chapters, we will describe life-cycle testing as one technique that can be applied at the system level and also at the individual component level.

For our purposes here, we will provide a chart, see Figure 3.21, that maps the use-case test plans to specific system tests. Most of the information required by the IEEE test plan format will have already been provided by the individual use case test plans.

System Test Plan

Use Case Number	Test Case Number	Reason for Selecting

Figure 3.21 System test plan

Iteration in Planning

The iterations in the development process affect how planning is carried out. Changes in product or increment requirements at least require that test plans be reviewed. In many cases they will also need to be modified. We keep traceability matrices to assist with this iterative modification.

If the development organization receives requirements in a traditional form, we build a requirements-to-use-case mapping matrix. This is often just a spreadsheet with requirement IDs in the vertical axis and use case IDs on the horizontal axis. An entry in a cell indicates that the use case provides functionality related to or constrained by the requirement.

We also maintain a second matrix in which we relate each use case to a set of packages of classes. An entry in a cell indicates that the package provides classes that are used to realize the use case. When a use case is changed, the owners of packages are informed. They check the functionality they are providing and make the necessary changes to their code. This triggers changes in several levels of test cases and perhaps test plans as well.

Planning Effort

The effort expended in planning depends on a few things:

- the amount of reuse that exists among the templates
- the effort required to complete each plan from the template
- the effort to modify an existing plan

Each of these values will require the establishment of a baseline on which to base estimates.

Test Metrics

Test metrics include measures that provide information for evaluating the effectiveness of individual testing techniques and the complete testing process. Metrics are also used to provide planning information such as estimates of the effort required for testing. To create these final measures we need measures of coverage and complexity to form the basis of effectiveness and efficiency metrics.

Coverage is a testing term that indicates which items have been touched by test cases. We will discuss a number of different coverage measures during the presentation of the testing techniques discussed in the book. Examples include the following:

- **Code coverage**—which lines of code have been executed.

- **Postcondition coverage**—which method postconditions have been reached.

- **Model-element coverage**—which classes and relationships in a model have been used in test cases.

Coverage metrics are stated in terms of the *product* being tested rather than the *process* we are using to test it. This gives us a basis by which we can describe how "thoroughly" a product has been tested. For example, consider the situation in which one developer uses every logical clause from every postcondition as a source for test cases, while a second developer only uses the "sunny-day" clauses[8] from the postconditions as the source for tests. The second developer is not testing as thoroughly as the first as evidenced by what fraction of the postcondition clauses are being covered.

Coverage can be combined with complexity to give an accurate basis for estimating the effort needed to test a product. That is, as the software becomes more complex, it will be much more difficult to achieve a specified level of coverage. Several measures of complexity are available:

- number and complexity of methods in the class
- number of lines of code
- amount of dynamic binding

By collecting performance data over time, a project or company can develop a baseline from which projections can be made for planning a new project.

The testing process is effective if it is finding faults. It is efficient if it is finding them with as few resources as possible. We will discuss a couple of measures that give information about both of these. The **number of defects/ developer-hour metric** determines the yield of the process while the

---

8. A **sunny-day clause** is an expected result, ignoring error conditions that might throw an exception or return an error code.

developer hours/number of defects metric provides a measure of the cost of the process. These numbers are dependent on the tools that are used to construct tests as well as the levels of coverage sought, so each company will need to baseline their process and collect actual performance data before using these numbers for planning purposes.

The effectiveness of the testing process is evaluated by collecting data over the complete development life cycle. Consider a fault that is injected into an application during design. The sooner that defect is detected, the more effective is the testing process. The efficiency of the testing process is measured by considering the intervals between the development phase in which the defect is injected and the phase in which it is detected for all defects. The perfectly effective testing process finds every defect in the same development phase in which it was injected. If defects injected at design time are not being detected until code testing, the testing technique used during the design of the system should be modified to search specifically for the types of faults that are not being detected in a timely manner.

Summary

In the competitive world in which complex software sells for $99.95 and companies pay a bounty to any employee finding a new software engineer, planning is an essential activity. The challenge is to balance time spent planning and documenting the plan, with the time available to produce software.

We have shown a series of templates that reduce the time required to complete the planning process. These documents are hierarchical where possible to further reduce the volume of documentation required to do an adequate job. The planning process will be a success if the developers who drive the process see benefit from it. It will be perfunctory at best if the attitude becomes one of "just get it done."

Exercises

3-1. Identify the documents and models that are available for a system you want to test. For those pieces that are missing, determine how you might provide the required information.

3-2. Prioritize the objectives for your project and product.

3-3. Continue the development of your test plan by building a chart that lists all of the "products" that will be available for testing. A second column could be used to list the testing techniques that will be applied to test the product. It will be left blank for now. Is your project iterative? Is it incremental? If it is iterative, there should be a column that summarizes the results of applying each technique during each iteration. If it is incremental, there should be a separate table for each increment of the system since they will be developed independently.

3-4. What risk level would you assign to the Sprite, PuckSupply, Puck, and Velocity classes for *Brickles*?

Testing Analysis and Design Models

☞ Want to learn how to inspect the semantics of UML models? See The Basics of Guided Inspection on page 116

☞ Need to set up an inspection session? See Organization of the Guided Inspection Activity on page 120

☞ Need a technique for testing a model for extensibility? See Testing Models for Additional Qualities on page 151

Developers model the software they are constructing because it assists in understanding the problem they are solving and because it helps manage the complexity of the system being developed. The models of analysis and design information will eventually be used to guide the implementation activities of the project. If the models are of high quality, they make a valuable contribution to the project, but if they contain faults, they are equally detrimental. In this chapter we present **guided inspection,** an enhanced inspection technique for verifying the models as they are created and for validating the completed models against project requirements. The principal shortcoming of standard review techniques is that they focus primarily on what *is* there (in the model) rather than what *should be* there. Reviews do not provide a means for systematically

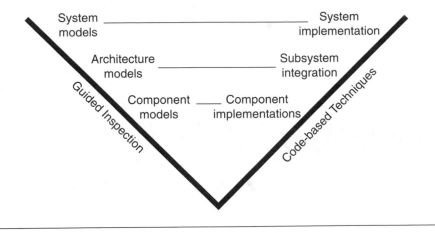

Figure 4.1 The new V model

searching for omissions from products. Even Fagan inspections [Faga86], which use checklists to make the process more detailed, do not provide a means for determining what is missing from a model.

Guided inspection applies the testing perspective very early in the development process. Traditionally, testing has begun at the unit implementation level and has continued as code segments are integrated into larger pieces until the entire system is available to be tested. In this chapter, we will begin "system testing" when the "system" is still represented only as analysis or design information. A new version of the traditional "V" testing model, shown in Figure 4.1, relates the repeated applications of guided inspections to the various levels of testing.

Guided inspection requires valuable resources, and the time and attention of project personnel. So is it worthwhile? Studies have reported widely varying savings ratios for finding and repairing faults early in the development process as opposed to during the compilation or system test phases. For example, repairing a fault found at system test time may cost as much as one hundred times the cost of repairing the same fault during analysis. So even a moderate effort at testing the models can result in big savings.

An Overview

Let's look at a quick example of using the guided inspection technique. To set the stage, we are in the initial stages of developing *Brickles*. The team has produced the design-level class diagram shown in Figure 2.18 and other diagrams such as the state diagram shown in Figure 2.19 and the sequence diagram shown in Figure 2.20. We are about to begin coding but want to validate the design model before spending extensive time coding the wrong definitions.

We begin by assigning the inspection team. The team includes the two of us who developed the model, a system tester from our company and our company's process person who will be the moderator. The tester will develop a set of test cases from the use case diagram. We developers will show how the classes in the design model handle each test case. The moderator will define the inspection boundaries, schedule the guided inspection session, distribute materials, keep the session moving forward, and then complete the final report.

In preparation for the session, the moderator defines the boundaries of the inspection by identifying the scope and depth of the information to be inspected. The scope is defined by a set of use cases. In our case, the scope covers all the use cases and thus the complete application. The depth is defined by identifying levels of containment in the composition hierarchies. In the case of *Brickles*, we will not inspect the objects that are aggregated within the BricklesView object. We will focus instead on those that represent the state of the match at any given time in a BricklesDoc object.

The tester writes test cases using the use cases found in Figure 2.11. We will focus on one test case, shown in Figure 4.2. Before the meeting, the developers complete the Design Model checklist shown in Figure 4.3. This exercise is completed individually by each developer. It requires that the developer compare the class diagram from the analysis model, shown in Figure 2.13, with the class diagram in the design model. Finally, the moderator sends out notice of the meeting along with either paper copies of the model or a URL to the Web version.

The test report from the guided inspection section notes the problems found during the symbolic execution of the test cases. With regards to the test case being considered here, the design is considered to have failed the test. The test report would reflect that it was not possible to determine how to complete the symbolic execution at this point in the algorithm. We do not want to confuse testing and debugging, but since we know exactly where execution terminated, it should be reported. The test report also includes the sequence diagram used to record the test execution, as shown in Figure 4.4.

The use case: A player stops a *Brickles* match by selecting Quit from the File menu.

Preconditions: The player has started the *Brickles* game, has moved the paddle, and has broken some bricks.

Test input: The player selects Quit.

Expected output: All game action freezes and the game window disappears.

Figure 4.2 Test case #1

UML Detailed Design Checklist Questionnaire	Yes	No
Analysis-to-design model transformation issues. Are all classes in the analysis model that are not in the design model outside the scope of the application?	✔	
Are all the states in the analysis-model statecharts also states in the statechart diagrams in the design model?		✔
Are the sequences of messages in all design-level sequence diagrams the same, even though additional messages may have been inserted between the analysis-level messages?		✔
Internal design model issues. Are all associations shown with no navigation information that is truly bidirectional?		✔
Are all composition relationships shown as unidirectional?		
Is every sequence diagram a subset of some activity diagram?		
Does every message sent in an interaction diagram appear as a method in the public interface of the class of the receiving object?		
Does every message sent in an interaction diagram go to the logically appropriate object?		
Are the transitions out of a state diagram mutually exclusive?		
Do all state machines, except for perpetual objects, contain initial and final states?		
Are all public modifier methods represented as transitions on each state even if they only result in staying in the same state?		
Is there a sequence diagram for each postcondition clause of each method that corresponds to use cases that meet the frequency/criticality threshold?		
Are all messages shown correctly as synchronous or asynchronous?		
Do the number of forks and joins balance in every activity diagram?		

Figure 4.3 Example design phase checklist

A Portion of a Session Transcript

MELISSA (moderator): OK, let's get started. Everyone has had a chance to look at the model and Dave and John have completed the checklists. Let me remind everyone that we are focusing on the locally designed classes and will ignore the standard user-interface classes such as menus. So let's begin with the first test case, Jason.

JASON (tester): Here is the first case [he hands out the first test case]. With John's help, I've laid out the beginnings of a sequence diagram for this test case based on the test case preconditions [see Figure 4.4]. So, the player selects Quit from the menu and...

JOHN (developer): My :BricklesView would receive the Quit message. And my object would send the Quit message to Dave's aBricklesDoc. [He draws these onto the sequence diagram.]

DAVE (developer): When :BricklesDoc gets the Quit message it will send the Stop message to aTimer. [He begins to draw this on the sequence diagram.]

JASON: Wait a minute! As I read the class diagram there is no association between those two classes.

DAVE: John, where is that Stop message supposed to go? I thought you said you were going to implement that method.

JOHN: [Busy shuffling between the sequence diagram and the class diagram with a confused look on his face.] Defect!

MELISSA: Sounds like we are ready for the next test case.

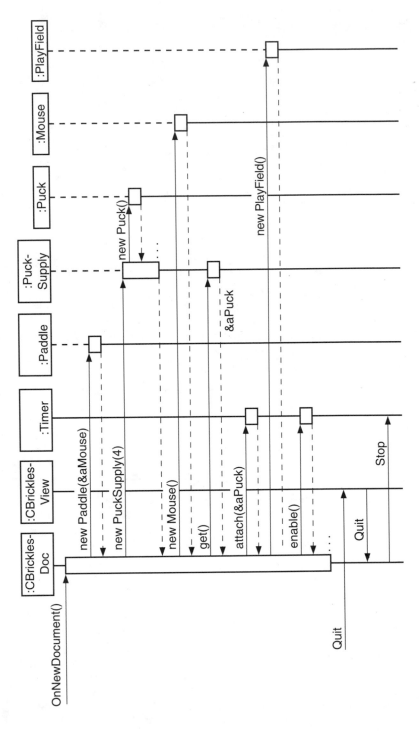

Figure 4.4 Partial sequence diagram for test case #1

Place in the Development Process

The last activity in each phase in the development process should be a verification that the work produced in the phase possesses the qualities we desire. That work is in the form of either a UML model or code in a programming language. (See A Development Process Overview on page 66.) The process is structured so that each development phase moves the product a step toward the final system, which results in a sequence of models in which the model produced in one development phase is more specific and more complete than the model from the previous phase. For example, during the application analysis phase, a model is created by filtering the information in the domain analysis model and the requirements model to eliminate information that is not specifically relevant to the application under development. Two of the differences between the succeeding models are the scope of the content and the level of abstraction. The requirements model filters the domain model so that any information not required for the immediate application is not included in the application analysis model. As the information in each succeeding model level becomes more specific, the inspection of each model can also become more specific and narrowly focused. This sequence of models described in Figure 4.5—actually it is just one model that is being transformed incrementally—provides an opportunity to establish a "chain of quality" in which each model is verified before moving to the next phase.

Phase/Model	Content	Transformed from...
Domain Analysis	Domain concepts, standard algorithms	The minds of the domain experts
Application Analysis	Concepts needed to explain the specific problem; standard algorithms	The domain analysis model and the requirements model
Architectural Design	Basic structure of interfaces and their interactions	Standard architectural patterns and creativity of designers
Detailed Design	Each interface in the architecture is implemented by one or more components	Architectural design model and standard design patterns and algorithms

Figure 4.5 Models and phases

The Basics of Guided Inspection

The **guided inspection** technique provides a means of objectively and systematically searching a work product for faults by using explicit test cases. This testing perspective means that reviews are treated as a test session. The basic testing steps are as follows:

1. Define the test space.

2. Select values from the test space using a specific strategy.

3. Apply the test values to the product being tested.

4. Evaluate the results and the percentage of the model covered by the tests (based on some criteria).

These steps are specialized to the following steps (we will elaborate on each of these in this chapter):

1. Specify the scope and depth of the inspection. The scope will be defined by describing a body of material or a specific set of use cases. For small projects, the scope may always be the entire model. The depth will be defined by describing the level of detail to be covered. It may also be defined by specifying the levels in aggregation hierarchies on certain UML diagrams in the model under test (MUT).

2. Identify the basis from which the MUT was created. The basis for all but the initial model is the set of models from the previous development phase. For example, the application analysis model is based on the domain analysis model and the use case model. Initial models are based on the knowledge in the heads of select groups of people.

3. Develop test cases for each of the evaluation criteria to be applied using the contents of the basis model as input (see Selecting Test Cases for the Inspection on page 123). The scenarios from the use case model are a good starting point for test cases for many models.

4. Establish criteria for measuring test coverage. For example, a class diagram might be well covered if every class is touched by some test case.

5. Perform the static analysis using the appropriate checklist. The MUT is compared to the basis model to determine consistency between the two diagrams.

6. "Execute" the test cases. We will describe the actual test session in detail later in this chapter.

7. Evaluate the effectiveness of the tests using the coverage measurement. Calculate the coverage percentage. For example, If 12 of the classes from a class diagram containing 18 classes have been "touched" by the test cases, the test coverage is 75%. The testing of analysis or design models is so high-level that 100% coverage is necessary to achieve good results.

8. If the coverage is insufficient, expand the test suite and apply the additional tests, otherwise terminate the testing. Usually the additional test cases cannot be written during the inspection session. The testers identify where the coverage is lacking and work with a developer to identify potential test cases that would touch the uncovered model elements. The tester then creates the full test cases and another inspection session is held.

Coverage in Models

In the UML models we use, the model elements are the usual object-oriented concepts: classes, relationships, objects, and messages. A test case "covers" one of these elements if it uses that element as part of a test case. Of course, a single test case using a particular element probably does not exhaust all possible values of the attributes of that element. For example, using an object from a class to receive a single message does not test the other methods in the same class.

As we move deeper into the development life cycle, the detail of the model increases and the detail at which coverage matters increases as well. For a domain analysis model, simply creating a single object from a class will be sufficient to consider that we have covered the class. Coverage for this level of model can be stated as a percentage of classes and relationships covered. At the design level, we would typically like to use every method in an interface before saying that a class is covered. Coverage for this level is more likely to be stated by counting all of the methods in the model rather than all of the classes.

The more abstract the classes, the higher the level of coverage that should be required. To omit a single abstract class from the coverage in testing overlooks the defects that could potentially be found in all of the concrete classes that eventually are derived from the abstract class. When testing at a concrete-class level, omitting a class during testing only overlooks the defects in that one class.

The higher the level of abstraction of the model, the higher the level of coverage that is required.

Reviews usually involve a discussion of the role of each piece of a model from a high level. The relationships between pieces are also explained in terms of the specified interfaces at the formal parameter level. The test cases created using this technique allow these same pieces and relationships to be examined at a much more concrete level that assigns specific values to the attributes of the objects. The test cases should be written at a level that is sufficiently specific to support tracing exact paths of execution through the logic of the algorithms, but not so specific that the code must be written first.

Should test cases be available to developers prior to the inspection session?

There has to be a balance between allowing developers to program to the tests and having the developers duplicate the effort of the testers by coming up with their own use scenarios. If the testers were going to develop all possible scenarios then giving those to the developers and sampling from them for model testing would be acceptable. Since the testers usually only create a small percentage of the possible scenarios, it is doubtful that they are duplicating the work of the developers who independently will (we hope) identify other scenarios. So, our general approach is to not let the developers have the scenarios prior to the inspection session.

Many object-oriented software development methods discuss using one or more diagrams within a model to evaluate the other diagrams. For example, a sequence diagram traces a path through the class diagram in which the messaging arrows in the sequence diagram are supposed to correspond to associations found in the class diagram. However, these development methods do not ensure a systematic coverage of the model. One step in guided inspection checks the internal consistency and completeness of the diagrams using the diagrams created during test execution.

Should testers only use test cases for the current increment in an inspection session?

No. Running a test scenario from a previous increment as a regression check on the model is a useful idea. The regression scenarios should be chosen to include those that failed in the previous increment and those that cover areas most likely to have been changed to incorporate the functionality of the current increment.

Evaluation Criteria

We are essentially trying to answer three questions as we inspect the MUT:

- Is the model correct?
- Is the model a complete representation of the information?
- Is the model internally consistent and consistent with its basis model?

Correctness is a measure of the accuracy of the model. At the analysis level, it is the accuracy of the problem description. At the design level, it is how accurately the model represents the solution to the problem. At both levels, the model must also accurately use the notation. The degree of accuracy is judged with respect to a standard that is assumed to be infallible (referred to as "the oracle"), although it seldom is. The oracle often is a human expert whose personal knowledge is considered sufficient to be used as a standard. The human expert determines the expected results for each test case.

Testing determines that a model is correct with respect to a test case if the result of the execution is the result that was expected. (It is very important that each test case have an expected result explicitly stated before the test case writer becomes biased by the results of the inspection.) The model is correct with respect to a set of test cases if every test case produces the expected result.

In the real world, we must assume that the oracle can be incorrect on occasion. We often separate the domain experts on a project into two teams who represent different perspectives or approaches within the company. One team constructs the model and at the same time, the second team develops the test cases. This check and balance doesn't guarantee correct evaluations, but it does raise the probability. The same is true for every test case. Any of them could specify an incorrect, expected result. The testers and developers must work together to determine when this is the case.

Completeness is a measure of the inclusiveness of the model. Are any necessary, or at least useful, elements missing from the model? Testing determines whether there are test cases that pose scenarios that the elements in the model cannot represent. In an iterative incremental process, completeness is considered relative to how mature the current increment is expected to be. This criteria becomes more rigorous as the increment matures over successive iterations.

One factor directly affecting the effectiveness of the completeness criteria is the quality of the test coverage. The model is judged complete if the results of executing the test cases can be adequately represented using only the contents of the model. For example, a sequence diagram might be constructed to represent a scenario. All of the objects needed for the sequence diagram must come from classes in the class diagram or it will be judged incomplete. However, if only a few test cases are run, the fact that some classes are missing may escape detection. For the early models, this inspection is sufficiently high level that a coverage of 100% of all use cases is necessary.

Consistency is a measure of whether there are contradictions within the model or between the current model and the model upon which it is based. Testing identifies inconsistencies by finding different representations within the model for similar test cases. Inconsistencies may also be identified during the execution of a test case when the current MUT is compared to its basis model or when two diagrams in the same model are compared. In an incremental approach, consistency is judged locally until the current increment is integrated with the larger system. The integration process must ensure that the new piece does not introduce inconsistencies into the integrated model.

Consistency checking can determine whether there are any contradictions or conflicts present either internal to a single diagram or between two diagrams. For example, a sequence diagram might require a relationship between two classes while the class diagram shows none. Inconsistencies will often initially appear as incorrect results in the context of one of the two diagrams and correct results in the other. Inconsistencies are identified by careful examination of the diagrams in a model during the simulated execution.

Additional qualities—defines a number of system attributes that the development team might wish to verify. For example, architectural models usually have performance goals to meet. The guided inspection test cases can be used as the scenarios for testing performance. Structural models used to compute performance can be applied to these scenarios, which are selected based on the use profile to estimate total performance and to identify potential bottlenecks.

If the architecture has an objective of facilitating change, test cases based on the change cases should be used to evaluate the degree of success in achieving this objective (see Testing Models for Additional Qualities on page 151).

Organization of the Guided Inspection Activity

Basic Roles

In the guided inspection activity there are three key roles that must be assumed by the available personnel.

1. **Domain expert**—The people in this role are the source of truth (or at least expected results). They define the expected system response for a specific input scenario. In many domains, the experienced developers are experts in their domain. They can provide a first line of validation. However, an additional, outside source of expertise is usually essential to the inspection process.

2. **Tester**—The people in this role conduct the analysis necessary to select effective test cases. Testers are often the creators of the basis model. When the scope of the inspection is at a system-wide level, the test case writers are often the system test team. They construct the input scenario specialized from the preconditions of a use case, the test actions as taken from the scenario, alternate paths, or exceptions sections of the use case, and the expected result as defined by the domain expert.

3. **Developer**—The creators of the MUT perform the role of "developer." They provide information that is not captured in the model. Except for those projects that generate code directly from a model, most develop-

ers leave many details out of the models, thus the necessary information is only available from the developers. The development staff walks the inspectors through the model, tracing actions on diagrams, showing the relationships between diagrams, and providing the actual system response at a level appropriate to the current maturity of the development.

Individual Inspection

Guided inspection begins with a **desk check** like traditional inspection techniques. Each tester completes a checklist specific to the type of model being inspected. Certain incompleteness and inconsistency faults can easily be found during this task. This also turns out to be the easiest task to automate. A number of tools offer some limited amount of static checks, which are basically syntactic. We have had success in expanding that capability with the scripting languages in some of the design environments. We won't name names since the landscape changes almost daily, but check out this feature as part of your next tool purchase evaluation.

Preparing for the Inspection

Specifying the Inspection

When a guided inspection is planned, the scope and depth of the material to be inspected should be specified. The earliest models, such as requirements and domain models, may be inspected in their entirety at a single session. Later models will usually be too large to allow this. In Realistic Models (below), we talk about ways of creating modular diagrams that can be grouped into different-sized pieces. Having modular models facilitates limiting an inspection to the work of a single group or even to a specific class hierarchy.

The **scope** of an inspection is defined by specifying a set of use cases, a set of packages, or abstract classes/interfaces. The scope determines starting points for scenarios, but other classes are pulled into scope as they are needed to support the scenarios.

The **depth** of the inspection is defined by specifying layers in aggregation hierarchies under which messages are not sent. The bottom layer classes simply return values with no indication of how the value was computed.

Realistic Models

It is usually not possible, or desirable to capture all of the details of an industrial-strength program in a few comprehensive diagrams in a single model. There will need to be multiple class diagrams, state diagrams, and, of course, multitudes of sequence diagrams. In preparation for the guided inspection, the developers should organize the model to facilitate the review by creating additional diagrams that link existing ones or by revising diagrams to conform to the scope of the inspection.

One basic technique that makes the model more understandable is to layer the diagrams. This results in more individual diagrams, but each diagram is sufficiently modular to fit within the scope of a specific inspection. The diagrams are easier to create because they follow a pattern.

Figure 4.6 illustrates one type of layering for class diagrams in which classes are grouped into packages and those packages may be enclosed in another package. Additionally, we often show all of the specializations from an abstract class as one diagram (see Figure 4.7) and all of the aggregation relationships for a class in another diagram.

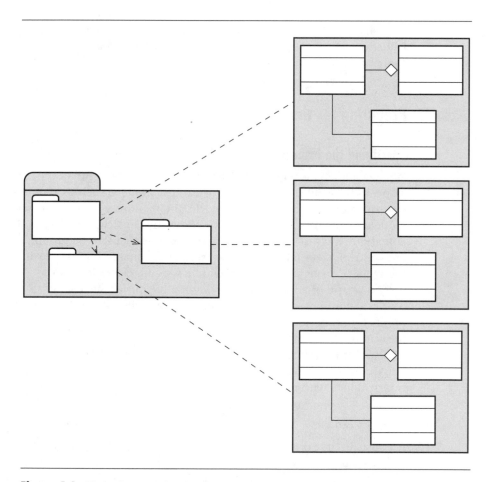

Figure 4.6 Class diagram layered into packages

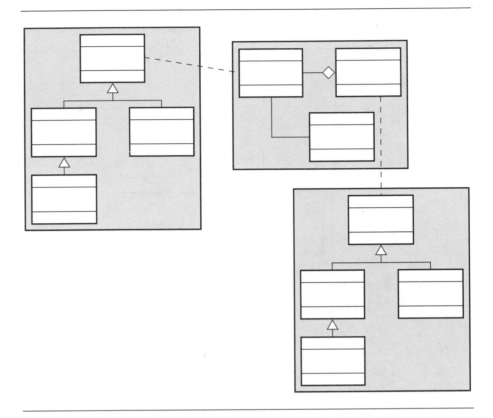

Figure 4.7 Separating relationships

Figure 4.8 shows a technique for linking class diagrams. The work of one team uses the work of other teams. This can be shown by placing a class box from the other team on the edge of the team's diagram and showing the relationships between the classes. An inspection would be limited to the classes in the team's diagram. Messages to objects from the "boundary classes" would not be traced further. The return value, if any, would simply be noted.

Figure 4.9 illustrates a layering for sequence diagrams. At one level, the diagram terminates at an interface or abstract class. A sequence diagram is then constructed for each class that implements the interface or specializes the abstract class.

Selecting Test Cases for the Inspection

There are usually many possible test cases that can be developed from any specific use case. Traditional testing techniques use techniques such as equivalence classes and logical paths through the program as ways to select effective test cases. Test cases can be selected to ensure that specific types of coverage

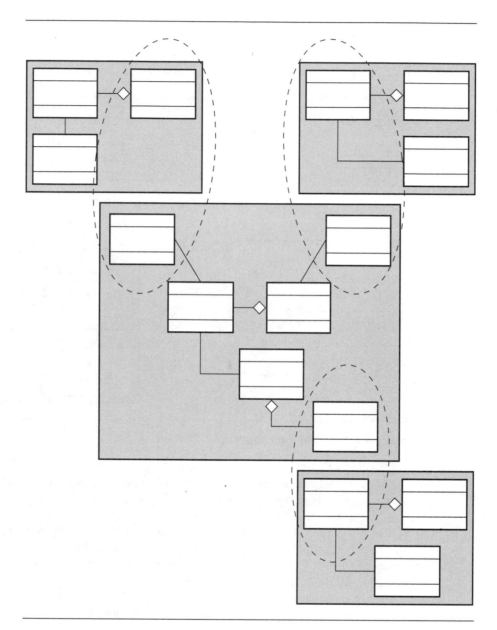

Figure 4.8 Links between class diagrams

are achieved or to find specific types of defects. We use *Orthogonal Defect Classification* to help select test cases that are most likely to identify defects by covering the different categories of system actions that trigger defects. We use a **use profile** to select test cases that give confidence in the reliability of the product by identifying which parts of the program are used the most.

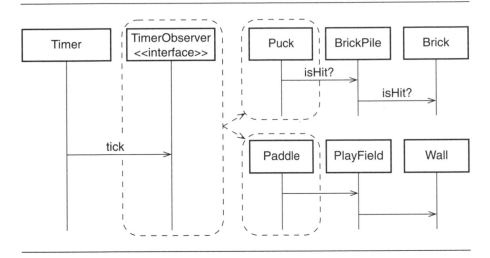

Figure 4.9 Sequence diagram per interface implementation

Orthogonal Defect Classification as a Test Case Selector

Orthogonal Defect Classification (ODC) [Chill92] is a scheme developed at IBM based on an analysis of a large amount of data. The activities that caused a defect to be detected are classified as "triggers." These are divided into groups based on when the triggers occurred, such as during reviews and inspections. Figure 4.10 is a list of attributes that trigger defects during reviews and inspections. The guided inspection technique uses several of these triggers as a guide to selecting test cases. We will delineate several of these triggers as we proceed, but we will address a few of these now.

1. Design conformance is addressed by comparing the basis model to the MUT as well as comparing the MUT to the requirements. This comparison is a direct result of the test case execution.

2. Concurrency is a trigger that will be visible in the design model and scenarios can be generated that explicitly explore thread interactions. The UML activity diagram will be the primary source for symbolic execution.

3. Lateral compatibility is activated by the trace of scenarios between objects on sequence diagrams.

By structuring the guided inspection process so that as many of these triggers as possible are encountered, you ensure that the tests that guide the inspection are more likely to "trigger" as many failures as possible.

Design conformance—comparison of basis and current model.

Operational semantics—tracing the logic.

Concurrency—examining the synchronization between threads/processes.

Backward compatibility—comparison to previous products.

Lateral compatibility—comparison with interfaces that use this one.

Rare situation—examining unspecified system behavior.

Side effects—examining behavior outside the scope of the current product.

Document consistency/completeness—examine for consistency/completeness.

Language dependencies—examining for language-specific details.

Figure 4.10 ODC review and inspection triggers

Use Profiles as a Test Case Selector

A *use profile* (see Use Profiles on page 130) for a system is an ordering of the individual use cases based on a combination of the frequency and criticality values for the individual use cases. The traditional operational profile used for procedural systems is based strictly on frequency-of-use information. Combining the frequency and criticality ratings to order the use cases provides a more meaningful criteria for ensuring quality. For example, we might paint a logo in the lower right-hand corner of each window. This would be a relatively frequent event, but should it fail, the system will still be able to provide important functionality to the user. Likewise, attaching to the local database server would happen very seldom but the success of that operation is critical to the success of numerous other functions. The number of test cases per use case is adjusted based on the position of the use case in the ranking.

Risk as a Test Case Selector

Some testing methods use risk as the basis for determining how much to test. This is useful during development when we are actively searching for defects. It is not appropriate after development when we are trying to achieve some measure of reliability. At that time, the use profile technique supports testing the application in the way that it will be used.

Our use case template captures the information needed for each of the techniques so that they can be used throughout the complete life cycle. We use the frequency/criticality information instead of the risk information for guided inspection because we are trying to capture the same perspective as the testing of the system after development. For situations in which the inspection is only covering a portion of the design, using the risk information may be equally relevant.

Technique Summary—Creating Test Cases from Use Cases

A test case consists of a set of preconditions, a stimulus (inputs), and the expected response. A use case contains a series of scenarios: the normal case, extensions, and exceptional cases. Each scenario includes the action taken by an actor and the required response from the system that corresponds to the basic parts of a test case. To construct a test case from the scenario, each part of the scenario is made more specific by giving exact values to all attributes and objects. This requires coordination between the use case diagram and the other diagrams. The "things" mentioned in the scenario should translate into some object or objects from the class diagram. Each of these objects should be in specific states defined in the state diagrams for those classes. The actions in the use case will correspond to messages to the objects.

Each scenario can result in multiple test cases by selecting different values (that is, states) for the objects used in the use case. The expected result part of the test case is derived from the scenario portion of the use case and the specific values provided in the input scenario. The following is a use case scenario and the corresponding test case.

- Subsystem use case: A `movablePiece` receives a tick() message. It must then check to determine whether it collided with a `stationaryPiece`.

- Test precondition: The puck is located within less than a tick of a brick and is headed for that brick.

- Test case: Input—The puck receives a tick message.

- Expected result: The puck has changed direction and the brick has changed its state from active to kaput, indicating that it has broken, and disappears.

Creating Test Cases

Test cases for a guided inspection are scenarios that should be represented in the MUT. Before the requirements model is verified, the scenarios come from a team of domain experts who are not producing the requirements. Later, we will see how this is done. For now we will focus on test cases that are based on the system requirements.

The use case template that we use (see an abbreviated version in Figure 4.11) has three sources of scenarios. The *Use Scenario* is the "sunny-day" scenario that is most often the path taken. The *Alternative Paths* section may list several scenarios that differ from the use scenario in a variety of ways, but still represent valid executions. The *Exceptional Paths* section provides scenarios that result in error conditions.

Use Case # 1

Actor: Player

Use Scenario: The user selects the Play option from the menu. The system responds by starting a match.

Alternative Paths: If a match is already in progress, the selection is ignored.

Exceptional Cases: If the match cannot open the display, an error message is displayed and the program aborts.

Frequency: Low

Criticality: High

Risk: Medium

Figure 4.11 An example of a use case

Completing Checklists

Prior to the interactive inspection session, the inspectors examine the models for certain syntactic information that can be evaluated just from the information contained in the model. This portion of the technique is not concerned with the content but only the form of the model. Figure 4.12 shows the checklist used during the design phase. The checklist is divided into two parts. One part addresses comparisons between the analysis model and the MUT. For example, the checklist reminds the inspector to check whether classes that have been deleted should have been deleted because of the differences between analysis and design information. The second part covers issues within the MUT. The checklist guides the inspector to consider whether the use of syntax correctly captures the information. For example, it guides the inspector to consider the navigability of the associations and whether they are correctly represented.

The Interactive Inspection Session

The testing portion of the guided inspection session is organized in one of two ways depending upon whether the model has been automated or not. If a prototype or other working model has been created, the session does not vary much from a typical code-testing session. The test cases provided by the testers are implemented, usually in some scripting language, and executed using the simulation facilities of the prototype of the model. These test cases must be more rigorously specified than the test cases that will be used in an interactive session with symbolic execution. The results of the execution are evaluated and the team determines whether the model passed the test or not.

UML Detailed Design Checklist Question	Yes	No
Analysis-to-design model transformation issues. Are all classes in the analysis model that are not in the design model outside the scope of the application?		
Are all the states in the analysis model statecharts also states in the statechart diagrams in the design model?		
Are the sequences of messages in all design-level sequence diagrams the same, even though additional messages may have been inserted between the analysis-level messages?		
Internal design model issues. Are all associations shown with no navigation information truly bidirectional?		
Are all composition relationships shown as unidirectional?		
Is every sequence diagram a subset of some activity diagram?		
Does every message sent in an interaction diagram appear as a method in the public interface of the class of the receiving object?		
Does every message sent in an interaction diagram go to the logically appropriate object?		
Are the transitions out of a state diagram mutually exclusive?		
Do all state machines, except for perpetual objects, contain initial and final states?		
Are all public modifier methods represented as transitions on each state even if they only result in staying in the same state?		
Is there a sequence diagram for each postcondition clause of each method that corresponds to use cases that meet the frequency/criticality threshold?		
Are all messages shown correctly as synchronous or asynchronous?		
Do the number of forks and joins balance in every activity diagram?		

Figure 4.12 Design phase checklist

If the model has not been prototyped, the testing session is an interactive session involving testers and developers. The developers cooperate to perform a symbolic execution that simulates the processing that will occur when actual code is available. That is, they walk the testers through the scenarios provided by the test cases.

Use Profiles

One technique for allocating testing resources determines which parts of the application will be utilized the most and then tests those parts the most. The principle here is "test the most used, most critical parts of the program over a wider range of inputs than the lesser used, least critical portions to ensure the greatest user satisfaction." A use profile is a ranking of the use cases based on the combined frequency/criticality values. This can be viewed as a double sort of the use cases based on the number of times that an end-user function (interface method) is used, or is anticipated to be used, in the actual operation of the program and the criticality of each of these uses. The criticality is a value assigned by the domain experts and recorded in each use case. The frequency information can be obtained in a couple of ways.

First, data can be collected from actual use perhaps during usability testing or during the actual operation if we will be testing a future version of the product. This results in a raw count profile. The count for each behavior is divided by the total number of invocations to produce a percentage. A second approach is to reason about the meanings and responsibilities of the system interface and then estimate the relative number of times each method will be used. The result is an ordering of the end-user methods rather than a precise frequency count. The estimated number of invocations for each behavior is divided by the total number of invocations to provide a percentage. The percentage computed for each use determines the percentage of the test suite that should be devoted to that use.

As an example, the Exit function for *Brickles* will be successfully completed exactly once per invocation of the program but the NewGame method may be used numerous times. It is conceivable that the Help function might not be used at all during a use of the system. This results in a profile that indicates an ordering of NewGame, Exit, and Help. We can assign weights that reflect the relative frequency that we expect. If on average we would estimate that a player would play 10 games prior to EXITing the system, the weights would be 10, 1, 1. The NewGame function should be exercised in 82.5% (10 out of 12) of the test cases while the Help function and Exit should each constitute 8.5%.

The following additional roles are assigned to individuals in an interactive testing session. A person may take on the following roles simultaneously.

■ *Moderator*—The moderator controls the session and advances the execution through the scenario. The session is not intended to debug, which the developers will want to do, nor to expand the requirements, which the domain experts will want to do. The moderator keeps the session moving over the intended material.

■ *Recorder*—This person, usually a tester, makes annotations on the reference models as the team agrees that a fault has been found. The recorder makes certain that these faults are taken into consideration in the latter parts of the scenario so that time is not wasted on redundant identification of the same fault. The recorder also maintains a list of issues that are not resolved during the testing session. These may not be faults. Information may need to come from a team in another part of the project or a team member who is absent during the inspection.

■ *Drawer*—This person constructs a sequence diagram as a scenario is executed. A drawer concentrates on capturing all of the appropriate details such as returns from messages and state changes. The drawer may also annotate the sequence diagram with information between the message arrow and the return arrow.

The guided inspection session can easily slip into an interactive design session. The participants, particularly the developers, will typically want to change the model during the testing session as problems are encountered. Resist this urge. This is the classic confusion between testing and debugging and diverts attention from other defects that are found. The recorder captures the faults found by the inspection so that they can be addressed later. This keeps attention focused on the search for faults and prevents a "rush to judgment" about the precise cause of the defect. If a significant number of problems are found, end the session and let the developers work on the model.

Testing Specific Types of Models

The basic guided inspection technique does not change from one development phase to another, but some characteristics of the model content and some aspects of the team do change.

■ The level of detail in the model becomes greater as development proceeds.

■ The amount of information also increases as development proceeds.

■ The exact interpretation of the evaluation criteria can be made more specific for a specific model.

■ The membership of the inspection team changes for different models.

We will now discuss models at several points in the life cycle.

Requirements Model

The requirements for an application are summarized by creating a model of the *uses* of the system. The UML construct used for this model is the use case developed by Jacobson [JCJO92], which is discussed in Chapter 2. Figure 4.13 is an abbreviated version of the text format used for a use case. Figure 4.14 shows

Use Case # 5

Actor: Player

Use Scenario: The user pauses the match by pressing the mouse button. The system responds by pausing the puck and not responding to mouse movement.

Alternative Paths:

Exceptional Cases: If the match is not in progress the mouse key press is ignored.

Frequency: Low

Criticality: Low

Risk: Medium

Figure 4.13 An example of a use case

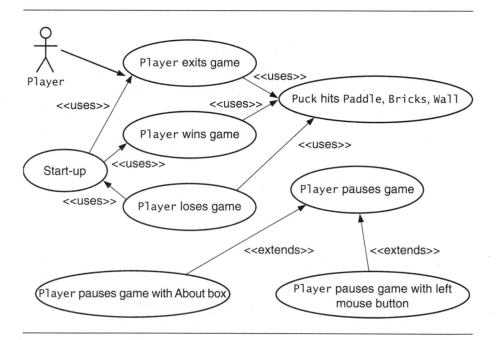

Figure 4.14 *Brickles* use case model

Criteria	Interpretation for Requirements
Completeness	The use cases represent all of the functionality needed for a satisfactory product. No use case is included that is not required functionality.
Correctness	Each use case accurately represents a requirement.
Consistency	Any system functionality is specified in the same manner everywhere it is described.

Figure 4.15 Criteria for requirements inspection

the UML use case diagram for the *Brickles* example, and Figure 4.16 through Figure 4.21 show the use-case text descriptions. The use case diagram captures relationships between the use cases. Individual use cases are broken into "sub-use cases" using the **uses** and **extends** relationships. Later, in Chapter 9, we will use these relationships to structure the system test cases. The text descriptions capture the majority of the information for each use case. While the relationships are used to structure tests, the text descriptions are used to provide most of the information for a test case.

Acceptance testing often finds faults that result from problems with the requirements. The typical problems include missing requirements (an incomplete requirements model), requirements that contradict each other (an inconsistent model), and scenarios in which the system does not behave as the client intended (an incorrect model). Many of these problems can be identified much earlier than the acceptance test phase using guided inspection.

The criteria for evaluating the models is interpreted specifically for the requirements model in Figure 4.15. Completeness is a typical requirements problem for which the iterative, incremental process model is a partial solution. Guided inspection can offer further help by requiring a detailed examination by an independent group of domain experts and product definition people. This examination will identify many missing requirements much earlier than the typical process.

The detailed examination will also search for correctness faults. The act of writing the test cases for the guided inspection will identify many requirements that are not sufficiently precise to allow a test case to be written. Running the test cases will provide an opportunity for the independent group to identify discrepancies between the expected results in the test cases and the actual content of the requirements model.

The larger the system, the more problem there is with the consistency of the requirements. In addition to contradictions, there is often the need to identify places where one use case supersedes another. For example, one use case calls for an action to happen at least within ten seconds while another expects the same action to occur within seven seconds. The use of the end-to-end scenarios that trace a complete action will help locate these inconsistencies.

Use Case #1

Actor: Player

Use Scenario: The player starts the *Brickles* executable, plays a match and then selects the Exit option on the File menu.

Alternative Paths:

Exceptional Cases:

Frequency: Low

Criticality: High

Risk: Low

Figure 4.16 An example of use case #1

One feature of the requirements model that affects how the inspection is organized is that there is no UML model on which the requirements are based. So comparisons to the basis model refer to documents produced by marketing, system engineering, or client organizations. Since this is a notorious source of defects, we will expend extra effort in verifying the requirements model.

The roles for this inspection are assigned as shown in Figure 4.22. You will want to adapt these to your situation. The domain expert provides the "correct" answers for test cases. In this case that means agreeing or disagreeing that a use case adequately represents the required functionality. Using the system testers in the tester role provides the system testers with an early look at the source of

---

Use Case #2

Actor: Player

Use Scenario: The player starts the *Brickles* executable, plays a match, breaks all of the bricks, and wins.

Alternative Paths:

Exceptional Cases:

Frequency: Medium

Criticality: High

Risk: Medium

Figure 4.17 An example of use case #2

Use Case #3

Actor: Player

Use Scenario: The player starts the *Brickles* executable, plays a match, loses all of the pucks, and loses the game.

Alternative Paths:

Exceptional Cases:

Frequency: Medium

Criticality: High

Risk: Medium

Figure 4.18 An example of use case #3

information for the system test cases and an opportunity to have input into improving the use cases. We also use a second group of domain experts and product definition people to work with the system testers. This provides a source of scenarios that is independent of the people who wrote the requirements. Some organizations will have the use cases written by developers rather than a separate organization of system engineers, and these developers will be the ones to execute test cases.

Use Case #4

Actor: Player

Use Scenario: The puck bounces against the paddle, breaks some bricks, hits a wall.

Alternative Paths:

Exceptional Cases:

Frequency: High

Criticality: High

Risk: Medium

Figure 4.19 An example of use case #4

Use Case #5

Actor: Player

Use Scenario: The player pauses play by holding down the left mouse button.

Alternative Paths:

Exceptional Cases:

Frequency: Low

Criticality: Low

Risk: Medium

Figure 4.20 An example of use case #5

Use Case #6

Actor: Player

Use Scenario: The player pauses play by selecting the About menu entry.

Alternative Paths:

Exceptional Cases:

Frequency: Low

Criticality: Low

Risk: Medium

Figure 4.21 An example of use case #6

Domain Expert	Domain expert, marketing representative, client, product-definition personnel
Tester	System tester, domain expert
Developer	System engineer

Figure 4.22 Roles in requirements inspection

> When dividing the domain experts into two groups, don't divide based on ideology. That just precipitates theoretical debates. Divide the experts so that each team has representation from as many "camps" as possible.

The basic outline of "testing" the requirements model is given in the following list along with an example using *Brickles.* The example is given in italics.

1. Develop the ranking of use cases by computing the combined frequency and criticality information for the use cases. Figure 4.23 gives the ranking for *Brickles*.

2. Determine the total number of test cases that can be constructed given the amount of resources available. It should be possible to estimate this number from historical data. *We will assume we have time for 15 test cases.*

3. Ration the tests based on the ranking. *Note how in Figure 4.23 only 14 of the 15 are assigned since it is impossible to evenly split the number of tests. The 15th test would be allocated to the category showing the most failures in the initial round of testing.*

4. Write scenarios based only on the knowledge of those in the domain expert's role. The number of scenarios is determined by the values computed in Step 3. *The player starts the game, moves the paddle, and has broken several bricks by the time he loses the puck. The system responds by providing a new puck.*

Use	Frequency	Criticality	Combined Value	Rank	Number of Test Cases
Start *Brickles*	Medium	High	High	1	3
Pause *Brickles*	Low	Low	Low	3	1
Stop *Brickles*	Medium	Low	Medium	2	2
Break brick	High	High	High	1	3
Wins	Medium	High	High	1	3
Loses	Medium	Low	Medium	2	2

Figure 4.23 *Brickles* use cases

5. In a meeting of the producers of the requirements and the test scenario writers, the writer presents each scenario and the requirements modelers identify the use case that contains the test scenario as either a main scenario, extension, exception, or alternative path that represents the scenario. If no match is found, it is listed as an incompleteness defect. If the scenario could be represented by two or more use cases (on the same level of abstraction), an inconsistency defect has occurred. In both of these cases, the first question asked is whether there is an incorrectness defect in the statement of a use case that, if corrected, would handle the scenario accurately. *In the scenario provided in Step 4 there is no mention of the limited number of pucks. The system may not be able to provide a puck if the supply is exhausted. The requirement should be explicit about a fixed number of pucks.*

Much of this effort will be reused in the testing of other models. Both the ranking of use cases and construction of test cases will produce reusable assets. The requirements model will serve as the basis for testing several other models, and therefore, these test cases can be reused.

Analysis Models

We will be concerned with two types of analysis models: domain analysis and application analysis models. The two types model existing knowledge. One models the knowledge in a domain while the other models knowledge about the product.

Domain Analysis Model

The domain analysis model represents information about a domain of knowledge that pertains to the application about to be constructed. As such, it is derived from the literature and knowledge about the domain as opposed to another UML model. Although many projects are satisfied with creating a domain model that is only a simple class diagram, most domains encompass standard algorithms and many refer to states that are characteristic of the concepts being represented. Figure 4.24 shows the interpretation of the evaluation criteria for a domain model.

The domain model is a representation of the knowledge in a domain as seen through the eyes of a set of domain experts. As is to be expected, there can be differences of opinion between experts. For this reason, we have found it useful to divide the available set of experts into two groups. One group, the larger, creates the domain model while the second group serves as the testers of that model. In Figure 4.25, group one is referred to as the developers and group two is referred to as both testers and domain experts. This check and balance between the groups provides a thorough examination of the model.

Criteria	Interpretation for Domain Modeling
Completeness	The concepts are sufficient to cover the scope of the content specified. Sufficient detail is given to describe concepts to the required depth.
Correctness	The descriptions of domain concepts are accurate; the algorithms will produce the expected results.
Consistency	Model elements should be consistent with the company's definitions and meanings.

Figure 4.24 Criteria for domain model inspection

Figure 4.26 relates portions of the class diagram from the domain models for *Brickles* to its application analysis model. Note that there are two domains represented, *Interactive Graphics* and *Games*. The test cases for this model will come from the second group of domain experts. They consider how these concepts are used in the typical applications in which they have had experience. The test cases will be written by a team composed of a system tester who knows how to write test cases, and the second group of domain experts. A test case only states details down to the level of the domain concepts. Any actions are domain algorithms.

A test case for the *Interactive Graphics* domain model would look like the following:

> *Assume that a canvas has been created and asked to display a shape. How will the canvas know where to locate the shape? It is expected that a* mouseEvent *would provide the coordinates to which a system user points.*

Role in Model Inspection	Role in Project
Domain Expert	Domain expert
Tester	System tester, domain expert
Developer	Domain expert

Figure 4.25 Roles in domain model inspection

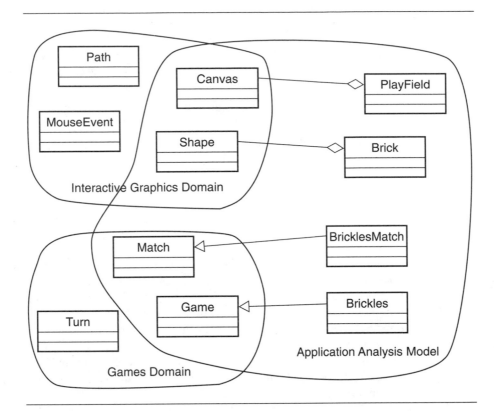

Figure 4.26 Mapping domain models onto application analysis models

Application Analysis Model

There will usually be multiple domain models for a large project. All of these contribute to the single application analysis model. Some parts of each domain model will be thrown away because they are outside the scope of this particular project. Some pieces of domain models will be merged to provide a single element in the application model. This makes judging completeness during the inspection more difficult since there is not a direct mapping from one model to another. Criteria and roles are shown in Figures 4.27 and 4.28.

An analysis model can be *too* complete. That is, it can contain design information that the project team has erroneously made part of the requirements. This leads to an overly constrained design that may not be as flexible as possible. As the inspection team measures the test coverage of the model, they examine pieces that are not covered to determine whether they should be removed from the model.

Figure 2.13 shows the class diagram for the application analysis model for *Brickles*.

Criteria	Interpretation for the Application Analysis Model
Completeness	The ideas expressed in each use case can be represented by the concepts and algorithms in the model. No design information is included in the model.
Correctness	Experts agree with the attributes and behaviors assigned to each concept; on the steps in each algorithm; major states for each conceptual entity.
Consistency	Where there are multiple ways to represent a concept of action, those ways are equivalent.

Figure 4.27 Criteria for application analysis model inspection

A test case for the application analysis model would look like the following:

Assume that a match has been started and the playfield has been constructed. How will a paddle prevent a puck from striking the floor boundary? It is expected that the paddle will move into the trajectory of the puck and collide with it. The collision will cause the puck to change direction by reflecting off the middle third of the paddle at the same angle from the point of impact.

Design Models

There are three levels of design in an object-oriented project: architectural, mechanistic, and detailed. We will focus on two basic design models that encompass those three levels: the architectural design model and the detailed class design model. The architectural model provides the basic structure of the application by defining how a set of interfaces are related. It also specifies the exact content of each interface. The detailed class model provides the precise semantics of each class and identifies the architectural interface to which the class corresponds.

Role in Inspection	Role in Project
Domain Expert	Domain expert; system engineer
Tester	System tester
Developer	Application developer

Figure 4.28 Roles in application analysis model inspection

Architectural Model

The architectural model is the skeleton of the entire application. It is arguably the most important model for the application so we will go into a fair amount of detail in this section. This is the model in which the nonfunctional requirements are blended with the functional requirements. This provides the opportunity to use the scenarios as a basis for modeling performance and other important architectural constraints.

An architectural design test case would look like the following:

Assume that the BricklesDoc and BricklesView objects have been constructed. A tick message is sent to every MovablePiece. How does the BricklesView receive the information necessary to update the bitmaps on the screen? It is expected that the BricklesDoc object will calculate the new position of each bitmap before it notifies the BricklesView that a change has occurred. The BricklesView object will call methods on the BricklesDoc object to obtain all of the information that it needs to update the display.

We will use the architecture of our game framework to illustrate the variety of techniques considered in this section. We first implemented the framework in C++ using the Microsoft Foundation Classes (MFC), which imposes an architecture known as Document/View and is a variant of the canonical Model/View/Controller (MVC) architecture [Gold89]. The framework was then implemented in Java using the java.awt package, which supports a slightly different form of MVC. In each of these efforts the user interface classes present the state of the game to the user. To achieve this, the user interface has to maintain some state itself. A typical fault for these systems would be for the state in the user interface to be different from the state maintained in the classes implementing the model.

A software architecture is the basic structure that defines the system in terms of computational components and interactions among those components [ShGa96]. We will use the terms **component** and **connector** to describe the pieces of an architecture. In the UML notation, components of the architecture are represented as classes with interfaces. If the connectors between components do not have any explicit behavior, they can be represented by simple relationships between classes. If the connectors do have state and/or meaningful behavior then they are represented by objects.

Representations for Architectures

There are three types of information that are widely used to represent an architecture: relationships, states, and algorithms. The basic UML modeling language has the advantage that it can be used for all three design models as well as the analysis models. Using the same notation for all three levels of models eliminates the need to learn multiple notations. Notations such as the UML are sufficiently simple in that no special tools are required, although for large models, tool support quickly becomes a necessity. Tools such as Rational Rose perform a variety of consistency checks on the static-relationship model. With this type of representation, the test cases are manually executed using the technique discussed previously. However, UML does not have specific syntax for describing architectures so the concept/token mapping between the architecture and UML symbols is ad hoc.

Tools such as ObjectTime [Selic94] and BetterState [BetterState00] provide facilities for "animating" design diagrams and provide automatic checking of some aspects of the model. In particular, they support a simulation mechanism that can be used to execute scenarios. The diagrams are annotated with detailed scenario information as well as special simulation information. The developer can "play" scenarios and watch for a variety of faults to be revealed. This approach makes the creation of new scenarios (and test cases) easier by providing a generalized template. One advantage of this approach is the combination of easy model creation with powerful simulation facilities. Usually however, these tools have a limited set of diagram types. BetterState, for example, focuses on building a state model as the specification for the system. This leaves incomplete those static portions of the system that do not affect the state. The obvious benefit is that the scenarios are executed automatically. This makes it easier to run a wide range of scenarios at the price of more time needed to create the model initially. This approach is best suited to small, reactive systems or those systems whose requirements change very little during development.

Often these tools will assist in finding some types of faults as the model is entered into the tool. Consistency checks will prevent certain types of connections from being established. Scenarios are represented in some appropriate format such as a sequential file of input values that are read at appropriate times. The actions of the simulation are often represented by events. Event handlers can be used to "catch" and "generate" events at a high level without the need to write detailed algorithms. This level of execution is sufficient for verifying that required interfaces are provided. It obviously is not sufficient for determining whether the functionality is correctly implemented.

Finally, architectural description languages provide the capability to represent a system at a high level of abstraction. Languages such as Rapide [Luckham95], which has developed at Stanford University, allow the modelers to be as specific as they would like to be. The flow of computation is modeled by events that flow between components. One advantage of this approach is the control that this approach provides to the modeler. The language is sufficiently descriptive to support any level of detail that the modeler wishes to use, unlike the tools previously discussed, which have a fixed level of representation. The disadvantage is that these models are programs with all of the problems associated with that level of detail.

When the model and test cases are represented in a programming language, the test execution can be performed automatically. The representation language may be a general purpose programming language used to implement a high-level prototype or a special purpose architectural description language such as Rapide, which is used to build a standard model. The level of detail represented in the prototype will determine how specific the testing can be.

Testing the Architecture

The Software Architecture Testing (SAT) [McGr96] technique is a special type of guided inspection that requires the following usual steps in testing any product: (1) test cases are constructed; (2) the tests are conducted on the product; and (3) the results of the test are evaluated for correctness. This technique is a "testing" technique because there are very specific test cases, and there is the concept of an execution even if the execution is sometimes manual. The team that is assigned to drive this activity is divided as shown in Figure 4.29. We will provide additional detail on each of the steps.

Constructing Test Cases

Test cases for the architecture are constructed from the use cases as described previously. Each use case describes a family of scenarios that specifies the different types of results that can occur during a specific use of the system. The test cases for the architecture are defined at a higher level than the more detailed design models. The results are used to evaluate the criteria shown in Figure 4.30.

The test cases are essentially defined at a level that exercises the interfaces between subsystems. For example, for the game framework, the essential interface is between a model and a view. The model is divided among the Puck, Paddle, and BrickPile classes. The view is concentrated in the BricklesView class.

The Model/View architecture calls for most of the interaction to be from the view but with the model notifying the view when a change has occurred to the model. Since *Brickles* requires animation, we modified the architecture so that when the BricklesView object is created it is sent a series of messages that provide it with handles to the pieces of the model.

The basic architectural model is given in Figure 4.31. With the analysis out of the way, the test cases can be selected. The two basic operations are (1) setup of the system and (2) repainting the screen after a move has occurred. Unlike many systems built on Model/View, there is no need to consider the ability to add additional views. We could define a test case for each operation; however, a single **grand tour**[1] case can be defined in this case. Usually grand tours are too large and give little information if they fail, but in this case the second operation cannot be realized without the first so it is a natural conjunction.

---

1. A grand tour is a test case that combines a number of separate test cases into one run.

Role in Inspection	Role in Project
Domain Expert	Domain expert; system engineer
Tester	System tester
Developer	Architect

Figure 4.29 Roles in the architectural design model inspection

Criteria	Interpretation for the Architectural Design Model
Completeness	A sufficient set of interfaces are defined to provide all of the services needed for the application's functionality. The relationship between the interfaces allows for the flow of control and data necessary to realize all of the uses described in the use case diagram.
Correctness	The architecture satisfies its constraints; uses the appropriate architectural patterns; represents the interactions between the interfaces.
Consistency	Each use of the system can be handled only in one set of interfaces.

Figure 4.30 Criteria for the architectural design model inspection

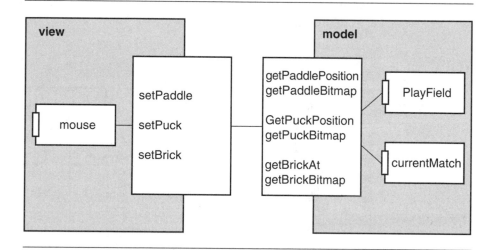

Figure 4.31 An architectural model for *Brickles*

Test Execution

The tests are executed as described for each specific type of representation. We have used the UML notation so this will be an interactive session.

We execute the test case by constructing a message-sequence diagram. The diagram reflects preconditions for a test case. The `BricklesView` object is created followed by a `BricklesGame` object. As the `BricklesGame` object is created, it creates a `PlayField` object that in turn creates `Puck`, `Paddle`, and `BrickPile` objects. The messages across the architectural boundaries are shown in bold italics in Figure 4.32.

Verification of Results

Usually for architectures, this step is fairly simple, even though for the detailed functionality of the final application it can be very difficult. When the output from the test is in the form of diagrams, the resulting diagrams must be verified after each test execution by domain experts. When the output is the result of an execution, the test results can be verified by having those domain experts construct event sequences that would be produced by an architecture that performs correctly. The interpretation of the evaluation criteria is given in Figure 4.29.

An Additional Example

The architecture of *Brickles* is obviously very simple so let's consider the typical three-layer architecture. Although the diagram in Figure 4.33 is greatly simplified, we can consider the types of test cases that would be effective. The client is intended to interact with a user, do computations needed to format presentations, and interact with the business model residing on the application server. The application server is intended to be the primary computational engine, and it also handles interactions with the client and database components. Finally, the database component provides persistence for the business objects from the application server.

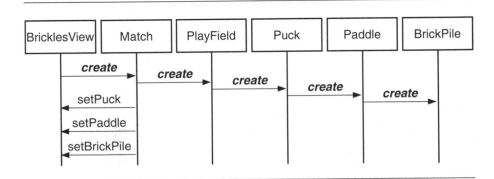

Figure 4.32 Test case execution

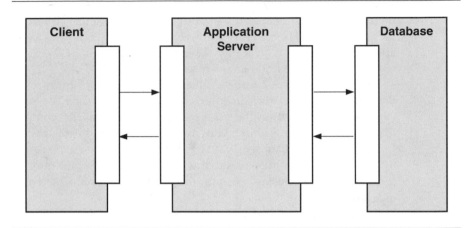

Figure 4.33 Three-tiered architecture

The most important scenarios for this type of architecture include multiple client/single server and multiple client/multiple server scenarios. The discussion in the next section provides a technique for structuring these tests so that they are repeatable and representative. Useful coverage of this architecture includes exercising various combinations of threads. Since these systems are usually distributed, we will defer further discussion until Chapter 8.

Evaluating Performance and Scalability

The architecture of a system should be evaluated beyond correctness, completeness, and consistency. Most architectures will have a specified set of quality attributes and these should also be evaluated. A system that presents animation, as does *Brickles*, must meet performance goals. The scenarios used as test cases for the basic inspection can also be used to analyze the expected performance for the architecture. The SAAM [Kazman94] approach uses a freeform analysis technique for analyzing performance. Software Architecture Testing (SAT) [McGr96] uses the testing perspective to ensure that the important features of the architecture are investigated.

The test cases are symbolically executed and the message-sequence diagrams can be analyzed from a performance perspective. For the analysis, each connection between components in the architecture is assigned a "cost" that reflects the type of communication used by the connection. The number of messages in each scenario gives an indication of the relative performance although by itself the technique gives an order of magnitude to quantified value rather than a specific quantity. A more exact value can be computed by the following string:

```
time to compute = n₁c₁ + n₂c₂ +... + nₘcₘ
```

$$\text{time to compute} = n_1c_1 + n_2c_2 + \ldots + n_mc_m$$

in which the c's are the connection types and the subscripts represent the number of each connection type in the scenario. If a use profile (see Use Profiles on page 130) is used to select a representative set of test cases, an accurate approximation to a typical user session can be computed. Worst and best case approximations can also be constructed.

Design alternatives can be evaluated by comparing the message sequence diagrams and the relative quantities of messages. By using the same set of test cases, selected based on the use profile, a fair and realistic comparison can be made as to how the system will perform if constructed using each alternative.

The performance of distributed systems can also be analyzed in this manner by annotating those messages that will be interprocess and interprocessor. The test case approach using a use profile produces a representative performance measure.

The sequence diagrams can also be used to evaluate the scalability of the architecture. The following use profile indicates several types of users and different frequencies of operations in each:

```
userType   = p₁s₁,  p₂s₂,  …,  pₙsₙ
useProfile = q₁ut₁, q₂ut₂, …, qₘutₘ
```

in which the p's and q's are the probability that a particular scenario and user type, respectively, will be selected.

A scalability test case is a hypothetical mix of actors that is different from the current use profile, that is, a set of values for the q's in the useProfile equation. Usually, the different types of users will remain constant, but the relative number changes. The computation given previously is used for each scenario and for each user type. Then the number of each user type is used to aggregate further. The resulting values can identify the intensity of use for specific messages.

Detailed Class Design Model

The detailed class design model populates the architectural model with classes that will implement the interfaces defined in the architecture. This model typically includes a set of class diagrams, the OCL pre- and postconditions for every method of every class, activity diagrams of significant algorithms, and state diagrams for each class. The detailed design model for *Brickles* is shown in Figure 2.18, and additional detail is shown in Figure 2.15 for one specific class.

The model evaluation criteria are specialized in Figure 4.34. The focus is on compliance with the architecture. This reinforces the idea that the architecture is the keystone of the product. This is also the place where components will be reused and inserted into the system. The specification of the component should be included in the execution trace to ensure there is no need for an adapter between the component and the application.

The roles are assigned in Figure 4.35. Notice that the architects have a role in testing the class diagram. The architects' responsibility to a project is to

Criteria	Interpretation for Class Design Model
Completeness	Classes are defined for each interface in the architecture. The preconditions for each method specify sufficient information so that the user can safely use the method. The postconditions for a method show error conditions as well as the normally expected result.
Correctness	Each class accurately implements the semantics of an interface. For those classes that correspond to interfaces in the architecture, the class's specification must correspond to the interface specified by the architecture.
Consistency	The behaviors in the interface of each class provides either a single way to accomplish a task or, if there are multiple ways, they provide the same behavior but with different preconditions.

Figure 4.34 Criteria for the class design model inspection

"enforce" the architecture. That is, the architect makes certain that developers do not violate the constraints imposed by the architecture. By selecting test cases and evaluating the results, the architects can gain detailed knowledge about the developers' implementation.

A detailed class design test case would look like this:

> Assume that a puck is moving to the left and up, but will hit the left wall before hitting a brick. How will the puck's direction and speed be changed when it hits the wall? It is expected that when the puck is found against the left wall, the wall will create a Collision object that will be passed to the puck. The puck will modify its velocity and begin to move to the right and up. It will be moving at the same speed.

Role in Inspection	Role in Project
Domain Expert	Domain expert; system engineer
Tester	Application developer; architect
Developer	Application developer

Figure 4.35 Roles in class design model inspection

The test cases at this level are very much like the final system test cases. There is so much detail available at this level that the testers have to be careful to record all the model elements that are touched by test cases. Figure 4.34 shows the diagram elements that must be coordinated during the guided inspection session. As the test progresses, the executors select methods that will be invoked, the state model of the receiver is checked to be certain that the target object can receive the message. The messages are then added to the sequence diagram and the state models are updated to reflect changes in state. When a state in a diagram is shaded, there is additional detail to the state but that information is not needed to evaluate the current test. Sequence diagrams will also have "dead-end" objects in which the testers will not attempt to examine the logic beyond that object.

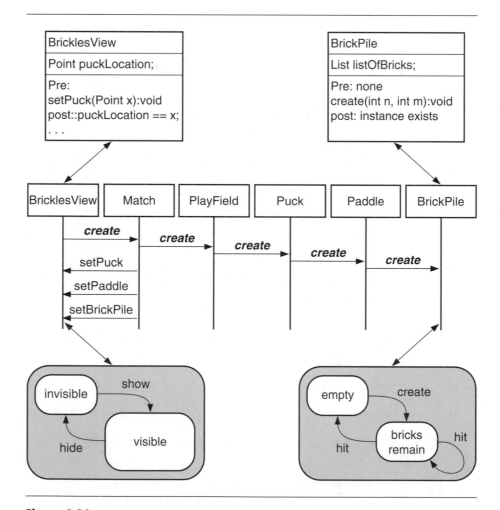

Figure 4.36 A test environment

This is the last step prior to implementation and code-based testing. Developers doing buddy testing of each other's code will benefit from coming back to the test cases created at this level of testing and translating these into class-level code tests.

Testing Again

We are assuming that you are using an iterative development process as we do. That means that these tests must be repeatable. We have tried to accomplish this by writing down formal test cases as opposed to simply thinking up scenarios during the inspection session.

On the second and succeeding iterations, we usually choose to reapply all those tests that were failed the last time and some of those that were passed. Tests may be added to cover the new features added. If any problems were discovered after the inspection was conducted, tests should be added to check for that problem as well.

Use guided inspection to transfer knowledge about the model under test. On a recent project, when the developer responsible for a specific piece of the design was leaving, we used a series of inspection sessions to bring other developers up to speed on their individual piece. A presentation by the developer, as opposed to an inspection, would have addressed the design in the way he knew it best, not in the way the other developers were viewing it.

Testing Models for Additional Qualities

Increasingly, projects are chartered to achieve more aggressive objectives such as the development of extensible designs, the design of reusable frameworks, or highly portable systems. The products of the analysis and design phases of these projects are most critical for achieving these types of objectives. In particular, the architecture is key to the success. Guided inspection can be used to ask metalevel questions about the system. In this mode, the test scenarios are developer actions on the system and not user actions. Instead of asking how the objects in the system would interact, the question is, "How must the classes of the system be changed to provide the newly required behavior?"

The changes to the design or the revisions needed to produce a framework from an existing application can be captured as **change cases** [EcDe96]. A change case is a use case that is not a requirement of the system, but it is an anticipated change to the system. Guided inspection applies correctness, completeness, and consistency criteria to the current analysis and design models with the change cases as the source of test scenarios.

Change Case #1

Actor: Player

Use Scenario: The player bounces the puck off several bricks. Some of the bricks break and disappear, but only two of the bricks crack.

Alternative Paths:

Exceptional Cases:

Frequency: Low

Criticality: Low

Risk: Medium

Figure 4.37 A change case for *Brickles*

For example, if the project is to build a framework upon which future development will be based, it is not sufficient to test against the current uses for the system. Consider the change case shown in Figure 4.37. Test cases can give insight into the effort required to extend the framework by testing how complete the existing model is relative to the new requirements. The second change case, as shown in Figure 4.38, could be used to test the architecture. It would be used to determine how completely the existing architecture covers the new requirement.

Change Case #2

Actor: Player

Use Scenario: The player directs the puck against a set of nonmoving, nonbreakable barriers. The player must move the paddle more quickly in order to catch the puck as it bounces off the closer obstacles.

Alternative Paths:

Exceptional Cases:

Frequency: Low

Criticality: Low

Risk: Medium

Figure 4.38 A second change case

The technique for testing these objectives can be viewed as a series of steps. Each of the steps is described and accompanied by an example.

■ Explicitly state the objective that the change case will address.

The design will be easily extensible to accommodate new games.

■ Construct a "change case" including a specific scenario that illustrates the objective.

The framework is to be used to implement pinball games that are user configurable. The obstacles to be available include posts, flippers, and bumpers.

■ Create test cases by sampling from the range permitted by the change case.

A pinball game is to be created. Figure 4.39 illustrates two new states that might be added to the Brickles *state machine.*

■ Enumerate the work needed to achieve the objective by specifying the differences in state and behavior required for the new objective. This can be accomplished by identifying the new subclasses that must be defined.

The StationarySprite *class will be subclassed to provide the new obstacles. A* Ball *class will extend* MovableSprite *and* CollideWith-Ball *methods would be required for all sprites. Attributes will be added to give a specific point value to each obstacle. The* PinBall *subclass of* ArcadeGame *would add a* Score *attribute.*

■ Evaluate the current design relative to the design required to achieve the objective. Answer the following questions: "Are there fundamental concepts missing that would have to be added?" and "Are there contradictions between what exists and what would be added?"

The necessary base classes and methods are present. The needed attributes can be added without conflict with existing attributes. However, the Sprite *class must be modified.*

■ Repeat with additional test scenarios until all proposed changes are examined.

The output of this process is a set of potential changes needed to achieve the desired system quality, such as extensibility. The inspection searches for missing concepts and contradictions between what exists in the model currently and what would need to be added to the model in order to achieve the new objective. This technique can provide early feedback to the development team about fundamental weaknesses in the design.

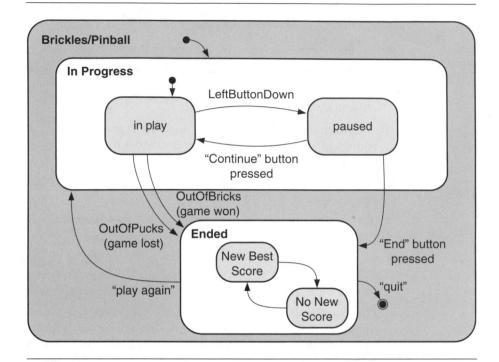

Figure 4.39 A state diagram for a pinball game

Summary

The techniques presented in this chapter are sometimes people intensive and scenarios should be systematically selected for maximum effectiveness. In particular choosing use cases that are less well understood or that represent high-risk situations is recommended. This maximizes the likelihood of finding errors and omissions that will have maximum impact on the quality of the system.

Figure 4.40 illustrates much of what we want you to get out of this chapter. The UML diagrams have been developed so that they are mutually supportive. The test cases developed in this chapter provide guidance for making a systematic search of the models for potential defects.

Why is this technique in a book on testing? First, it uses a testing perspective to focus the examination of the models. Second, much of this testing uses a system-wide scope and thus it is a natural role for the system testers. They can participate in the development process from the earliest phases if they have responsibility for developing test cases from the use cases. In this chapter, we have presented an approach that will identify defects early in the development process and will support the early involvement of the test community, and the class integration and system testers in the development project.

The checklist in Figure 4.41 summarizes the tasks described in this chapter.

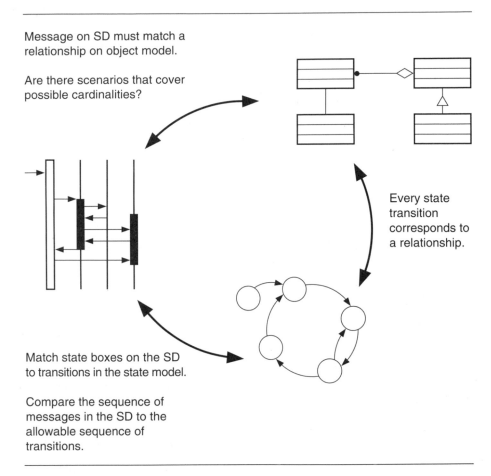

Message on SD must match a relationship on object model.

Are there scenarios that cover possible cardinalities?

Every state transition corresponds to a relationship.

Match state boxes on the SD to transitions in the state model.

Compare the sequence of messages in the SD to the allowable sequence of transitions.

Figure 4.40 Consistency between diagrams (SD = sequence diagram)

Model-Testing Checklist

The steps in this checklist are intended to ensure that all of the required activities in the guided inspection process are completed. A detailed process is defined in the addendum to this chapter.

Guided Inspection Process Checklist Step

Decide how completeness, consistency and correctness will be judged for the particular use in the model under test (MUT).

Determine which scenarios to sample from the use case model to use as test cases.

Create test cases by supplementing the scenarios with specific data.

Select the model/notation that will record the results of each execution.

Conduct tests.

Evaluate the results of the test executions to determine which tests the model passed and which it failed.

Record the results for use in guiding the repair and testing processes in the next iteration.

Figure 4.41 A guided inspection process checklist

Exercises

4-1. Using the use cases of your project as a starting point, you add the Frequency and Criticality fields to them. Perform the risk analysis for the use cases and fill in that field for each use case. Develop an ordering of uses that reflects how intensely each should be tested. Write test cases for the use cases in the model. Write one test case for the least important use case. Write additional test cases for each of the use cases.

4-2. Conduct a guided inspection session for the initial analysis model for your project. Generate a report that lists the discrepancies between the models.

4-3. Develop three scenarios from the use cases given in this chapter. Then, using the models given in Chapter 2 and Chapter 4, identify examples of incompleteness, inconsistency, and incorrectness.

4-4. Select the phase in your software development process in which, in your estimation, more defects are created than any other. Design a guided inspection checklist that will lead developers to finding the types of defects created in that phase.

Addendum: A Process Definition for Guided Inspection

Goal: To identify defects in artifacts created during the analysis and design phases of software construction.

Steps in the Process

1. Define the scope and depth of the guided inspection.
2. Identify the basis model(s) from which the material being inspected was created.
3. Assemble the guided inspection team.
4. Define a sampling plan and coverage criteria.
5. Create test cases from the bases.
6. Apply the tests to the material.
7. Gather and analyze test results.
8. Report and feedback.

Detailed Step Descriptions

1. Define the scope and depth of the guided inspection.

   Inputs:

   The project's position in the life cycle.

   The materials produced by the project (UML models, plans, use cases).

   Outputs:

   A specific set of diagrams and documents that will be the basis for the evaluation.

   Method:

   Define the scope of the guided inspection to be the set of deliverables from a phase of the development process. Use the development process information to identify the deliverables that will be produced by the phase of interest.

   Example:

   The project has just completed the domain analysis phase. The development process defines the deliverable from this phase as a UML model containing domain level use cases, static information such as class diagrams, and dynamic information such as sequence and state diagrams. The guided inspection will evaluate this model.

2. Identify the basis model(s) from which the material being inspected was created.

Inputs:

The scope of the guided inspection.

The project's position in the life cycle.

Outputs:

The material from which the test cases will be constructed (the model under test—MUT).

Method:

Review the development process description to determine the inputs to the current phase. The basis model(s) should be listed as inputs to the current phase.

Example:

The inputs to the domain analysis phase is the "knowledge of experts familiar with the domain." These mental models are the basis models for this guided inspection.

3. Assemble the guided inspection team.

Inputs:

The scope of the guided inspection.

Available personnel.

Outputs:

A set of participants and their roles.

Method:

Assign persons to fill one of three categories of roles: Administrative, Participant in creating the model to be tested, Objective observer of the model to be tested. Choose the objective observers from the customers of the model to be tested and the participants during the creation of the basis model.

Example:

Since the model to be tested is a domain analysis model and the basis model is the mental models of the domain experts, the objective observers can be selected from other domain experts and/or from application analysts. The creation participants are members of the domain modeling team. The administrative personnel can perhaps come from other interested parties or an office that provides support for the conduct of guided inspections.

4. Define a sampling plan and coverage criteria.

Input:

The project's quality plan.

Outputs:

A plan for how test cases will be selected.

A description of what parts of the MUT will be covered.

Method:

Identify important elements of this MUT. Estimate the effort required to involve all of these in the guided inspection. If there are too many to cover, use information such as the RISK section of the use cases or the judgment of experts to prioritize the elements.

Example:

In a domain model there are static and dynamic models as well as use cases. At least one test case should be created for each use case. There should be sufficient test cases to take every "major" entity through all of its visible states.

5. Create test cases from the bases.

Inputs:

The sampling plan.

MUT.

Output:

A set of test cases.

Method:

Obtain a scenario from the basis model. Determine the preconditions and inputs that are required to place the system in the correct state and to begin the test. Present the scenario to the "oracle" to determine the results expected from the test scenario. Complete a test case description for each test case.

Example:

A different domain expert than the one who supported the model creation would be asked to supply scenarios that correspond to uses of the system. The experts also provide what they would consider an acceptable response.

6. Apply the tests to the material.

Inputs:

Set of test cases.

MUT

Output:

Set of test results.

Method:

Apply the test cases to the MUT using the most specific technique available. For UML models in a static environment, such as Rational Rose, an interactive simulation session in which the Creators play the roles of the model elements is the best approach. If the MUT is represented by an executable prototype then the test cases are mapped onto this system and executed.

Example:

The domain analysis model is a static UML model. A simulation session is conducted with the Observers feeding test cases to the Creators. The Creators provide details of how the test scenario would be processed through the model. Sequence diagrams document the execution of each test case. Use agreed-upon symbols or colors to mark each element that is touched by a test case.

7. Gather and analyze test results.

Inputs:

Test results in the form of sequence diagrams and pass/fail decisions. The marked-up model.

Outputs:

Statistics on percentage pass/fail.

Categorization of the results.

Defect catalogs and defect reports.

A judgment of the quality of the MUT and the tests.

Method:

Begin by counting the number of test cases that passed and how many have failed. Compare this ratio to other guided inspections that have been conducted in the organization. Compute the percentage of each type of element that has been used in executing the test cases. Use the marked-up model as the source of this data. Update the defect inventory with information about the failures from this test session.

Categorize the failed test cases. This can often be combined with the previous two tasks by marking paper copies of the model. Follow the sequence diagram for each failed test case and mark each message, class, and attribute touched by a failed test case.

Example:

For the domain analysis model we should be able to report that every use case was the source of at least one test case, and that every class in the class diagram was used at least once. Typically, on the first pass, some significant states will be missed. This should be noted in the coverage analysis.

8. Report and feedback.

Inputs:

Test results.

Coverage information.

Outputs:

Information on what new tests should be created.

Test report.

Method:

Follow the standard format for a test report in your organization to document the test results and the analyses of those results. If the stated coverage goals are met then the process is complete. If not, use that report to return to Step 5 and proceed through the steps to improve the coverage level.

Example:

For the domain analysis tests, some elements were found to be missing from the model. The failing tests might be executed again after the model has been modified.

Roles in the Process

Administrator

The administrative tasks include running the guided inspection sessions, collecting and disseminating the results, and aggregating metrics to measure the quality of the review. In our example, the administrative work could be done by personnel from a central office.

Creator

The persons who created the MUT. Depending on the form that the model takes, these people may "execute" the symbolic model on the test cases or they may assist in translating the test cases into a form that can be executed with whatever representation of the model is available. In our example the modelers who created the domain model would be the "creators."

Observer

Persons in this role create the test cases that are used in the guided inspection. In our example they would be domain experts and preferably experts who were not the source of the information that was used to create the model initially.

Class Testing Basics

☞ Want to know what to consider when testing a class? See Class Testing on page 164.

☞ Want to know how to identify test cases for testing a class? See Constructing Test Cases on page 168.

☞ Want to know a good way to implement a test driver for a class? See Constructing a Test Driver on page 183.

Chapter 5

In this chapter we describe how to test a single class. The techniques we describe in this chapter will be applied in later chapters when we discuss testing object interactions and testing classes in an inheritance hierarchy. For this discussion, we assume the code for a class has been written and needs to be tested. Our primary focus is on classes whose instances do not collaborate extensively with any other instance. We will use the Velocity and PuckSupply classes from *Brickles* to illustrate. We will address the testing of more complex classes in the next two chapters.

Class Testing

The fundamental unit of an object-oriented program is a class. **Class testing** comprises those activities associated with verifying that the implementation of a class corresponds exactly with the specification for that class. If an implementation is correct, then each of the class's instances should behave properly.

Class testing is roughly analogous to unit testing in traditional testing processes and has many of the same problems that must be addressed (see sidebar). Class testing must also address some aspects of integration testing since each object defines a level of scope in which many methods interact around a set of instance attributes. Some of the most critical issues will be discussed in the context of concurrent issues in Chapter 8. The focus of this chapter is execution-based testing of classes. Our primary objective is to describe basic elements and strategies of testing classes, and we will focus on relatively simple classes. The testing of more complex classes will be addressed in the next two chapters.

We assume that a class to be tested has a complete and correct specification, and that it has been tested within the context of the models.[1] We assume the specification is expressed in a specification language such as the Object Constraint Language (OCL) [WK99] or a natural language, and/or as a state transition diagram. If more than one form of specification is used for a class, we assume all forms are consistent and that information may be taken from whichever form is most useful as the basis for developing test cases for the class. We prefer to use the most formal specification for generating test cases.

Ways to Test a Class

The code for a class can be tested effectively by review or by executing test cases. Review is a viable alternative to execution-based testing in some cases, but has two disadvantages over execution-based testing:

- Reviews are subject to human error.
- Reviews require considerably more effort with respect to regression testing, often requiring almost as many resources as the original testing.

While execution-based testing overcomes these disadvantages, considerable effort can be required for the identification of test cases and the development of test drivers. In some cases, the effort needed to construct a test driver for a class can exceed the effort of developing that class by several orders of magnitude. In that case, the costs and benefits of testing the class "outside" the system in which it will be used should be evaluated. This situation is not peculiar

---

1. Consistency is primarily a design consideration. When class testing is underway, design for the class should be finished—at least as far as the current development iteration is concerned.

Traditional Unit Testing

The purpose of unit testing is to ensure that each unit meets its specification. If each unit meets its specification, then any bugs that appear when units are integrated together are more likely caused by incorrect interfacing of units than by incorrect implementations of the units. Debugging efforts can then be concentrated on the interfaces, not on the units themselves.

Unit testing is done as units are developed. In the procedural paradigm, a unit is a procedure (or function) or sometimes a group of procedures that implement an abstract data type. Units are typically tested by a combination of code inspections and execution testing, with most emphasis being placed on the latter. A simple unit test plan can be developed that identifies the test cases needed, and then a test driver can be constructed in a straightforward manner.

This all sounds good in theory, but in practice a number of stumbling blocks can arise. Typically, only the simplest of units—those that appear as terminal nodes in a structure chart—can be tested without significant effort. Test cases for such units tend to be easy to identify, and test drivers tend to be easy to construct if parameters do not have much structure to them.

Even units that have parameters with significant structure can sometimes be unit tested without significant effort if the driver can initialize the actual parameters with a relatively few assignment or read operations. Note, however, that this increases the amount of coupling between the unit and its test driver, which can increase maintenance costs if the structure changes over time.

While units at the lower levels in a structure chart can be unit tested in a straightforward way, at some point—perhaps two or three levels from the bottom—the interactions between units become so interwoven that unit testing becomes impractical. The effort required to produce a test driver can be greater than testing the unit in the context of testing a larger assembly. In some cases, the code for a test driver can be significantly larger than the code in the unit under test. This introduces an issue of unit testing the test driver itself.

to object-oriented programming. The same situation arises in traditional procedural development with respect to many of the subprograms invoked at upper levels in a structure chart.

Once we have identified executable test cases for a class, we must implement a test driver to run each of the test cases and report the results of each test case run. The test driver creates one or more instances of a class to run a test case. It is important to keep in mind that classes are tested by creating instances and testing the behavior of those instances (see Definitional versus Operational Semantics of Objects on page 19). The test driver can take a number of forms that we will describe later in this chapter. We favor the form of a separate "tester" class over the others because it offers a convenient organization for managing drivers and inheritance, and can be used to capture commonality among them. More benefits arise in testing class hierarchies, as we show in Chapter 7.

Dimensions of Class Testing

For each class, we must decide whether to test it independently as a unit or in some way as a component of a larger part of the system. We base that decision on the following factors:

- The role of the class in the system, especially the degree of risk associated with it.

- The complexity of the class measured in terms of the number of states, operations, and associations with other classes.

- The amount of effort associated with developing a test driver for the class.

If a class is to be part of a class library, extensive class testing is appropriate even though the cost of developing a test driver might be high because its correct operation is essential. In the context of *Brickles*, we associate high risk with some of the most basic classes, such as Velocity and PuckSupply. If they are not implemented correctly, the game program will not work. Writing code to test these classes is straightforward because in the system design, they do not have to collaborate with other *Brickles* classes. We associate high risk with other classes, such as Puck, but we recognize these might not be easy to write a test driver for. They have associations in the design with many other classes, primarily because much of Puck's behavior is graphical. Puck associates with PlayField and any of the kinds of sprites in a playfield. We can foresee a significant effort in writing a test driver for Puck because all test cases will require an instance of a PlayField and some that are used for testing collision processing will require instances of Brick, BrickPile, and Paddle. Testing Puck, therefore, relies on an assumption that all these other classes work correctly. (We will examine this further in Chapter 6.) We might decide to test some or all of Puck in the context of cluster testing since we need instances of other classes to build environments around pucks suitable for testing them.

Let us now consider the five dimensions of testing in the context of testing a class.

Who

Classes are usually tested by its developer, just as subprograms traditionally are unit tested by their developer. Having a class developer also play the role of a class tester minimizes the number of people that have to understand a class's specification. It also facilitates implementation-based testing since the tester is intimately familiar with the code. Finally, the test driver can be used by the developer to debug the code as it is written.[2]

The main disadvantage of test drivers and code being developed by the same person is that any misunderstandings of the specifications by the developer will be propagated to the test suite and test drivers. These potential problems are headed off by formal reviews of the code, and/or by requiring a test plan to be written by another class developer, and by allowing the code to be reviewed independently.

It is not unusual for independent testers to discover problems with the specifications for a class, so time should be allowed during testing to resolve them.

What

We primarily want to ensure that the code for a class *exactly* meets the requirements set forth in its specification. The amount of attention given to testing a class to ensure it does nothing *more* than what it is specified for depends on the risk associated with the class supplying *extra* behaviors. Incomplete coverage of code after a wide range of test cases have been run against the class could be an indication that the class contains extra, undocumented behaviors. Or it could merely suggest that the implementation must be tested using more test cases.

When

A test plan—or at least some form of identification of test cases—should be developed soon after a class is fully specified and ready for coding. This is particularly true when a class's developer is also responsible for its testing because early identification of test cases will help a developer to understand the specification and, as we mentioned, get feedback from an independent review. Take care when a class's developer is also responsible for its testing. A class developer who identifies incorrect or insufficient test cases will produce an implementation that passes all test cases, but that causes significant problems when the class is integrated into a larger part of a system.

Class testing can be done at various points in its development. In an incremental, iterative development process, the specification and/or the implementation for a class might need to be changed over the course of a project. Class testing should be performed prior to the use of the class in other portions of the software. Regression class testing should be performed whenever the implementation for a class has changed. If the changes resulted from the discovery of bugs in the code for the class, then a review of the test plan must be performed and test cases must be added or changed to detect those bugs during future testing.

---

2. A goal of testing is to find bugs, not to fix bugs. However, a useful component of class testing is in helping to isolate errors in the code.

How

Classes are usually tested by developing a test driver that creates instances of the class and sets up a suitable environment around those instances to run a test case. The driver sends one or more messages to an instance as specified by a test case, then checks the outcome of those messages based on a reply value, changes to the instance, and/or one or more of the parameters to the message. The test driver usually has responsibility for deleting any instances it creates if the language, such as C++, has programmer-managed storage allocation.

If a class has **static** data members and/or operations, then testing of those is required. These data members and methods belong to the class itself rather than to each instance of the class. The class can be treated as an object—for example, in Java an instance of the class Class—and tested according to what we describe in this chapter.

If the behavior of the **instances** of a class is based on the values of class-level attributes, then test cases for testing these class-level attributes must be considered as an extension of the state of the instances.

How Much

Adequacy can be measured in terms of how much of the specification and how much of the implementation has been tested. For class testing, we usually want to consider both. We want to test operations and state transitions in all sorts of combinations. Recall that objects maintain state and typically that state affects the meaning of operations. However, you need to consider whether exhaustive testing is feasible or even necessary. If not, then selective pair-wise combinations can be effective, especially when done in conjunction with risk analysis so that the most important test cases can be used and less important test cases can be sampled.

Constructing Test Cases

Let us investigate how to identify and construct test cases for a class. First, we will look at how to identify test cases from a class specification expressed in OCL. Then we will look at test case construction from a state transition diagram.

Test cases are usually identified from the class specification, which can be expressed in a variety of ways. These include OCL, natural language, and/or state transition diagrams. Test cases can be identified from a class implementation, but using only that approach will propagate errors the class developer has made in interpreting the specification during implementation to the test software. We prefer to develop test cases initially from the specification and then augment them with additional cases as needed to test boundaries introduced by the implementation. If a specification does not exist for a class to be tested, then we "reverse engineer" one and have it reviewed by the developers before we start testing.

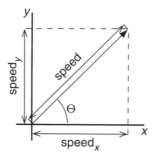

Figure 5.1 A velocity is a vector characterized by a speed and a direction Θ

Most of the examples in this chapter will be based on testing the Velocity and PuckSupply classes from *Brickles*. A *puck supply* is a collection of pucks that have not yet been put into play. A *velocity* represents the movement of a movable sprite on a playfield based on attributes of a *speed* (expressed in playfield units per unit time) and a *direction* (expressed as an angle in degrees, with 0 designating *east* or *right*, 90 designating *north* or *up*, and so on) (see Figure 5.1). The speed attribute is broken into two components: $speed_x$—speed in the *x* direction (*left-right*)—and $speed_y$—speed in the *y* direction (*up-down*). While the *speed* attribute is always a non-negative value, the components of a velocity's speed can be negative. The value of $speed_x$ is negative if a velocity's direction is heading left. The value of $speed_y$ is negative if the direction is down. *Speed* and *Direction* are abstract types ultimately defined as integer values.

A class model for Velocity is shown in Figure 5.2. Its OCL specification is shown in Figure 5.3. The invariant for the class constrains the value for direction and speed as well as the relationships between the values of those attributes, including the $speed_x$, and $speed_y$ components. Because these attributes are integer-valued, the invariant relaxes the ideal relationship described by the Pythagorean theorem.

The design of Velocity includes the setSpeed() and setDirection() modifiers to improve runtime efficiency by eliminating the need to create a new instance every time one or both attribute values change.

Test Case Construction from Pre- and Postconditions

The general idea for identifying test cases from preconditions and postconditions for an operation is to identify requirements for test cases for all possible combinations of situations in which a precondition can hold and postconditions can be achieved. Then create test cases to address these requirements. From the requirements, create test cases with specific input values, including

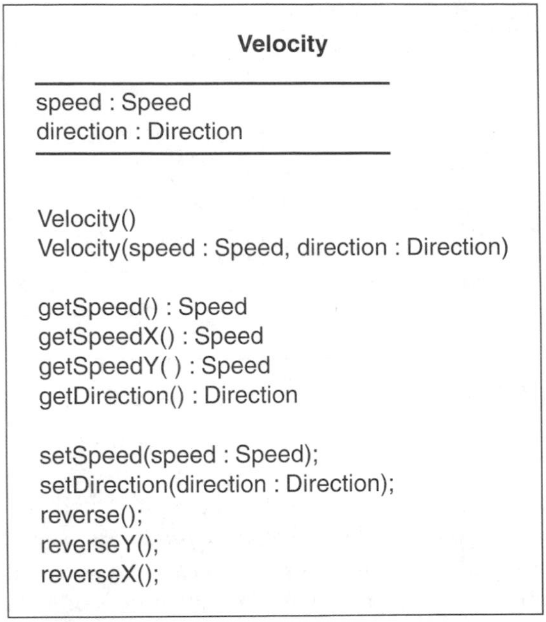

```
                            Velocity

            speed : Speed
            direction : Direction


            Velocity()
            Velocity(speed : Speed, direction : Direction)

            getSpeed() : Speed
            getSpeedX() : Speed
            getSpeedY( ) : Speed
            getDirection() : Direction

            setSpeed(speed : Speed);
            setDirection(direction : Direction);
            reverse();
            reverseY();
            reverseX();
```

Figure 5.2 The Velocity class as specified in the UML model

typical values and boundary values, and determine the correct outputs. Finally, add test cases to address what happens when a precondition is violated (see sidebar).

To identify general test case requirements from pre- and postconditions, we can analyze each of the logical connectives in an OCL condition and list the test cases that result from the structure of that condition. Figure 5.4 and Figure 5.5 list the requirements for test cases that result from various forms of logical expressions in preconditions and postconditions, respectively. Figure 5.4 identifies additional test cases that result from an implicit use of defensive programming. Notice the significant increase in the number of test case requirements over the contract approach.

Use these two figures to find requirements for the minimum number of test cases[3] needed to test an operation specified using all combinations of preconditions and postconditions. Follow these steps:

1. Identify a list of precondition contributions specified in the entry in Figure 5.4 that matches the form of the precondition.

2. Identify a list of postcondition contributions specified in the entry in Figure 5.5 that matches the form of the postcondition.

---

3. *Minimum* because they typically do not account for cases in equivalence classes of values.

Test Cases for Failed Preconditions

Our discussion of class specification in Chapter 2 described defensive programming and contracts. Under defensive programming, a class implementation includes code in each method to verify the associated precondition holds. Under the contract approach, no such code is included because any client requesting an operation is assumed to have ensured that the precondition holds for that request.

In many cases, the defensive programming approach is implicit in a specification—that is, the class specification is written using the same preconditions, postconditions, and invariants as would be used for a contract approach. There is an understanding that each violated precondition results in some standard action, such as abnormally terminating program execution, throwing a standard exception, or displaying a message in an error log.

Testers must be aware of any implicit handling of violated conditions. If implicit handling is part of a class specification, testers should generate test cases to verify the correct processing of that implicit part of the specifications. In testing `Velocity::setDirection()`, for example, we would need to add additional test cases for the operation to cover the possibilities that a direction is negative or greater than 359. If the designers take a contract programming perspective on a class, the implementers still might include code for debugging purposes to perform runtime checking of preconditions and/or postconditions. If test cases are needed to check this debugging code, take care to identify such test cases in the test driver so that they can be disabled when the debugging code is disabled.

3. Form test case requirements by making all possible combinations of entries from the contributions lists. One way is to substitute each input constraint from the first list for each occurrence of *Pre* in the second list.

4. Eliminate any conditions generated by the table that are not meaningful. For example, a precondition of, say, *(color = red)* or *(color = blue)* will generate a test case in which *(color = red)* and *(color = blue)*, which cannot satisfied.[4]

If a precondition or a postcondition has a more complex form than is shown in the table—for example, involving three disjuncts—then the processes described in Steps 1 and 2 will have to be applied recursively—that is, broken into smaller pieces with the rules applied to the pieces, and then applied together as the pieces are recombined with operators. Fortunately, widely accepted object-oriented design principles keep most preconditions and postconditions simple.

---

4. It could be argued that a more accurate precondition is *(color = red)* xor *(color = blue)*, which states that one or the other, but not both, must be true. In this case, a tester might suggest such a change to the developers to improve the specification.

Velocity::Velocity

    0 <= direction and direction < 360 and speed >= 0 and
        speedX = ((2 * PI * direction / 360.0).cos * speed).floor and
        speedY = ((2 * PI * direction / 360.0).sin * speed).floor and
        speedX*speedX + speedY*speedY <= speed*speed

Velocity::Velocity();

pre: true
post: self.speed = 0 and self.direction = 0

Velocity::Velocity(speed : Speed, direction : Direction);

pre: speed >= 0 and (0 <= direction and direction < 360)
post: self.speed = speed and self.direction = direction

Velocity::getSpeed() : Speed

pre: true
post: result = self.speed

Velocity::getSpeedX() : Speed

pre: true
post: result = speedX

Velocity::getSpeedY( ) : Speed

pre: true
post: result = speedY

Velocity::getDirection() : Direction

pre: true
post: result = direction

Velocity::setSpeed(speed : Speed)

pre: speed >= 0
post: self.speed = speed and direction = direction@pre

Velocity::setDirection(dir : Direction)

pre: 0 <= dir and dir < 360
post: direction = dir and speed = speed@pre

Velocity::reverse()

pre: true
post: self.speed = speed@pre and speedX = -speedX@pre and speedY =
          -speedY@pre

Velocity::reverseY()

pre: true
post: self.speed = speed@pre and speedY = -speedY@pre and
          direction = (360 - direction@pre).mod(360)

Velocity::reverseX()

pre: true
post: speed = speed@pre and direction =
        if direction@pre <= 180 then (180 - direction@pre)
        else (540 - direction@pre).mod(360)

Figure 5.3 OCL specification for the Velocity class

Logical Expression	Contribution	
true	(*true*, *Post*)	
①	(①, *Post*)	
	(not ①, *Exception*)	❋
not ①	(not ①, *Post*)	
	(①, *Exception*)	❋
① **and** ②	(① and ②, *Post*)	
	(not ① and ②, *Exception*)	❋
	(① and not ②, *Exception*)	❋
	(not ① and not ②, *Exception*)	❋
① **or** ②	(①, *Post*)	
	(②, *Post*)	
	(① and ②, *Post*)	
	(not ① and not ②, *Exception*)	❋
① **xor** ②	(① and not ②, *Post*)	
	(not ① and ②, *Post*)	
	(① and ②, *Exception*)	❋
	(not ① and not ②, *Exception*)	❋
① **implies** ②	(not ①, *Post*)	
	(②, *Post*)	
	(not ① and ②, *Post*)	
	(① and not ②, *Exception*)	❋
if ① **then** ② **else** ③ **endif**	(① and ②, *Post*)	
	(not ① and ③, *Post*)	
	(① and not ②, *Exception*)	❋
	(not ① and not ③, *Exception*)	❋

Notes

1. ①, ②, and ③ represent components in an OCL expression.

2. If defensive programming is implicit in a specification, then the test cases marked by ❋ must also be addressed. If defensive programming is explicit in the specification, then the test cases will be identified.

Figure 5.4 Contribution to the test suite by preconditions

Postcondition	Contribution
❶	(*Pre*, ❶)
❶ and ❷	(*Pre*, ❶ and ❷)
❶ or ❷	(*Pre*, ❶) (*Pre*, ❶) (*Pre*, ❶ and ❷)
❶ xor ❷	(*Pre*, ❶ and not ❷) (*Pre*, not ❶ and ❷)
❶ implies ❷	(*Pre*, not ❶ or ❷)
if ❶ then ❷ else ❸ endif	(*Pre* and ✪, ❷) (*Pre* and not ✪, ❸)

Notes

1. ❶, ❷, and ❸ represent components in an OCL expression.

2. For postcondition if ❶ then ❷ else ❸ endif, if expression ❶ does not depend on the effect of the test case, then ✪ = ❶ else ✪ is a condition that will make ❶ true at the time the postcondition applies.

Figure 5.5 Contribution to the test suite by postconditions

Figure 5.6 and Figure 5.7 show examples of how to use these tables for two of the operations in the Velocity class.

Test Case Construction from State Transition Diagrams

State transition diagrams show the behavior associated with instances of a class graphically. These diagrams can supplement written specifications or comprise the entire specification. A state transition diagram for the PuckSupply class is given in Figure 5.8. A puck supply holds the pucks that have not yet been put into play during a *Brickles* match. OCL for the class is also shown in the figure so you can compare the forms of specification.

Velocity::setDirection(dir : Direction)
pre: 0 <= dir and dir < 360
post: direction = dir and speed = speed@pre

In setDirection(), ① represents 0 <= dir, ② represents dir < 360, ❶ represents direction = dir, and ❷ represents speed = speed@pre. The table entries for precondition of the form ① and ② and postcondition of the form ❶ and ❷ combine to yield requirements for test cases.

(① and ②, ❶ and ❷)   (0 <= dir and dir < 360,
                                   direction = dir and speed = speed@pre)

(not ① and ②, *Exception*) ✸ (not (0 <= dir) and dir < 360, *Exception*) ✸
(① and not ②, *Exception*) ✸ (0 <= dir and not (dir < 360), *Exception*) ✸
(not ① and not ②, *Exception*)✸ ~~((not (0<=dir) and not (dir<360), *Exception*)~~

We eliminated the last case because no value for *dir* can be both less than zero and greater than or equal to 360. We keep the second and third cases because for example, the implementers are checking preconditions with assertions during development and we want to test that those assertions work correctly.

We can now satisfy these test case requirements by providing values for *dir*, *direction*, and *speed@pre*. From a testing perspective, we can see how a programmer might try to use memoizing and/or trigonometric identities to speed the computation of sine and cosines used in computing component speeds. Consequently, we decide to do exhaustive testing because a change in direction affects both the component speeds. We use a speed of 1000 for all directions between 0 and 359, inclusive. Even though a puck in *Brickles* is not likely to have that velocity, 1000 gives us three digits of accuracy when computing sines and cosines as integer values, improving our ability to check the implementation. For the second test case, we use speed 1000 and direction -1. For the third test case, we use 360 (a boundary value) and 540, an arbitrary value above 360. With exhaustive testing, we have 363 test cases for the setDirection() operation.

While boundary values can also be associated with speed, we associate low risk with them and do not generate test cases using a speed of zero or a speed of the largest positive integer value. From a testing perspective, if the code works correctly with a speed of 1000, it will most likely work correctly with any value. We can analyze coverage of code for the method to confirm our position. If every code statement is executed at least once over runs of all these test cases, and the test cases all pass, then we can be almost certain the code is correct.

Figure 5.6 Identifying test cases for Velocity::setDirection()

Velocity::reverseX()
pre: true
post: speed = speed@pre and direction =
              if direction@pre <= 180 then (180 - direction@pre)
              else (540 - direction@pre).mod(360)

Because the postcondition involves both *and* and *if-then-else* operators, we need to apply the table expansions recursively. At the first level, ❶ represents *speed = speed@pre* and ❷ represents *if direction@pre <= 180 then (180 - direction@pre) else (540 - direction@pre).mod(360)*. At the second level, ❶ represents direction@pre <= 180, ❷ represents (180 - direction@pre), and ❷ represents (540 - direction@pre).mod(360). We will use subscripts to show the levels. The table entries for precondition of the form *true* and postcondition of the form ❶$_1$ *and* ❷$_1$ applies first, yielding

(*Pre*, ❶$_1$ and ❷$_1$)   (true, speed = speed@pre and ❷$_1$)

Using the table to expand *if* ❶ *then* ❷ *else* ❸ *endif* and combining with what we have above yields requirements for test cases

(*Pre* and ✪$_2$, ❷$_2$)   (true and direction@pre <= 180,
                                         speed = speed@pre and (180 - direc-
                                         tion@pre)

(*Pre* and not ✪$_2$, ❷$_2$)   (true and not (direction@pre <= 180),
                                         speed = speed@pre and
                                     (540 - direction@pre).mod(360))

Note *Pre* = true and ✪$_2$ = direction@pre <= 180 since that condition involves only a constant value and an attribute value *@pre*.

We can now satisfy these test case requirements by providing values for *direction@pre* and *speed@pre*. Because we have decided to test setDirection() exhaustively, we decide to test reverseX() with boundary values and some in-between values. For this operation, boundaries lie at directions 0 (right), 90 (up), 180 (left), and 270 (down). We pick one value between boundaries at, say, 30, 135, 188, and 275. The speed can be chosen arbitrarily. We will choose 10 for each test case. The first general test case, then, produces test cases involving speed 10 and directions 0, 30, 90, 135, and 180. The second general test case produces test cases involving speed 10 and directions 188, 270, and 275.

Figure 5.7 Identifying test cases for Velocity::reverseX()

Describing Test Cases

While it is easy to define a test case as a pair (*input, output*), it is not so easy to describe in a succinct way what *input* and *output* are for a specific test case. An input involves an object under test (OUT) in a given state with values specified for all attributes; for zero or more objects in specified states that are in associations with the OUT (perhaps helping to define that object's state); for a sequence of one or more messages (or other events) to be sent to the OUT; and for zero or more objects (and values) that serve as parameters to messages. An output involves the resulting state of the OUT, the resulting state of any objects in association with the OUT, a result returned from the last message sent as input, and the resulting state of any objects passed as parameters to messages. Note that the class of an OUT can be one of the objects associated with it.

We use a text-based notation for describing test cases. We use a table having a column for inputs and one for outputs. Each column is subdivided as shown. The text in each column except for *Events* is an adaptation of OCL. The *Events* column uses programming language notation. Events include messages and object creation.

Input		Output	
State	**Events**	**State**	**Exceptions Thrown**
none	OUT = new Velocity;	OUT.speed = 0 and OUT.direction = 0 and OUT.speedX = 0 and OUT.speedY = 0	none
OUT:Velocity [speed=100, direction=90]	OUT.setDirection(45)	OUT.speed=1000, OUT.direction=45, OUT.speedX=707, OUT.speedY=707	none

The first test case listed is for the default constructor. The second is for setDirection(). By convention, we use the name OUT to refer to the object under test. The notation OUT:Velocity[speed=100, direction=90] denotes that OUT is an instance of Velocity with attribute values as specified in the brackets. If attribute values are unspecified, then they are irrelevant for the test case.

We can generate code for a test case in a straightforward way. For each test case, write code to achieve the input state, then write code to generate the events, and then write code to check the result.

We can use the same general approach to generating test cases that we described for using pre- and postconditions. Each transition on the diagram represents a requirement for one or more test cases. The diagram in Figure 5.8 has six transitions between states, one transition representing construction, and two representing destruction—nine transitions total.[5] Thus, we have nine

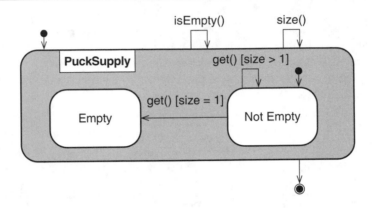

PuckSupply
    size >= 0

PuckSupply::PuckSupply();
pre: true
post: size = 3 and Puck->size() = Puck@pre->size() + 3 and
           pucks->forAll(puck: Puck | not puck.inPlay())

PuckSupply::~PuckSupply();
pre: true
post: Puck->size() = Puck@pre->size() - size@pre

void PuckSupply::size() const;
pre: true
post: result = size

Puck * PuckSupply::get();
pre: not self.isEmpty()
post: result = pucks->asSequence->first and size = size@pre - 1

bool PuckSupply::isEmpty() const;
pre: true

    result = (size = 0)

Figure 5.8 The PuckSupply class's state transition diagram and OCL specification

5. A transition on the superstate PuckSupply distributes to each of the two substates, yielding two transitions.

requirements for test cases. We satisfy these requirements by selecting representative values and boundary values on each side of a transition. If a transition is guarded, then you should select boundary values for the guard condition, too.

Boundary values for states are determined based on the range of attribute values associated with a state. Each state is defined in terms of attribute values. In PuckSupply, the *Empty* state is associated with a *size* attribute value of zero. The *Not Empty* state is associated with a nonzero *size* attribute value. We want to be sure to include a test case to check that a PuckSupply instance does not behave as though it is empty when its *size* is one.

For most of us, generating test cases from state transition diagrams is more intuitive than generating them from pre- and postconditions. The behavior associated with a class is more evident from the diagrams, and it is easy to identify the requirements for test cases since they come directly from the transitions. However, we must be careful to understand completely the way states are defined in terms of attribute values, and how events affect specific values within a given state. Consider, for example, the *Not Empty* state in PuckSupply. From the diagram alone, we are left to guess that each time a puck is removed, the size decreases by one. This is explicit in the OCL specification. At the extreme, consider Velocity, which has only one state and twelve transitions. It is difficult to identify all test cases from that simple diagram alone. When testing based on state transition diagrams, make sure you investigate the boundaries and results of each transition as you generate test cases.

Adequacy of Test Suites for a Class

Ideally, we could exhaustively test every class, that is, test with all possible values to ensure each class meets its specification. In practice, exhaustive testing is either impossible or requires considerable effort. Nonetheless, it is wise to exhaustively test certain classes. Consider, for example, the Velocity class in *Brickles*. If it does not operate correctly, the system has no chance of operating correctly. The benefits of exhaustive testing in this case outweigh the cost of writing a test driver to run more test cases.

Exhaustive testing is usually infeasible or impractical under time and resource constraints, so we need to test a class *enough*. Without exhaustive testing, we cannot be sure every aspect of a class meets its specification, but we can apply some measure of adequacy to give us a high level of confidence in the quality of the test suite. Three commonly used measures of adequacy are *state-based coverage, constraint-based coverage, and code-based coverage*. Meeting these measures minimally will result in different test suites. Using all three measures for a test suite will improve the level of confidence in testing adequately.

State-Based Coverage

State-based coverage is based on how many of the transitions in a state transition diagram are covered by the test suite. If one or more transitions is not covered, then the class has not been tested adequately and more test cases should

Boundary Conditions

In testing a component, it is often the case that a small change in input value results in a significant change in the response of the software. The input value at which a large change occurs is referred to as a **boundary**. Boundaries must be identified when test cases are identified. Test cases must be generated to check input values close to each boundary. The response of the system to inputs occurring between two adjacent boundaries is generally equivalent. A relatively small number of test case inputs can be taken from that set for adequate testing, but a test case must be generated for each side of and (possibly) for each boundary.

Some boundaries are easy to identify from a state transition diagram from the guards placed on state transitions—a test case for the *true* condition and one for the *false* condition. Other boundaries are not so obvious from a state transition diagram because they do not effect a state change, but do affect a response. Consider, for example, a method to compute a Julian date. Clearly, the value associated with March 1 depends on whether the year is a leap year.

Some boundaries can only be identified from code itself because they are derived from an algorithm used to implement a specification and not from the specification itself. A standard example is a function to sort an array of integer values in nondecreasing (*ascending*) order. With respect to the size of an array to be sorted, boundary conditions are as follows:

- an array containing no elements
- an array containing exactly one element
- an array containing exactly two elements—the smallest array that can actually be sorted
- an array of a large number of elements

With respect to the ordering of elements in an array to be sorted, they can be arranged as follows:

- in a random order
- as the same value
- in a sorted order
- in reverse of their sorted order

Finally, we can consider the aspect of the actual values in an array to be sorted, which can be unique, the same, or partly unique and partly the same.

The values can range from the smallest boundary value to the largest. These three aspects generate a fairly large number of test cases.

be generated to cover those transitions. If test cases are generated from a state transition diagram as we described, then the test cases achieve this measure. If test cases were generated from pre- and postconditions, then analyzing the test cases in terms of which transitions they cover is quite useful for finding missed test cases.

Even if all transitions are covered once, adequate testing is doubtful because states usually embrace a range of values for various object attributes. We need to test values over those ranges. Testing is needed for typical values and boundary values.

We must also be concerned about how operations interact with respect to transitions. If there are two transitions T_1 and T_2 into a state and one transition T_3 out of a state, then the test cases for T_3 might pass when the input state is set up using T_1, but not when T_2 is used. We can address this problem using a measure of adequacy based on coverage of all *pairs* of transitions in the state transition diagram. In our example, we would test the combinations of T_1-T_3 and T_2-T_3.

Constraint-Based Coverage

Parallel to adequacy based on state transitions, we can express adequacy in terms of how many pairs of pre- and postconditions have been covered. If for example, the preconditions for an operation are pre_1 or pre_2 and the postconditions are $post_1$ or $post_2$, then we make sure the test suite contains cases for all the valid combinations—pre_1=true, pre_2=false, $post_1$=true, $post_2$=false; pre_1=false, pre_2=true, $post_1$=true, $post_2$=false, and so on.

Recall the steps we described earlier for finding test case requirements when generating test cases from pre- and postconditions. If one test case is generated to satisfy each requirement, then the test suite meets this measure of adequacy.

In a way similar to what we described for using pair-wise sequences of transitions in state-based coverage, we can use sequences of operations based on analysis of preconditions and postconditions. For each operation *op* that is not an accessor, identify the operators op_1, op_2, and so on, for which the preconditions are met when the postconditions for *op* hold. Then execute the test cases for op-op_1, op-op_2, and so on.

Code-Based Coverage

A third measure of adequacy can be based on how much of the code that implements the class is executed across all test cases in the suite. It is a good idea to determine that every line of (or path through) the code implementing a class was executed at least once when all test cases have completed execution. Tools for making such measurements are available commercially. If certain lines of code (or paths) have not been reached, then the test suite needs to be expanded with test cases that do reach those lines (paths)—or the code needs to be corrected to remove unreachable lines.

Even with full code coverage, the test suite for a class might not be adequate because it might not exercise interactions between methods as we described in state-based and constraint-based coverage. Use of one of those other metrics to determine adequacy is important. However, measuring in terms of code coverage is also important (see sidebar). One implementation-level technique for determining the adequacy of a test suite is measuring code coverage for sequences of operations. If all statements (paths) are not executed, generate more test cases to reach them.

A Need for Implementation-Based Testing

In testing a function to sort an array (see Boundary Conditions on page 180), we might want to use a sampling of test cases in order to reduce the testing effort. (Pair-wise sampling is discussed in the next chapter.) The following test case inputs provide a good cross section of the possibilities:

- an array of zero elements
- an array of exactly one element
- an array containing exactly two elements that are out of order
- an array of 100 elements that contain 100 different values, some negative and some positive, arranged in a random order
- an array of 101 elements that all contain the same value
- an array of 50 elements that contain values that are already sorted
- an array of 72 elements that contain values that are in exactly the reverse of their sorted order

The choices of sizes 101, 100, 50, and 72 are arbitrary. An array of any reasonable size would seem to suffice. We decided to use different sizes just to get a better sampling. Some inputs are ordered randomly, already ordered, and reverse ordered. These cases seem to cover the specification reasonably well. If the function can pass these test cases, then we can be reasonably confident that it can sort any array. Of course, exhaustive testing would make us more confident.

However, we cannot ever be fully confident a component meets its specification based purely on test cases derived from a specification. Consider a scenario in which this sort function has been implemented so that all arrays of a size under 1024 are sorted using a bubble-sort algorithm, and all larger arrays are sorted using a quicksort algorithm. Then, by using these test cases, the code for this function would not be tested adequately. A size of 1024 comprises a boundary imposed by the implementation that is not identifiable from the specification. Thus, more test cases that use arrays containing 1024 and more elements are needed.

Constructing a Test Driver

A test driver is a program that runs test cases and collects the results. We describe three general approaches to writing test drivers. There are probably others and certainly there are many variations on what we present. We recommend one approach over the others and will develop it in detail.[6]

Consider three ways to implement a test driver for the Velocity class. We will use C++ to illustrate the structure of the test driver design.

1. Implement a function main() that can be compiled conditionally (with #define TEST) when compiling the member function definitions (in the *Velocity.cpp* file) and then executed (see Figure 5.9).

2. Implement a static member function within the class that can be invoked to execute and collect the results for each of the test cases (see Figure 5.10).[7]

```
// File: Velocity.h
#ifndef VELOCITY_H
#define VELOCITY_H

#include "direction.h"
#include "speed.h"

class Velocity {
public:
    Velocity();
    Velocity(Speed speed,
             Direction dir);
...
private:
    Speed _speed;
    Direction _direction;
...
};
```

```
// File: Velocity.cpp
#include "Velocity.h"

Velocity::Velocity()
    : _speed(0), _direction(0), … { }

Velocity::Velocity(Speed speed,
                    Direction dir)
    : _speed(speed), _direction(dir), … { }

...
#ifdef TEST
// Test driver code
int main() {
    // run and report test cases
    // …
}
#endif
```

Figure 5.9 A conditionally compiled test driver for the Velocity class embedded in the source file

6. If the behavior of the class calls for program termination as a postcondition—for example, when an implementation based on a defensive programming approach uses the assert() library function to check preconditions—then multiple test drivers might be needed or the test driver needs to support some way of running individual test cases.

7. In Java, this could be a class method named main(), thereby making execution of the test driver as simple as running a class file on the Java virtual machine.

```
// File: Velocity.h
#ifndef VELOCITY_H
#define VELOCITY_H

#include "direction.h"
#include "speed.h"

class Velocity {
public:
    Velocity();
    Velocity(Speed speed, Direction
    dir);
    ...
private:
    Speed _speed;
    Direction _direction;
    // ...
};
```

```
// File: Velocity.cpp
#include "Velocity.h"

Velocity::Velocity()
    : _speed(0), _direction(0),
    ...{ }

Velocity::Velocity(Speed speed, Direction
    dir)
    : _speed(speed), _direction(dir), ...{ }
    ...

int Velocity::main() {
    // run and report test cases.
    // ...
}
```

Figure 5.10 A test driver embedded as a class operation for Velocity

3. Implement a separate class whose responsibility is to execute and collect the results for each test case (see Figure 5.11). A main() function instantiates this class and sends it a message to run all test cases. Note: in Java, main() can be a static method of the VelocityTester class.

```
// File: VelocityTester.h
#ifndef VELOCITYTESTER_H
#define VELOCITYTESTER_H

#include "Velocity.h"

class VelocityTester {
public:
    VelocityTester();

    void runTestSuite();

private:
    ...
};
```

```
// File: VelocityTester.cpp
#include "VelocityTester.h"
VelocityTester::VelocityTester()
    : ... { ... }

void VelocityTester::runTestSuite() {
    // code to run and report test cases.
    ...
}
```

```
// File: VelocityTesterMain.cpp
#include "VelocityTester.h"
int main()
    VelocityTester tester;
    tester.runTestSuite();
}
```

Figure 5.11 A test driver for the Velocity class implemented as a separate "tester" class

All three designs are equivalent with respect to their support for running the same test cases and reporting the results. Some of the strengths and weaknesses of each are summarized in Figure 5.12.

The second and third designs are attractive because they can be implemented using standard features of most object-oriented programming languages. We prefer the third design.[8] Although it separates test code from production code, the relationship between a class and a driver for testing it is easy to remember—each class C has a **tester class** called CTester. The use of a separate class is not necessarily a disadvantage. The proximity of a driver's code to the code for a class it tests is advantageous if the code for both is being developed by the same person. Otherwise it is a disadvantage. This tester class design allows some flexibility since in most programming languages two classes can be defined in the same file or in different files.

Method	Strengths	Weaknesses
1. Conditionally compiled driver.	Driver code maintained closely with (in the same file as) class code.	Hard to reuse code for driver to test a subclass without cloning. Requires support for conditional compilation.
2. Static method serves as test driver.	Driver code maintained closely with class code. Easy to reuse code for driver (by inheritance) to test a subclass.	Care must be taken to strip driver code from delivered software.
3. Separate "tester" class.	Easy to reuse code for driver to test a subclass. Production code is as small as possible. Production code is as fast as possible.	New class must be created. Care must be taken to reflect changes in the class in the tests.

Figure 5.12 Strengths and weaknesses of the test driver designs

---

8. It has even more strengths in association with testing inheritance hierarchies, as we will describe in Chapter 7.

We will concentrate on the tester class design, although most aspects of development of such a driver can be adapted in a straightforward manner to the other designs.

Test Driver Requirements

Before looking at tester classes in more detail, consider the requirements for a test driver for execution-based testing of a class.

The main purpose of a test driver is to run executable test cases and to report the results of running them. A test driver should have a relatively simple design because we seldom have time or resources to do execution-based testing of driver software. We rely primarily on code reviews to check driver code. In support of reviews and to facilitate maintenance, we should be able to readily trace the testing requirements in a test plan to the code in a driver. A test driver must be easy to maintain and adapt in response to changes in the incremental specification for the class it tests. Ideally, we should be able to reuse code from the test drivers for existing classes in creating new drivers.

Figure 5.13 shows a model for a class Tester that satisfies these requirements. The public interface provides operations to run various test suites—or all of

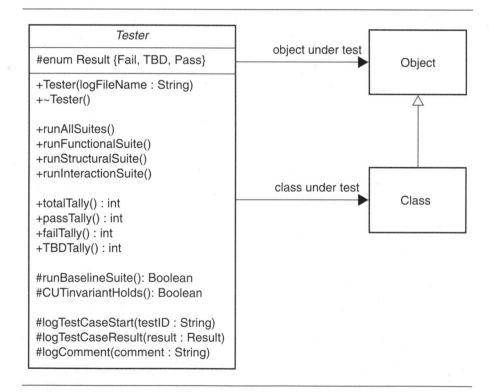

Figure 5.13 A class model for requirements of a Tester class

them. The test cases are organized into suites based on their origin—*functional* if they were identified from the specification, *structural* if they were identified from the code, and *interaction* if they test the correct operation of sequences of events on an object, such as pairs of input/output transitions. We identify these categories to facilitate maintenance of tests. The lines between these categories are sometimes hard to draw, but the general criterion for putting a test case in a category concerns how the test case was initially identified and what impact changes to a class have on a test case. Interaction test cases are usually generated to augment other test cases to achieve some level of coverage. Implementation-based test cases are generated to test some behavior of the code that arises from the implementation rather than the specification. If the implementation for a class changes, but not the specification, then we should be able to update the driver code just by modifying code to run implementation-based test cases. We refer to the set of test cases in a particular category as a *test suite* for that category. Thus, we identify a **functional** (specification-based) **test suite**, a **structural** (implementation-based) **test suite**, and an **interaction test suite**.

The tally operations on a tester can be used to check how many test cases have passed so far. A driver keeps a log of test case execution and the results in a file whose name is specified at the time it is instantiated. The protected logTestCaseStart(), logTestCaseResult(), and logComment() operations place information in the log file. The protected runBaselineSuite() operation verifies the correctness of methods in the class under test (CUT) that are used by the test driver in checking the results of test cases. Accessor and modifier methods are usually tested as part of the baseline test suite for a class. The CUTinvariantHolds() operation evaluates the invariant of the CUT using the state of the current object under test (OUT).

The Tester class is abstract. Code for the class can provide default implementations for operations common to all (concrete) testers. These include operations for logging test case results and performing other functions common to all class test drivers, such as measuring heap allocation and providing support for timing execution of individual test cases. The methods to run the test suites and to check a class invariant must be implemented for each specific CUT.

We now look at the typical design for a concrete Tester class. A design for VelocityTester is shown in Figure 5.14. The figure shows a little more detail about the Tester class than is shown in Figure 5.13, including some operations to manipulate an OUT and some factory methods for creating instances of the CUT. We will describe these in the next section. A concrete Tester class is responsible primarily for implementing methods for test cases and running them as part of a suite.

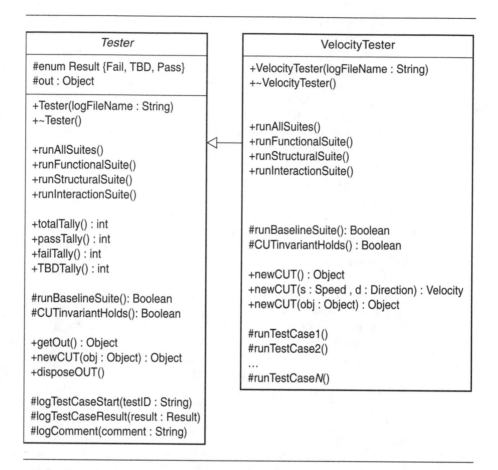

Figure 5.14 Class model for a VelocityTester class

Tester Class Design

Since the Tester class provides operations to help report test case results, the primary responsibility of a concrete Tester class, such as VelocityTester, is to run test cases and report results. The main components of the class interface are operations to set up test cases, to analyze the results of test cases, to execute test cases, and to create instances of the CUT to be used in running test cases. Our design has proven both flexible and maintainable. It has proven quite useful when instances of a class are needed to test another class, as we will show in the next chapter.

Within a concrete tester class, we define one method for each of the test cases. We refer to these as **test case methods**. These provide traceability to the test plan—one method per test case or group of closely related test cases. The purpose of a test case method is to execute a test case by creating the input state, generating a sequence of events, and checking the output state.

Test Case Methods

In a Tester class, each test case is represented by a single method. The name of the method should reflect the test case in some way. For small numbers of test cases, we can sequentially number the test cases identified in the test plan and name the operations runTestCase01(), runTestCase02(), and so on. Sequential numbering is simple, but can result in problems if test cases in a plan are ordered in some way and test cases are inserted or deleted. Usually a naming convention can be developed based on the derivation of the test cases (see sidebar).

The responsibility of a test case method is to construct the input state for a test case—for example, by instantiating an OUT and any objects to be passed as parameters, and then by generating the events specified by the test case. A test case method reports the status of the result—*pass*, *fail*, or *TBD*[9] to indicate some action is needed to determine the result. A test case method verifies that the CUT's invariant holds for the OUT.

In our code, a test case method has a general structure shown in pseudocode in Figure 5.15.

Implement a **test script method** for each test case when creating a **Tester** class for classes in which there are many interaction test cases. A test script method is responsible for creating the OUT for use by a test case method, invoking the test case method, and then checking postconditions and the class invariant. It also reports the results. The test case method handles only the event sequence on the OUT. An interaction test case can then be coded as a single test script method that invokes a sequence of test case methods and then checks and reports the results.

OUT Factory Methods

Classes are tested by creating instances and checking their behaviors against a set of test cases. We have referred to an instance to which a test case is being applied as the **object under test** (OUT). The main requirement with respect to the OUT is that attributes be specified for the inputs to the test case so that

---

9. *To be determined.* Some results require human reaction, such as verifying generation of a sound or a change in what is displayed on a monitor screen. For example, testing an overloaded stream insertion operator for a class in C++ might require a tester to open a file and verify that the data is printed correctly. For such test cases, we like to include directions as comments in the log.

Naming Test Cases

Naming test cases well is an interesting problem. We would like the names to somehow reflect what is being tested. In an environment in which paragraph numbers are associated with each piece of a specification, the name of a test case can include some encoded reference to that paragraph that gives rise to the test case. This is desirable because it gives traceability to the test case and is commonly used to name system test cases. However, paragraph numbers are not associated with OCL specifications or state transition diagrams, which are used to specify classes.

For naming specification-based test cases, a naming scheme can be based on an operation name and pre- and postcondition numbering. Assume an operation is specified with the following pre- and postconditions:

> operation
> pre: ① or ②

Based on a goal of testing each combination of precondition and postcondition, then the combinations in the following table are possible:

①	②	❶	❷	Test Case Name
F	T	T	F	op1F2T1T2F
T	F	T	F	op1T2F1T2F
T	T	T	F	op1T2T1T2F
F	T	F	T	op1F2T1F2T
T	F	F	T	op1T2F1F2T
T	T	F	T	op1T2T1F2T
F	T	T	T	op1F2T1T2T
T	F	T	T	op1T2F1T2T
T	T	T	T	op1T2T1T2T

The test case name is derived by numbering the disjuncts in the precondition and the postcondition, and incorporating those numbers in the name followed immediately by a "T" or an "F" to indicate the truth value associated with that test case. If several equivalence classes, as determined by boundary values, exist for a particular test case, then a suffix can be added to the name—for example, op1F2T1T2Fa, op1F2T1T2Fb, and so on. An explanation of these test cases should be included in documentation for the code or the test plan.

This scheme works for naming test cases that address a single operation. Test cases involving interactions can be named based on concatenating names for each of the operations in a sequence comprising an interaction.

Checking Postconditions and Invariants

Postconditions and invariants can be checked in a straightforward manner, assuming the CUT defines public operations for accessing state and/or attribute values.

We have identified two general approaches to writing code to check postconditions and invariants. One is to write code to compute attribute values in the tester code when they are needed. The other is to use a database of some form—including as a file or array in memory—from which values can be retrieved when needed. Consider checking the values of speedX and speedY attributes in the invariant for Velocity. The condition involves sines and cosines of angles. We can compute these values as test cases execute using the sin() and cos() functions in a standard library, assuming we are using reliable functions. Alternatively, we can precompute values of the attribute for various values of direction and speed used in test cases, and then retrieve that information when it is needed. We have used spreadsheet programs to perform such computations.

A tricky part of checking postconditions is in coding expressions that use *@pre*, meaning the value at the start of the method execution. The method must store such values in a local "temp" whose value is used once the test case output is available for checking. Use the factory method in the Tester class that corresponds to a copy constructor to facilitate *@pre* checking. For example, in checking the postcondition for setDirection(Direction dir), use

```
Velocity *OUTatPre = newCUT( *getOUT() ); // remember state
...
if ( OUT.getSpeed() == OUTatPre.getSpeed() &&
     OUT.getDirection() == dir ) ...
```

If postconditions relate to the state of the OUT, then invoke operations to check the state. If no such operations are defined by the CUT, then define them in the tester class as protected member functions. Note well: *If the test case method is relying on operations defined in the CUT, then make sure tests for those operations are included in the baseline suite.*

OCL allows state names to be used as Boolean-valued attributes in specifications [WK99]. A class need not define an operation to explicitly return the state of an instance. We believe classes should always include some way of observing the current state of an object based on state names, not just ranges of attribute values—for example, in the PuckSupply class we defined the isEmpty() operation. If the CUT does not completely support in its interface the operations needed to test postconditions and invariants in terms of states, approach the developers to add them to the CUT rather than coding methods in the Tester class. After all, a client (in this case the Tester class) should be able to *observe* all the behavior of an object if that behavior is referenced by the specification. Certainly a class must have in its public interface all the operations necessary for a client to check the preconditions for any public operation.

```
void tc_testCaseID() {
  report start of test case;

  create a new instance I of the CUT using a factory method;
  put I into the correct input state;
  setOUT(I);

  generate the prescribed sequence of events on the OUT;

  check post-conditions and class invariant against OUT;
  report results;
  disposeOUT()
}
```

Figure 5.15 Pseudocode for a typical test case method

preconditions associated with a test case to be applied are met. The Tester class includes setOUT() and getOUT() operations that are used by test case methods to access the current OUT (see Figure 5.14). A disposeOUT() is available to end an association of the OUT with its current instance.

A tester interface includes a set of operations to construct instances of the CUT. These operations include newCUT(Object), which is a factory method used to create an instance of the CUT that is a *copy* of the object passed as its argument—a factory method resembling a copy constructor in C++. A concrete Tester class should implement a factory method corresponding to each constructor defined in the CUT. Test case methods use these factory methods to create an OUT instead of constructors for the CUT. Test case methods use getOUT() to access a current OUT. In the case of VelocityTester, we define operation newCUT() to create an instance of Velocity constructed with the default constructor and setOUT() to make that instance the current OUT. We also define the newCUT(s: Speed, d: Direction) operation to create a new instance using the Velocity::Velocity(s: Speed, d: Direction) constructor. The test case methods *must* use these factory methods to create new instances of the CUT for reasons that will be apparent when we look at testing class hierarchies in Chapter 7.[10]

---

10. Here is a preview. For any subclass (of the CUT) designed in accordance with the substitution principle, test cases for the CUT still apply to that subclass. We will create a tester for the subclass that is a subclass of the tester for the CUT. Since the test case methods in the tester for CUT rely on factory methods, we can just override those same methods in the subclass's tester to create instances of the subclass. As we mentioned at the start of the book, object-oriented technologies improve testing as well as development.

It is not uncommon for a Tester class to define additional factory methods for the convenience of test cases that need to create an OUT in some specific state. For example, the PuckSupplyTester class might provide a newPuckSupply-OfOne() operation to construct a PuckSupply instance containing a single puck. Such factory methods should be public since they are very useful when instances of the CUT are needed to test another class. The test case methods for the other class can use an instance of this Tester class as a helper to create the instances in the necessary states. In implementing such methods, however, take care to use the other factory methods in the Tester and not the constructors for the CUT.

Objects under test should be allocated from the heap because the use of a single object shared by all test cases will not work in the general case. It is also easier to understand test driver code that is written so that each test case method creates its own OUT and then disposes it. Sharing such objects between test case methods increases coupling. Keep test driver code as simple as possible, even at the expense of some time and/or space inefficiency. One of the most frustrating aspects of developing test drivers is testing and debugging them. The more straightforward the code, the better the driver.

In using a language such as C++ in which a programmer must manage the heap, make each test case method responsible for deleting objects it allocates. The disposeOUT() method can delete the current OUT.

Baseline Testing

Test case methods contain code to establish an OUT, which might require a series of modification requests to be sent to an instance of the CUT. Test case methods use accessor operations in the process of checking postconditions. If the constructors, modifier methods, and accessor methods for the CUT are incorrect, then the results reported by a tester are unreliable. The first thing a tester must do is check that such constructors and methods are themselves correct by executing test cases for them. We call this set of test cases a **baseline test suite**.[11]

A baseline test suite is a set of test cases that tests the operations of the CUT that are needed for the other test cases to verify their outcomes. This suite includes testing constructors and accessors. Most likely, all the test cases in the baseline test suite will be replicated in the functional test suite.

---

11. Thorough testing of the most basic operations needed to check test results is critical. We once worked on a compiler for which the programs in the test suite always checked for failure of each test case—that is, of the form *set up test case input; execute test case input; if (some condition not true) then report failure*. A compiler could pass the executable test suite if it generated code so that all conditions evaluate to true so that no failure would be reported. This is clearly a weakness of the testing approach. We needed a baseline test suite that checked for correct evaluation of conditional expressions in *if* statements.

We have identified two basic approaches to baseline testing, one that's specification-based and one that's implementation-based:

1. Check that all the constructors and accessors are self-consistent. Create a test case for each constructor and verify that all attributes are correct by invoking accessors.

2. Check that all the constructors and accessors use the *variables* in an object correctly. This requires a tester to know how attributes are implemented in a CUT. Its implementation relies on visibility features of programming languages that allow a tester class to have access to the implementation of the class it tests. These features include *friends* in C++ and package visibility in Java.

Base your approach on how closely you want to couple the code for a tester to the code for the class it tests. We have found the second approach to produce more reliable results, although it requires more programming effort and tightly couples the code between the two classes—for example, in C++ the CUT must declare its Tester class a friend. The second approach usually requires fewer test cases in the baseline suite than does the first approach.

Assertion Checking in a Class Under Test

While the primary mechanism for execution-based testing is implementing a test driver, bugs can also be found by inserting assertion checks in code for a class as it is developed. This can include assertions to check preconditions, postconditions, and invariants. An implementer can identify an implementation-oriented set of invariants in addition to the invariants specified for a class. Consider, for example, the Sprite class in *Brickles*. For efficiency reasons, each instance maintains in its local state both the bounding rectangle (as a corner point, a width, and a height) and the points that form the upper left and lower right points of the bounding rectangle. This redundancy is a potential source of bugs because the values can become inconsistent. This design introduces an *implementation-level* class invariant constraining the point at the lower right corner of the bounding rectangle to be the lower right point stored in an instance. A SpriteTester class cannot contain code to check such implementation-level invariants unless it has access to the implementation of Sprite. To facilitate testing, an implementer should include an assertion to check this implementation-level class invariant in every member function that modifies the bounding rectangle of an instance. This facilitates debugging and testing without increasing the coupling between a tester class and its CUT.

Tip

Implement a protected method in a Tester class to check postcondition clauses. The same postcondition often appears in the specification of more than one operation defined for a class. Invoke these protected methods rather than coding the same postcondition checks in each test case method.

Similarly, define a factory method to return an OUT in a state required for a test case. It is not uncommon for a number of test cases to specify the same preconditions for an OUT and to have a convenient method to create an instance and reduce the amount of code in a test driver.

If test script methods are being used to facilitate interaction testing in a class, write each test case method so that it verifies the input state for the test case before generating events on the OUT. Since tester classes are seldom formally tested themselves (by Tester classes), a little defensive programming can help in debugging them.

Running Test Suites

The abstract Tester class includes in its protocol some operations to run all test cases or selected suites. These methods for these operations are straightforward to implement. Each calls a sequence of test case methods. Take care to ensure that the baseline test suite is executed before any of these other suites are executed. A possible design calls for executing the baseline test suite when a concrete tester class is instantiated—that is, as part of its initialization.

If the CUT contains static member functions and/or data members, then the Tester class should to incorporate code that ensures that code has already been tested and works correctly or at least warns that the class itself might need testing before its instances can be tested. This is not critical since the goal of test-

Is it possible to design a class to make testing easier?

Yes. Ensure that the public interface includes operations that enable all conditions within preconditions, postconditions, and class invariants to be checked by clients. Furthermore, enable the current *observable state* to be observed without a client having to determine that state based on current attribute values. If a class is not designed with such methods, approach the class designer about adding them to the interface.

Providing a public operation in a class to check the class invariant is useful to a Tester class and to developers for debugging. Be wary, however, of relying on that code to check postconditions in test case methods. We prefer to code up an independent CUTinvariantHolds() method in each Tester class we implement.

ing a class is to uncover bugs, not diagnose the source of those bugs. However, such a reminder can serve to ensure that a test driver is written for those static members.

> Be sure to rerun all test cases after debugging code is removed from the code for a class. Sometimes developers add code to help in debugging a class—for example, assertion checks and statements that write trace information to streams. In many shops, debugging code is removed before software is deployed. (To support this, for example, C++'s assert() macro (library header file *assert.h*) checks assertions only if NDEBUG is not defined.) Under some circumstances, code that includes debugging information can have behaviors different from the same code without the debugging support. Consequently, take care to run test cases in both debugging and nondebugging modes.

Reporting Test Results

A test case method determines the success of a test case. In our design, test case methods report results to the tester instance itself, which tallies test suite run statistics. It is useful for each test case method to identify itself as part of its report. A string denoting the script name or purpose is useful.

Keep in mind that the purpose of testing is not to debug a class, but to see if it meets its specification. Since a class's tester is usually its developer, writing code in a driver that attempts to diagnose problems with the CUT is very appealing. Extensive effort put into diagnostic code is almost always misplaced. Symbolic debuggers and other tools are better for such activities. Such debugging can, of course, be done in the context of the test driver.

Example of Test Driver Code

We illustrate the design of a Tester class by showing the representative parts[12] of VelocityTester written in C++ and in Java. Features and restrictions in the two languages result in different designs. A test plan for Velocity is shown in Figure 5.16. A set of test case descriptions is shown in Figure 5.17. Some test cases are determined by combinations of values for attributes over a range of values.

---

12. The code is quite lengthy. The sections omitted follow the pattern set forth by the code shown in the example.

Component Test Plan

Component Name Velocity	Tracking Number CTP102895

Developer(s) David Sykes	Tester(s) David Sykes

Objectives for This Component

This class plays a central role in implementing sprites that move in *Brickles*—or any other arcade game. It is more generally useful in representing anything that moves in a plane represented as a grid of coordinates having integer values.

Guided Inspection Requirements

As this is a critical component, 100% of its code shall be inspected.

A risk analysis has shown that all operations in the interface are likely used by other components of the system and consequently all must be tested.

Building and Retaining Test Suites

The test suites shall be prepared in accordance with project standards. Thus, the test driver shall take the form of a VelocityTester class and shall include operations to execute functional, structural, and interaction test cases.

Reporting of results shall conform to project standards as set forth in the documentation for the abstract Tester class.

Specification-Based Test Cases

Test cases for each operation shall address the equivalence classes of speed (*zero*, *slow*, *moderate*, and *fast*) and direction (*east, northeast, north, northwest, west, southwest, south,* and *southeast*). Pair-wise combinations shall be used.

Implementation-Based Test Cases

Execute test cases needed to cover any code not executed by test cases in the specification-based suite.

Interaction Test Cases

Execute test cases that test the interactions of the **reverse()**, **reverseX()**, and **reverseY()** operations.

State-Based Test Cases

Execute test cases that cover every transition in the state representation.

Figure 5.16 A component test plan for the Velocity class

Description	Input		Output	
	Setup	**Event(s)**	**Result State**	**Exceptions**
test default constructor	none	OUT = new Velocity;	OUT.speed=0 and OUT.direction=0	none
test constructor {spd = 6, 12, 1000; dir = 0..359}	none	OUT = new Velocity(spd, dir)	OUT.speed = spd and OUT.direction = dir	none
test setDirection {spd = 1000; dir = 0..359}	OUT:Velocity[speed=1000, direction=dir]	OUT.setDirection(dir+1)	OUT.direction = dir and OUT.speed = spd	none
test setSpeed {spd = 0, 1, 5, 10, 1000; dir = 0, 30, 90, 135, 180, 182, 270, 335}	OUT:Velocity[speed=100, direction=dir]	OUT.setSpeed(spd);	OUT.direction = dir and OUT.speed = spd	none
test reverse()	OUT:Velocity[speed = 10, direction = 0]	OUT.reverse()	OUT.speed = 10 and OUT.direction = 180	none
	OUT:Velocity[speed = 10, direction = 30]	OUT.reverse()	OUT.speed = 10 and OUT.direction = 210	none
	OUT:Velocity[speed = 10, direction = 90]	OUT.reverse()	OUT.speed = 10 and OUT.direction = 270	none
	OUT:Velocity[speed = 10, direction = 135]	OUT.reverse()	OUT.speed = 10 and OUT.direction = 315	none
	OUT:Velocity[speed = 10, direction = 180]	OUT.reverse()	OUT.speed = 10 and OUT.direction = 0	none
	OUT:Velocity[speed = 10, direction = 182]	OUT.reverse()	OUT.speed = 10 and OUT.direction = 2	none
	OUT:Velocity[speed = 10, direction = 270]	OUT.reverse()	OUT.speed = 10 and OUT.direction = 90	none
	OUT:Velocity[speed = 10, direction = 335]	OUT.reverse()	OUT.speed = 10 and OUT.direction = 155	none
reverseX()	OUT:Velocity[speed = 10, direction = 0]	OUT.reverse()	OUT.speed = 10 and OUT.direction = 180	none
	OUT:Velocity[speed = 10, direction = 30]	OUT.reverse()	OUT.speed = 10 and OUT.direction = 150	none
	OUT:Velocity[speed = 10, direction = 90]	OUT.reverse()	OUT.speed = 10 and OUT.direction = 90	none
	OUT:Velocity[speed = 10, direction = 135]	OUT.reverse()	OUT.speed = 10 and OUT.direction = 45	none
	OUT:Velocity[speed = 10, direction = 180]	OUT.reverse()	OUT.speed = 10 and OUT.direction = 0	none
	OUT:Velocity[speed = 10, direction = 182]	OUT.reverse()	OUT.speed = 10 and OUT.direction = 358	none
	OUT:Velocity[speed = 10, direction = 270]	OUT.reverse()	OUT.speed = 10 and OUT.direction = 270	none
	OUT:Velocity[speed = 10, direction = 335]	OUT.reverse()	OUT.speed = 10 and OUT.direction = 205	none
reverseY()	...			

Figure 5.17 Test case descriptions for some of the Velocity operations

C++ code for the Tester and VelocityTester is shown first, followed by the Java code. First, we will make some observations about the code.

- In the C++ version, we have used a template parameterized by the CUT to generate the Tester abstract class. By using a template, we can produce a class at the root of the tester hierarchy for each CUT. Consequently, for example, operations such as getOUT() return a pointer to an instance of the CUT and not a pointer of type void * or of a pointer to some abstract Object class.

    In the Java version, we defined Tester as an abstract class and used Object to represent the class of the OUT. This requires each test case method to dynamically cast a reference to the OUT to a reference to the CUT.

- The Tester class in both implementations have the same functionality. This includes code to tally and report test results to a log file. This design could be enhanced significantly to maintain a database of test results and do more elaborate reporting.

- Notice how the factory methods in VelocityTester return an instance of the Velocity class. A tester should always declare such factory methods to return a pointer or a reference to the CUT.

- The baseline test suite implemented in TestVelocity is minimal. It merely checks that the attribute values returned by accessors are correct for a single object. More extensive testing of accessors is part of the functional test suite.

- The CUTInvariantHolds() method in VelocityTester relies on the math library functions sin() and cos(). We trust those functions to return the correct value. In the C++ version, we use the arc cosine of -1 to compute a value for PI. Java provides Math.PI to use.

- To save space, we have not included all test case methods. The test case method tc_Velocity() tests the default constructor. The tcs_VelocitySpeedDirection() and tcs_setDirection() methods run the sets of test cases described in Figure 5.17 for the nondefault constructor and setDirection() operation.

C++ code for the Tester **class.** This code was compiled using Metrowerks CodeWarrior Pro 5.

```cpp
#include <fstream>
#include <iomanip>
#include <ctime>
using namespace std;

enum TestResult {Fail, TBD, Pass};

template<class CUT>
class Tester {
public:
  Tester<CUT>(string CUTname, string logFileName)
    : _CUTname(CUTname), _logStream(logFileName.c_str()),
      _OUTPtr(0), _passTally(0), _failTally(0), _TBDTally(0) {
      time_t systime = time(0);
      _logStream << ctime(&systime) << endl;
  }

  virtual ~Tester<CUT>() { // Summarize results in log
    _logStream << endl << "Summary of results:" << endl
               << '\t' << totalTally() << " test cases run" << endl
               << fixed << showpoint << setprecision(2)
               << '\t' << setw(7) << "Pass:" << setw(5)
               <<passTally() << endl
               << '\t' << setw(7) << "Fail:" << setw(5)
               << failTally() << endl
               << '\t' << setw(7) << "TBD :" << setw(5)
               <<  TBDTally() << endl;
    _logStream.close();
  }

  virtual void runAllSuites() {
    runFunctionalSuite();
    runStructuralSuite();
    runInteractionSuite();
  }

  virtual void runFunctionalSuite() = 0;
  virtual void runStructuralSuite() = 0;
  virtual void runInteractionSuite() = 0;

  int passTally() const { return _passTally; }
  int failTally() const { return _failTally; }
  int TBDTally() const  { return _TBDTally; }
  int totalTally() const {
    return _passTally + _failTally + _TBDTally;
  }

  virtual CUT *getOUT() { return _OUTPtr; } // Current OUT
  virtual void disposeOUT() { // Finish use of current OUT
```

```
      if ( ! _OUTPtr ) {
        delete _OUTPtr;
        _OUTPtr = 0;
      }
    }
    virtual CUT *newCUT(const CUT &object) = 0;

protected:
    virtual bool runBaselineSuite() = 0;
    virtual bool CUTinvariantHolds() = 0;

    void setOUT(CUT *outPtr) { _OUTPtr = outPtr; }
            // used by factory methods

    void logTestCaseStart(string testID) {
      _logStream << "Start test case " << testID << endl;
    }

    void logSubTestCaseStart(int caseNumber) {
      _logStream << "Start sub test case " << caseNumber << endl;
    }

    void logTestCaseResult(TestResult result) {
      _logStream << "RESULT: ";
      switch ( result ) {
      case Fail:  ++ _failTally;
                  _logStream << "FAIL";
                  break;
      case TBD:   ++ _TBDTally;
                  _logStream << "To be determined";
                  break;
      case Pass:  ++ _passTally;
                  _logStream << "Pass";
                  break;
      default:
                  _logStream << "BAD result (" << int(result) << ')'
                             << endl;
      }
      _logStream << endl;
    }

    void logComment(string comment) {
      _logStream << "\t* " << comment << endl;
    }

    TestResult passOrFail(bool condition) {
      // Utility for a result that cannot be TBD.
      // This checks the invariant, too.
      if ( condition && CUTinvariantHolds() )
        return Pass;
      else
        return Fail;
    }
```

```
    private:
      string _CUTname;  // name of the class under test
      ofstream _logStream;// log stream
      CUT *_OUTPtr;      // pointer to current object under test
      int _passTally;    // number of test cases passing so far
      int _failTally;    // number of test cases failing so far
      int _TBDTally;     // number of test cases provisionally
                          // passing so far
  };
```

C++ code for the VelocityTester class.

```
// VelocityTester.h
#include "Tester.h"
#include "Velocity.h"

class VelocityTester : public Tester<Velocity> {
public:
  VelocityTester(string logFileName)
    : Tester<Velocity>("Velocity", logFileName) {
    runBaselineSuite();
   }

  virtual void runFunctionalSuite() {
    tc_Velocity();
    tcs_VelocitySpeedDirection();
    tcs_setDirection();
  }
  virtual void runStructuralSuite() { }
  virtual void runInteractionSuite() { }

  virtual Velocity *newCUT() { return new Velocity(); }
  virtual Velocity *newCUT(const Velocity &v) {
    return new Velocity(v);
  }
  virtual Velocity *newCUT(const Speed speed, const Direction dir)
  {
    return new Velocity(speed, dir);
  }

protected:
  virtual bool runBaselineSuite() {
    // Verify that the accessor operations are consistent
    logComment("Running baseline test suite.");
    Velocity v(1000, 321);
    if ( v.getSpeed() == 1000 && v.getDirection() == 321 &&
         v.getSpeedX() == 777 && v.getSpeedY() == -629 ) {
      logComment("Baseline suite passed");
      return true;
    }
    else {
      logComment("Baseline suite FAILED");
      return false;
    }
  }
```

```
virtual bool CUTinvariantHolds() {
  const Velocity &OUT = *getOUT();
  const Direction direction = OUT.getDirection();
  const Speed speed = OUT.getSpeed();
  const Speed speedX = OUT.getSpeedX();
  const Speed speedY = OUT.getSpeedY();
  static const double PI = 3.14159265;
  const double radians = 2.0 * PI * direction / 360.0;

  bool result =
    0 <= direction && direction < 360 && speed >= 0 &&
    speedX == int(cos(radians) * double(speed)) &&
    speedY == int(sin(radians) * double(speed)) &&
    (speedX*speedX + speedY*speedY) <= speed*speed;
  if ( ! result ) {
    logComment("Invariant does not hold");
  }
  return result;
}

void tc_Velocity() {  // test default constructor
  logTestCaseStart("Velocity()");
  setOUT(newCUT());
  Velocity &OUT = *getOUT();

  logTestCaseResult(passOrFail(OUT.getSpeed() == 0 &&
                    OUT.getDirection() == 0));
  disposeOUT();
}

void tcs_VelocitySpeedDirection() {
  // test Velocity(Speed, Direction)
  //This  runs 360 test cases
  logTestCaseStart("Velocity(Speed, Direction)");
  const Speed fixedSpeed = 1000;

  for ( Direction dir = 0 ; dir < 360 ; ++dir ) {
    logSubTestCaseStart(dir);

    setOUT(newCUT(fixedSpeed, dir));
    Velocity &OUT = *getOUT();

    logTestCaseResult(passOrFail(OUT.getDirection() == dir &&
                      OUT.getSpeed() == fixedSpeed));
    disposeOUT();
  }
}

void tcs_setDirection() {
  logTestCaseStart("setDirection");
  const Speed fixedSpeed = 1000;

  setOUT(newCUT(fixedSpeed, 359)); // any dir value != 0
  Velocity &OUT = *getOUT();
```

```
    for ( Direction dir = 0 ; dir < 360 ; ++dir ) {
      logSubTestCaseStart(dir);

      OUT.setDirection(dir);

      logTestCaseResult(passOrFail(OUT.getDirection() == dir &&
                        OUT.getSpeed() == fixedSpeed));
    }
    disposeOUT();
  }
};
```

The main program creates an instance of the Tester class and runs all the suites. Results are logged to the *VelocityTestResults.txt* file.

```
#include <iostream>
using namespace std; //introduces namespace std
#include "VelocityTester.h"

int main ( void )
{
  VelocityTester vt("VelocityTestResults.txt");

  vt.runAllSuites();
  return 0;
}
```

Java code for the Tester class. We define a TestResult class to represent three possible outcomes of a test case.

```
import java.io.*;
import java.util.*;

/**
  A class that defines three possible test case outcomes:
    Fail - failure
    TBD  - unknown ("To be determined"), usually because
           result requires further analysis or observation
    Pass - success
  @see Tester
*/
public class TestResult {
  public TestResult(String value) { _value = value; }
  public String toString() { return _value; }

  private String _value;

  static public final TestResult Fail = new TestResult("Fail");
  static public final TestResult TBD  = new TestResult("TBD");
  static public final TestResult Pass = new TestResult("Pass");
}
```

```java
/**
   An abstract class that represents a class tester. The
   responsibilities of a tester for a class C include:
      1. running test suites,
      2. creating instances of the class it tests
      3. logging test results
*/
abstract class Tester {
   /**
      Constructs a new instance.

      @param CUTname     the name of the class under test
      @param logFileName the name of the file into which results
                         are logged
   */
   public Tester(String CUTname, String logFileName) {
      _CUTname = CUTname;
      try {
         _log = new FileWriter(logFileName);
      }
      catch (IOException e) {
         System.err.println("Could not open file " + logFileName);
      }
      _OUT = null;
      _passTally = 0;
      _failTally = 0;
      _TBDTally = 0;
      try {
         String line = new Date().toString()+'\n';
         _log.write(line);
      }
      catch (IOException e) {
         System.err.println("Error writing to log file");
         e.printStackTrace();
      }
   }

   public void dispose() { // Summarize results in log
      try {
         int total = totalTally();
         _log.write("\n");
         _log.write("Summary of results:\n");
         _log.write("\t" + total + " test cases run\n");
         _log.write("\t" + "Pass:" + " " + passTally() + '\n');
         _log.write("\t" + "Fail:" + " " + failTally() + '\n');
         _log.write("\t" + "TBD :" + " " + TBDTally() + '\n');
         _log.close();
      }
      catch (IOException e) {
         System.err.println("Error writing to log file");
         e.printStackTrace();
      }
   }
```

```java
public abstract Object newCUT(Object object); //copy object

public void runAllSuites() {
  runFunctionalSuite();
  runStructuralSuite();
  runInteractionSuite();
}

public abstract void runFunctionalSuite();
public abstract void runStructuralSuite();
public abstract void runInteractionSuite();

public int passTally() { return _passTally; }
public int failTally() { return _failTally; }
public int TBDTally()  { return _TBDTally; }
public int totalTally() {
  return _passTally + _failTally + _TBDTally;
}

public Object getOUT() { return _OUT; }
public void disposeOUT() { _OUT = null; }

protected abstract boolean runBaselineSuite();
protected abstract boolean CUTinvariantHolds();

protected void setOUT(Object outPtr) { _OUT = outPtr; }

protected void logTestCaseStart(String testID) {
  try {
    _log.write("Start test case " + testID + '\n');
    _log.flush();
  }
  catch (IOException e) {
    System.err.println("Error writing to log file");
    e.printStackTrace();
  }
}

protected void logSubTestCaseStart(int caseNumber) {
  try {
    _log.write("Start sub test case " + caseNumber + '\n');
    _log.flush();
  }
  catch (IOException e) {
    System.err.println("Error writing to log file");
    e.printStackTrace();
  }
}

protected void logTestCaseResult(TestResult result) {
  if ( result == TestResult.Fail ) {
    ++ _failTally;
```

```
      try {
        _log.write("\tOUT: " + getOUT().toString() + '\n');
        _log.flush();
      }
      catch (IOException e) {
        System.err.println("Error writing to log file");
        e.printStackTrace();
      }
    }
    else if ( result == TestResult.TBD ) {
      ++ _TBDTally;
    }
    else if ( result == TestResult.Pass ) {
      ++ _passTally;
    }
    try {
      _log.write("RESULT: " + result.toString() + '\n');
      _log.flush();
    }
    catch (IOException e) {
      System.err.println("Error writing to log file");
      e.printStackTrace();
    }
  }

  protected void logComment(String comment) {
    try {
      _log.write("\t* " + comment + '\n');
      _log.flush();
    }
    catch (IOException e) {
      System.err.println("Error writing to log file");
      e.printStackTrace();
    }
  }

  protected TestResult passOrFail(boolean condition) {
    // Utility for a result that cannot be TBD.
    // This checks the invariant, too.
    if ( condition && CUTinvariantHolds() )
      return TestResult.Pass;
    else
      return TestResult.Fail;
  }

  private String _CUTname;   // name of the class under test
  private FileWriter _log;   // log stream
  private Object _OUT;       // pointer to current object under test
  private int _passTally;    // number of test cases passing so far
  private int _failTally;    // number of test cases failing so far
  private int _TBDTally;     // number of test cases provisionally
                             // passing so far
};
```

Java code for the VelocityTester class.

```java
//import java.util.*;
import Tester;
import Velocity;
/**
  A class to test class Velocity.
*/
class VelocityTester extends Tester {

  public static void main(String args[]) {
    VelocityTester vt = new VelocityTester("VelTest--Java.txt");
    vt.runAllSuites();
    vt.dispose();
  }

  public VelocityTester(String logFileName) {
    super("Velocity", logFileName);
      runBaselineSuite();
   }

  public void runFunctionalSuite() {
    tc_Velocity();
    tcs_VelocitySpeedDirection();
    tcs_setDirection();
  }

  public void runStructuralSuite() { }
  public void runInteractionSuite() { }

  // Factory methods for creating an instance of CUT
  public Object newCUT(Object object) {
    Velocity v = (Velocity)object;
    return new Velocity(v.getSpeed(), v.getDirection());
  }
  public Velocity newCUT() {
    return new Velocity();
  }
  public Velocity newCUT(int speed, int dir) {
    return new Velocity(speed, dir);
  }


  protected boolean runBaselineSuite() {
    // Verify that the accessor operations are consistent
    logComment("Running baseline test suite.");
    Velocity v = new Velocity(1000, 321);
    if ( v.getSpeed() == 1000 && v.getDirection() == 321 &&
           v.getSpeedX() == 777 && v.getSpeedY() == -629 ) {
      logComment("Baseline suite passed");
      return true;
    }
```

```
    else {
      logComment("Baseline suite FAILED");
      return false;
    }
  }

  protected boolean CUTinvariantHolds() {
    Velocity OUT = (Velocity)(getOUT());

    int direction = OUT.getDirection();
    int speed = OUT.getSpeed();
    int speedX = OUT.getSpeedX();
    int speedY = OUT.getSpeedY();
    final double radians = Math.toRadians(direction);

    if ( direction > 90 ) {
      double dx = Math.cos(radians) * (double)(speed);
      dx = Math.floor(dx);
      int expectedSpeedX = (int)dx;
      int expectedSpeedY =
        (int)Math.floor(Math.sin(radians) * (double)(speed));
      boolean rest =
        (speedX*speedX + speedY*speedY) <= speed*speed;
      rest = rest;
    }
    boolean result =
      0 <= direction && direction < 360 && speed >= 0 &&
      speedX == (int)(Math.cos(radians) * (double)(speed)) &&
      speedY == (int)(Math.sin(radians) * (double)(speed)) &&
      (speedX*speedX + speedY*speedY) <= speed*speed;
    if ( ! result ) {
      logComment("Invariant does not hold");
    }
    return result;
  }

  protected void tc_setDirection001() {
    logTestCaseStart("setDirection001");

    setOUT(newCUT(1000, 0));
    Velocity OUT = (Velocity)(getOUT());

    OUT.setDirection(01);

    logTestCaseResult(passOrFail(OUT.getDirection() == 01));
    disposeOUT();
  }

  void tc_Velocity() {  // test default constructor
    logTestCaseStart("Velocity()");
    setOUT(newCUT());
    Velocity OUT = (Velocity)getOUT();
```

```
                    logTestCaseResult(passOrFail(OUT.getSpeed() == 0 &&
                                      OUT.getDirection() == 0));
        disposeOUT();
    }

    void tcs_VelocitySpeedDirection() {
      // test Velocity(Speed, Direction)
      logTestCaseStart("Velocity(Speed, Direction)");
      final int speedValue[] = { 6, 12, 1000 };

      for ( int i = 0 ; i < 3 ; ++i ) {
        int speed = speedValue[i];
        for ( int dir = 0 ; dir < 360 ; ++dir ) {
          logSubTestCaseStart(dir);

          setOUT(newCUT(speed, dir));
          Velocity OUT = (Velocity)getOUT();

          logTestCaseResult(passOrFail(OUT.getDirection() == dir &&
                                OUT.getSpeed() == speed));
          disposeOUT();
        }
      }
    }

    void tcs_setDirection() {
      logTestCaseStart("setDirection");
      final int fixedSpeed = 1000;

      setOUT(newCUT(fixedSpeed, 359)); // any dir value != 0
      Velocity OUT = (Velocity)getOUT();

      for ( int dir = 0 ; dir < 360 ; ++dir ) {
        logSubTestCaseStart(dir);

        OUT.setDirection(dir);

        logTestCaseResult(passOrFail(OUT.getDirection() == dir &&
                              OUT.getSpeed() == fixedSpeed));
      }
      disposeOUT();
    }
};
```

Summary

Class testing corresponds to unit testing in a traditional testing process. Execution-based class testing requires the identification of test cases, the development of a test driver to apply the test cases against instances of the CUT, and the execution of the test driver. So far we have described testing of fairly simple classes—those whose instances do not interact significantly with other instances.

Test cases are identified and generated from the class specification and implementation. We have shown how to identify test case requirements from preconditions and postconditions as well as from state transition diagrams. Adding interaction test cases improves code coverage.

We have presented a design for a test driver based on the implementation of a tester class for each class to be tested. We have described in detail a design based on Tester classes that we have used successfully. Benefits of our design include a clean organization using an abstract Tester class to capture behavior and code common to all class test drivers, and support for different people working on testing and development. As we will show in Chapter 7, the use of tester classes provides an additional benefit in the context of testing classes related by inheritance.

Exercises

5-1. Identify test requirements for the constructors and   reverse() operators for the Velocity class (see Figure 5.3). Consider the difference in requirements between the contract and defensive programming approaches. Construct the test cases for the requirements you identify.

5-2. Do the same for an elementary class that you have.

5-3. Write a test driver to implement the test cases you constructed in either of the previous exercises. If you are implementing in C++ or Java, you can start with the Tester abstract classes described at the end of this chapter.

5-4. Write a specification for an abstract   Tester class that would be useful in your organization.

5-5. Consider the dilemma of baseline testing. In a specification-based approach, the Tester class must make judgments based solely on the apparent consistency of all attributes of an object when it is in some given state. On the other hand, an implementation-based approach strongly couples the code between a Tester and its CUT so that a   Tester's implementation cannot be completed until the CUT's code is mostly completed. Under what circumstances would you support testing based solely on specification? Under what circumstances would you insist on using both approaches?

Testing Interactions

Chapter 6

An object-oriented program comprises a collection of objects that collaborate to solve some problem. The ways in which those objects collaborate determine what a program does and, consequently, the correctness of a program's execution. An instance of a trusted primitive class, for example, may contain no faults, but if the services of that instance are not used correctly by other program components, then the program contains faults. Thus, the correct collaboration—or *interaction*—of objects in a program is critical to the correctness of the program.

Most classes have collaborators—that is, the methods in the class interact with instances of other classes. In Chapter 5, we addressed finding faults within the implementation of an individual class that had no such interactions. In Chapter 7, we address interactions between the definition of a subclass and the definition of its superclass. In this chapter we will expand our scope and address testing classes that do have interactions with other classes. The interactions being tested are between objects at runtime—for example, when one object is passed to another as a parameter or when an object maintains a reference to another object as part of its state. Interactions always involve unidirectional messaging. Some interactions involve bidirectional messaging between the objects. In this chapter we will assume that the interactions are sequential. In Chapter 8, we will consider more complex relationships such as concurrent interactions among distributed objects that use concurrent interactions.

The focus of **interaction testing** is ensuring that messaging occurs correctly with objects whose classes have already been tested separately. Interaction testing can be performed with the interacting objects embedded in an application program or by interacting the objects in an environment provided by a separate test harness, such as a Tester class. We will examine both approaches in this chapter.

First, we will present details about what object interactions are and how interactions are identified in a class interface. Then we will look at testing interactions outside the context of a particular application program. Finally, we will consider some of the difficult issues that arise in testing interactions within the context of an application program and how these issues can be addressed.

Object Interactions

An **object interaction** is simply a request by one object (the *sender*) to another (the *receiver*) to perform one of the receiver's operations and all of the processing performed by the receiver to complete the request.[1] In most object-oriented languages, this covers the vast majority of activity in a program. It includes messages between an object and its components and between an object and other objects with which it is associated. We assume these other objects are instances of classes that have already been tested in isolation to the extent that the class's implementation is complete.

Since multiple object interactions can occur during the processing of any single method invocation on a receiving object, we want to consider the impact of these interactions both on the internal state of the receiving object and on those objects with which it has an association. These effects can range from "no change" to changes in certain attribute values in one or more of the objects involved to state changes in one or more of the objects, including the creation of new objects and the deletion of existing objects.

---

1. We assume a class interface is defined solely using operations and not data. If data is accessible by collaborators, then approach the testing of that access as if operations existed to *set* and *get* the value of the data.

Partial Class Testing

In an iterative, incremental development approach, a class is often developed in stages. Only the functionality needed to satisfy the requirements of the current increment are specified and/or implemented. The relationships between classes often are such that it is not possible to sequence the development of a class so that all the classes it needs to interact with are totally developed and tested. Lower level—that is, more primitive implementation—classes are more likely to be completely developed at one time and tested as a complete unit. Other classes are therefore developed and tested incrementally.

Classes are tested to the extent that they are developed. Evolve tester classes toward completeness just as the production software does. Identify the test cases you can and then implement a Tester class to implement those test cases. Keep a record, by test case naming conventions or other documentation, of the origin of each test case so that for the next round of testing you can identify the effect changes in specification and implementation of a class under test has on the test cases and its Tester class.

Basing interaction testing solely on specifications of public operations is considerably more straightforward than basing it on implementations. We will limit interaction testing to just associated, peer-to-peer objects and take a public interface approach. This is reasonable because we assume the associated classes have already been adequately tested. However, this approach does not remove the obligation to look *behind* the specification to verify that a method completed all of the computation required. That means verifying the values of the receiver's internal state attributes, including any aggregated attributes—that is, attributes that are themselves objects. Our focus will be to select tests based on the specification of each operation in a class's public interface.

Identifying Interactions

Interactions are implied by a class specification in which references are made to other objects. In Chapter 5, we discussed the testing of primitive classes. A **primitive class** can be instantiated and the instance used without any need to create any other instance of any other class, including the primitive class itself. Such objects represent the simplest components of a system and certainly play an important role in any program execution. However, there are relatively few primitive classes in an object-oriented program that truly model the objects in a problem and all the relationships between those objects. **Nonprimitive classes** are common in and indeed essential to well-designed object-oriented programs.

Nonprimitive classes support—or perhaps *require*—the use of other objects in some or all of their operations. Identify the classes of these other objects based on association (including aggregation and composition) relationships in the class diagram. These associations translate into class interfaces and the way a class interacts with other classes[2] in one or more of the following ways:

1. A public operation names one or more classes as the type of a formal parameter. The message establishes an association between the receiver and the parameter that allows the receiver to collaborate with that parameter object. The attach() and detach() operations in the Timer class shown in Figure 6.1 illustrate this kind of relationship. A Timer instance can receive a request to attach a TimerObserver instance. The notify() method in Timer will send a message to the attached Timer-

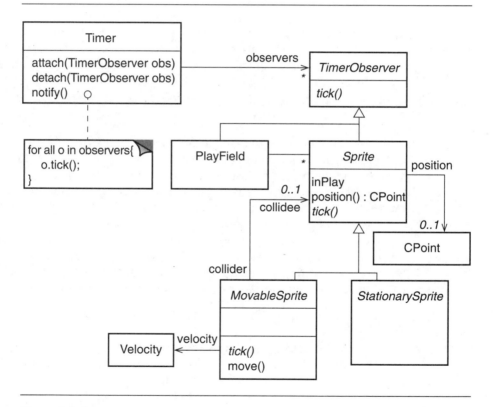

Figure 6.1 Parameter interaction

2. The proper way to state this concept is that an *instance* of a nonprimitive class collaborates with one or more *instances* of other classes. Since the specification and implementation for a class determine the full behavior of any instance, we will use the more prevalent expression of this relationship in terms of classes. However, keep in mind that collaboration is an object relationship, not a class relationship.

Observer instances to invoke a method—in this case, tick(). In this example, a receiver saves the association as part of its state and messages these other objects in subsequent operations. Another scenario is for the receiver to message the parameter, directly or indirectly, as part of the processing of a message.

2. A public operation names one or more classes as the type of a return value. The position() operation of class Sprite shown in Figure 6.1 is an example of this type of interaction. The specifying class may be responsible for creating the returned object or may be passing back a modified parameter. In an environment such as C++ in which heap storage management is programmed explicitly, the specification should detail whether the receiver retains responsibility for any storage management of a returned object or delegates that to the sender. Tester class methods should observe such responsibilities.

3. The method for a class creates an instance of another class as part of its implementation. In Figure 6.1, MovableSprite has a method to process a collision with another sprite. The code for this method needs to create some instances of CPoint and other classes to use as temporaries to determine what happens in a particular collision. Objects such as PlayField to which MovableSprite has a peer-to-peer relationship are not allowed to know about these other objects. Remember, we will not analyze any further down a composition hierarchy. However, when executing tests, there may be a failure in the instance of some class C within a subobject, such as a CPoint instance. Validating the results of the test will include checking the state of C.

4. The method for a class refers to a global instance of some class. Of course, good design principles reduce the use of globals to a minimum. If a class's implementation references some global object, treat it as an implicit parameter to the methods that reference it.

These interactions can be implemented in a variety of ways in programming languages. Collaborators may be addressed directly—for example, using a variable name—or they may be addressed by a pointer or a reference. If a pointer or a reference is used, the dynamic type of the object may be different from the static type associated with the pointer or reference. In other words, pointers and references are polymorphic, thus they are bound to an instance of any number of classes. In the context of Figure 6.1, a C++ implementation for Timer most likely stores pointers to instances of any of the subclasses of TimerObserver. A Java implementation stores references to instances of any class that is a subclass of TimerObserver or implements a TimerObserver interface. Polymorphism increases the number of the kinds of objects that could interact with a class under test.

The pre- and postconditions for operations in the public interface of a class typically refer to states and/or specific attribute values of any collaborating objects. We can categorize a nonprimitive class based on properties of interaction—that is, based on a degree of interaction with other instances. Some classes maintain associations with instances of other classes, but never actually interact with those instances. We refer to such a class as a **collection class**. We refer to a class with more extensive interactions as a **collaborating class**. A much smaller number of classes will "collect" other objects. Next, we will describe how to test these collection objects, and then we will discuss testing collaborating classes.

Collection Classes

Some classes use objects in their specifications, but never actually collaborate with any of them—that is, they never request any services from them. Instead, they do one or more of the following:

- store references (or pointers) to these objects, typically representing one-to-many relationships between objects in a program
- create instances of these objects
- delete instances of these objects

Collection classes can be identified by a specification that refers to other objects, but that does not refer to values computed based on the state or attribute value of those objects. Within the design of *Brickles*, the PuckSupply class (see Figure 6.2) is a collection class. A PuckSupply object, as part of its construction, instantiates an appropriate number of Puck instances and returns a pointer to one of those instances upon request. A PuckSupply instance never uses operations associated with a Puck except for constructors. By contrast, for example, the Timer class stores references (pointers) to implementers of the TimerObserver interface, such as a Puck, when they are attached. A Timer sends a tick() request to each attached observer whenever a Timer event occurs during execution.

Class libraries that accompany compilers and development environments usually include a set of container classes. C++ has the standard template library (STL) and Java has a set of collection classes. The classes in these libraries include lists, stacks, queues, and maps (dictionaries). These collection classes hold the objects they are handed and return them in specific orders or find them based on specific criteria.

Collaborating Classes

Nonprimitive classes that are not collection classes are collaborating classes. Such classes use other objects in one or more of their operations and as part of their implementation. When a postcondition of an operation in a class's interface refers to the state of an instance of an object and/or specifies that some attribute of that object is used or modified, then that class is a collaborating class.

```
// PuckSupply.h

/*
A puck supply is a set of pucks that can be retrieved one at a time.
These pucks are created by a supply using a default constructor.
When a puck supply is deleted, any pucks remaining in it are deleted.

Eventually a way to increase a supply might be added.
*/

class PuckSupply {
public:
  PuckSupply();
  ~PuckSupply();

  Puck* get();
  int count() const;

private:
  int _count;
  Puck* _store[N];
};
```

Figure 6.2 The PuckSupply class

The BrickPile class in *Brickles* (see Figure 6.3) is a collaborating class. This class models the rectangular arrangement of bricks in the game and is responsible for identifying, but not processing, any collisions between the puck in play and a brick. It serves as a container for bricks, but collaborates with a playfield, a hint (in which all changes to the brick pile are recorded so the image of the brick pile can be rendered efficiently on the display), and sprites—particularly a puck that moves into the brick pile. When a brick pile is constructed, it is positioned at a point in some playfield. The classes with which BrickPile collaborates are as follows:

■ PlayField. A brick pile occupies part of a play field.

■ Hint. A brick pile records broken bricks in a hint.

■ CPoint. A brick pile's location in a playfield is specified by a point that determines the upper left corner of the brick pile.

■ Brick. A brick pile creates bricks as part of its own construction and tracks which bricks are broken and which are unbroken.

■ MovableSprite. A brick pile recognizes collisions between its bricks and a puck, which is a kind of movable sprite.

```
class PlayField;
class Hint;
#include "Brick.h"

const int ROWS = 6;
const int COLS = 10;

class BrickPile {
public:
BrickPile(PlayField* playField_p, const CPoint& position,
         Hint& hint);
~BrickPile();
void broken(Brick* brick_p);
int unbrokenCount() const;
Brick* overlaps(Sprite* sprite_p);

protected:
  static const BrickColor evenBrickColor;
  static const BrickColor oddBrickColor;

  PlayField* _playField_p;
  Brick* _pile[ROWS][COLS];
  int _count;
  CPoint _origin;
  CRect _boundingRect;
}
```

Figure 6.3 The BrickPile class header file

Testing basic interactions between two objects is only the beginning. The number of potential collaborations can become impossibly large quickly. Often the bugs that are most serious do not arise from the interaction of two objects, but from the interactions between a complete set of objects. A BrickPile object may work perfectly well when tested with a PlayField object, but failure can result when BrickPile interacts with Hint to record the breaking of a brick. The question that arises then is whether to test each interaction individually or as a group.

Choosing the correct "chunk" size for testing depends on the following three factors:

1. We distinguish between those objects that have a composition relationship with an object under test and those that are merely associated with that object. During a class test, the interaction of the composing object with its composed attributes is tested. The interaction between an object and its associated objects are tested as successive layers of aggregation are integrated.

2. The number of layers of aggregations created between interaction tests is closely related to the visibility of defects. If too large a chunk is chosen, there may be intermediate results that are incorrect, but they are never seen at the level of test-result verification. This may not be a problem for the chosen test parameters. However, a slight change in test parameters would result in a failure. More layers of aggregation introduces more possible test parameters.

3. The more complex the objects, the fewer that should be integrated prior to a round of testing. This complexity is seen in the number of parameters for each method, the number of methods and the number of state attributes in each object. As with the layers of aggregations, trying to test a chunk that is too complex often results in defects that successfully hide from the tests.

Specifying Interactions

In the discussion in the next section on testing interactions, we will assume that operations defined by a class are specified by preconditions, postconditions, and class invariants. We will use the Object Constraint Language (OCL). From a testing perspective, it is important to know whether *defensive design* or *design by contract* has been used in creating the specification of the particular interface to be tested. These approaches change the way senders and receivers interact. We will make a simplifying assumption that for any given class, all of the operations in the interface have been specified using only one of these approaches. If a class you want to test mixes the approaches, then you can mix the techniques we describe in a straightforward way.

Implications of Defensive and Contract Designs for Testing

Defensive design assumes that little or no checking of parameter boundaries occurs prior to a message being sent. This reduces the number of clauses in preconditions, requires checks internally for violations of attribute constraints, and increases the number of clauses in postconditions. A larger number of postcondition clauses results from a larger number of exceptions that arise to identify the different constraint violations. This translates into more interaction test cases oriented toward checking boundaries around inputs that produce exceptions.

Design by contract assumes that appropriate preconditions are checked prior to a message being sent and that the message is not sent if any of the parameters are outside acceptable limits. This increases the number of clauses in preconditions, requires no checking internally for violations of attribute constraints, and reduces the number of clauses in the postcondition clause. This means more test cases are needed to try to get an object under test to send a message for which preconditions are violated. Alternatively, we use code reviews to prove to ourselves that preconditions indeed cannot be violated, thereby eliminating the need for more test cases at the cost of a manual review.

Testing Object Interactions

Testing Collection Classes

Collection classes are tested using techniques for primitive classes (see Chapter 5). A test driver will create instances[3] that are passed as parameters in messages to a collection being tested. Test cases center primarily around ensuring that those instances are correctly incorporated into and removed from the collection. Some test cases address any limitations placed on the capacity of the collection. The precise class of each of the objects used in testing a collection class is insignificant in determining the correct operation of the collection class since there is no interaction between a collection instance and the objects in a collection. If forty or fifty items might be added to a collection during actual use, then generate test cases that add at least fifty items. If no estimate on a typical upper bound is possible, then test with a very large number of objects in the collection.

The behavior of a collection object under circumstances in which it cannot allocate memory to add the new item to itself should be tested. Structures such as growable arrays often allocate the space for several items at one time. Tools are available to help the tester to limit the amount of memory available during the execution of test cases that check the allocation of a larger-than-available block of memory. An object under test should return the appropriate exception to the requestor of the action. We will address this issue in the Testing Exceptions section on page 245.

If the defensive design approach has been used, negative tests should be a part of the test suite. Some collections have a finite capacity specified, and all collections have some practical limit such as available memory that should be tested with tests that exceed the specified limits. If a collection class uses an array as its storage, then the usual test cases for filling the array and then attempting to add one more item should be included. The appropriate exception should be generated by the object under test and caught by the object that sent the message. If a contract approach has been used, such tests are meaningless.

An important aspect of testing collection classes—and testing collaborator classes as well—is testing *sequences* of operations—that is, the way modifier operations on a single object interact with one another. The techniques associated with state-based testing (see Chapter 5) can be applied to testing this aspect of collections.

---

3. The factory methods for creating an object under test (see OUT Factory Methods on page 189.) are useful in creating instances used in interaction tests.

Testing Collaborator Classes

The complexity of testing a collaborating class is greater than that of testing a collection class or a primitive class. Consider the class BrickPile in the *Brickles* application. A brick pile is an aggregation of bricks arranged in a rectangular fashion. The BrickPile class is similar to a collection class, but the BrickPile sends semantically meaningful messages to the individual Bricks—for example, to determine a brick's position on a playfield or to break a brick. It is impossible to test BrickPile without using instances of Brick. It will be hard to identify faults in BrickPile if certain types of faults exist in Brick. A brick pile is responsible for detecting collisions between the bricks it contains and movable sprites (namely pucks), but it is not responsible for processing those collisions. It is also responsible for recording hints associated with breaking bricks so that the screen can be updated efficiently by the *Brickles* view object.[4]

In order to test class BrickPile, we must use one or more instances of each of these classes. In fact, an instance of BrickPile cannot be constructed without an instance of a PlayField, a CPoint, and a Hint because these must be passed as parameters to a constructor (see Figure 6.3). Of course, it will need to use instances of Brick to create a brick pile.

Hint, CPoint, and Brick are all primitive classes and can be tested using the techniques presented in Chapter 5. The CPoint class used in *Brickles* is one of the Microsoft Foundation Classes (MFC) and is consequently "trusted," meaning that we won't test it at all. PlayField and BrickPile are not primitive and must be tested in the context of their interactions with the code in other classes using techniques discussed in this chapter.

Friend Functions

Ordinarily, a class interface comprises all the operations—and, heaven forbid, data—declared public. However, when using a language such as C++ that also supports *friend functions,* which are nonmember functions that can access the hidden parts of a class, we include any such functions in the interface. For example, many classes have defined an associated insertion operator (operator<<) that allows an instance's state to be streamed, that is, written outside the current program to a file or some other sequential structure. Treat such functions as operations in the public interface for a class. This is also the perspective taken by a programmer using the class.

---

4. A hint is directed at the system components that draw the playfield, thus it provides information about the damaged parts of the playfield.

The Interaction between Testing and Design Approach

The differences between contract and defense design techniques (see Implications of Defensive and Contract Designs for Testing, on page 221) extend to testing. Contract design places more responsibility on the human designer than on error-checking code. This reduces the amount of class-level testing since there are fewer paths due to a smaller amount of error-checking code. However, at the interaction level, there is more testing required for contract-designed code in order to be certain that the human designer has complied with the client side of the contract using precondition constraints.

A focus of interaction testing for contract design is whether the preconditions of methods in a receiving object are being met by the sending object. It is not legitimate to build test cases that violate these preconditions. It is usually legitimate to set the receiving object into a certain state and then begin a scenario with the sending object, which requires the receiving object to be in another state. The intention is to determine that the sending object checks the preconditions of the receiving object before sending the message inappropriately. The test should also check whether the sending object aborts correctly, probably by throwing an appropriate exception.

BrickPile::BrickPile(PlayField* playField_p, const CPoint& position, Hint& hint);
pre: playField_p <> 0 and playField_p->boundingRect().contains(position)
post: self.boundingRect.TopLeft() = position

BrickPile::~BrickPile();
pre: true
post: bricks->isEmpty

void BrickPile::broken(Brick* brick_p);
pre: brick_p <> 0 and not brick_p->isBroken()
post: brick_p->isBroken() and
              self.unbrokenCount() = self@pre.unbrokenCount + 1 and
              bricks = bricks@pre->excluding(*brick_p)

int BrickPile::unbrokenCount() const;
pre: true
post: result =(bricks->select(b : not isBroken(b))).size

Brick* BrickPile::overlaps(Sprite* sprite_p);
pre: sprite_p <> 0
post: result =
              if (bricks->collect(b : b.boundingRect.intersect(sprite_p->
              boundingRect()))->isEmpty) then 0
              else bricks->collect(b : b.boundingRect.intersect(sprite_p->
              boundingRect()))->asSequence->first

Figure 6.4 An OCL specification for the `BrickPile` class

For example, consider the following specification for the broken() method from BrickPile in which a brick pile interacts with Brick objects (see Figure 6.4). If a design by contract approach is being used, a test case in which brick_p is 0 (null) is meaningless. A test case in which brick_p points to a specific brick instance should be used and the test case should clearly verify that the postcondition has been satisfied.

In testing BrickPile, we need test cases that exercise interactions with a PlayField. In this context, there should be a test case in which PlayField is told to "break" a specific brick that is already broken. The test case is checking to be certain that PlayField is checking and will not send the broken() message to a BrickPile instance in violation of the precondition.

Sampling Test Cases

Exhaustive testing—that is, running every possible test case covering every combination of values—is obviously a reliable testing approach. However, in many situations the number of test cases is too large to handle reasonably. If there are more possible test cases than there is time to construct and execute them, a systematic technique is needed for determining which ones to actually use. If we have a choice then we would prefer to select the ones that will find the faults in which we are most interested. If we have no prior information, then a random selection is probably as good as we can do. In this section we will consider the general concept of sampling, and then we will apply it to interaction testing.

With any testing approach we are interested in ways that the level of coverage can be increased systematically. If a tester simply creates test cases without sufficient analysis, then creating more cases later often repeats some of the functionality already tested. With the techniques presented here, there is a well-defined set of cases and a well-defined technique for increasing coverage.

There are a number of possibilities for determining which test cases to select. The technique we will discuss first uses a simple selection process based on a probability distribution. A **probability distribution** defines, for each data value in a **population**, a set of allowable values, and the probability that value will be selected. Under a **uniform probability distribution**, each value in the population is assigned the same selection probability.

We define the population of interest to be all possible test cases that could be executed. This includes all preconditions and all possible combinations of input values. A **sample** is a subset of a population that has been selected based on some probability distribution. One approach is to base the probability distribution on the user profile. If the uses of the system are ranked by frequency, the ranks can be transformed into probabilities. The higher the frequency of use, the larger the probability of selection. But more about this later (see Use Profile on page 313).

We can select a **stratified sample** in which tests are selected from a series of categories. A stratified sample is a set of samples in which each sample represents a specific subpopulation—for example, we might select test cases that we are certain exercise each component of the architecture. A population of tests is divided into subsets so that a subset contains all of the tests that exercise a specific component. Sampling occurs on each subset independent of the others.

An approach that works well is to use the actors from the use case model as the basis for stratifying the test cases. That is, we select a sample of test cases from the uses of each actor. Each actor uses some subset of the possible uses with some frequency (see Use Profiles, on page 130). Stratifying the test case samples by each actor provides an effective means of increasing the reliability of the system. Running the selected tests uses the system the way that it will be used in typical situations and finds those defects that are most likely to be found in typical use. Removing these defects produces the largest possible increases in reliability with the smallest effort.

The sampling technique provides an algorithm for selecting a test suite from a set of possible test cases. This does not mandate how the population of test cases is determined in the first place. The test process is intended to define the population of tests in which we are interested—for example, functional test cases—and then to define a technique for selecting which of these test cases will be constructed and executed.

A test suite for a component may be constructed using a combination of techniques. Consider the Velocity class we used in Chapter 5 in which we did an exhaustive test of *direction* values, but only a few *speed* values. We can reduce the number of tests by first using the specification as a source of test cases, and then applying a sampling technique to supplement those tests.

The specification of Velocity includes a modifier operation called setDirection(const Direction &newDirection) whose precondition requires newDirection to be in the range 0 through 359, inclusive. The postcondition specifies that the receiver's direction has been modified to the value of newDirection. We first generate test data for this method using the specification as a basis. First, note that Direction is a typedef for int so we are selecting from the set of integers rather than a set of objects. Rather than sample for every test case (0 through 359), we first select values based on boundary values. So we can have three tests around the boundary of zero, perhaps -1, 0, and 1. If this were a "design by contract" project, the -1 value would not be a legitimate test case. There should be a similar set of values around the other boundary, so perhaps 358, 359, and 360. Again, 360 is not legitimate in a contract context. There should be tests in the intervals between 1 and 358 and here is where sampling plays a useful role. The values in the two intervals could be sampled using something like int(random() * 360) and int(-1 * random() * 360). The random() function generates a pseudo random value between 0.0 and 1.0 in accordance with a uniform distribution, so each value is within the interval and each value has an equal chance of being selected.

The advantage of using the random value generator in the test case is that over iterations and reapplications of test cases, many values in the intervals will be tested rather than the same ones over time. The disadvantage is that now the test cases are not being reproduced since a different value is used every time. By having the test driver record the generated values as part of the test log, we can re-create any failed test case. Any randomly chosen value that causes a failure is explicitly added to the test suite and is used to test the repaired software. After the fault has been repaired, those values can be used to validate the repair. The regression suite consists mainly of those tests that originally produced failures but were ultimately passed by the software.

Now let us consider the interaction between two classes: Sprite and MoveableSprite in the collideInto() operation (see Figure 6.5). Both Sprite and MoveableSprite classes are abstract, so we have an opportunity to design tests that can be reused by their subclasses. The precondition places no restriction on the parameter so we need to find some other way to determine the population from which we will sample. There are three dimensions along which we can sample.

First, Sprite is the base class in a very large **class family**, which is a set of classes related by inheritance. An object from any one of the classes in the family can be substituted for the sprite parameter. Therefore, we should sample from this set for possible parameters. This is one of the problems we mentioned earlier about testing object-oriented systems. At some time in the future, a new member of the family can be created and passed to this routine without any recompilation of the MoveableSprite class. Traditional techniques for triggering regression tests do not work in this environment. They should be controlled in the configuration management tool or perhaps the development environment. Each new class definition stimulates a round of regression testing. Usually however only the overridden methods will need to be tested if most of the methods are inherited.

Tip Use the class diagram to identify the classes that should be involved in a regression test resulting from the creation of a new class. Examine the parent classes for this new class and identify interactions in which those classes participate. Execute the tests that interact those parents with other classes, but substitute the new class for the parent class in the test.

void MoveableSprite::collideInto(Sprite& sprite);
pre: none
post: sprite.collideWith(self)

Figure 6.5 Specification for operation collideInto()

The second dimension for sampling is to consider that each member of the family may have *different states* that can cause two objects from the same class to behave differently. Obviously the Puck and Wall classes probably have some interesting differences in their states. In the case of families of classes, the state machines are related along the lines of the inheritance hierarchy. Our experience and a number of published papers have shown that as we look down the inheritance hierarchy, there will be the same number of states or more states in the derived class as there are in the base class. We should cover the states defined for each class with special emphasis on the new states added at that level in the inheritance hierarchy.

A third dimension relates to the class family associated with Moveable-Sprite. This is a subset of the Sprite family. Once these tests are designed, they can be applied to any of the classes in the family, assuming the substitution principle has been followed during design.

Given these three dimensions, we have the possibility of a combinatorial explosion in the number of test configurations. In this scenario, a test case would have a member of the MoveableSprite family sending a message to a member of the Sprite family, which may be in any one of its states.

Orthogonal Array Testing

Orthogonal arrays provide a specific sampling technique that seeks to limit the explosion by defining pair-wise combinations of a set of interacting objects. Most of the faults resulting from interactions are due to two-way interactions. One specific technique for selecting a sample is **orthogonal array testing system** (OATS). An **orthogonal array** is an array of values in which each column represents a **factor**, which is a variable in an experiment. In our case it

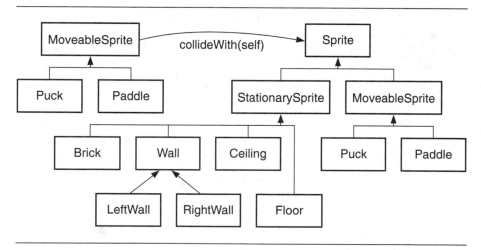

Figure 6.6 Explosion of test cases

will represent a specific class family[5] in the software system. Each variable can take on a certain set of values called **levels**. In our testing work, each level will be a specific class in the family. There will also be a parallel factor and set of levels that correspond to the *states* of these classes. The value entered into a particular cell in the array is an instance of the specific class or is a specific state of an object.

In an orthogonal array, the factors are combined pair-wise rather than representing all possible combinations of the levels for the factors. For example, suppose that we have three factors—say, A, B, and C—each with three levels—say, 1, 2, and 3. There are 27 possible combinations of these values—3 for A times the 3 for B times the 3 for C. If pair-wise combinations are used instead—that is, if we consider only those combinations in which a given level appears exactly twice—then there are only 9 combinations as shown in Figure 6.7.

OATS uses a balanced design. Every level of a factor will appear exactly the same number of times as every other level of that factor. If we think of the rows of a table as test cases, then 18 of the possible 27 tests are not being conducted. This is a systematic way of reducing the number of test cases. If we later decide that additional tests should be run, we will know exactly which combinations have not been tested. This is also a logical way of doing the reduction. Most of the errors that are encountered are between pairs of objects rather than among several objects. In this way, we are testing those situations that are most likely to reveal faults. To demonstrate OATS, we will work through a general example and then a *Brickles*-specific example. The general example comprises interactions between senders in a class family A, receivers in a class family C, and parameters in a class family P (see Figure 6.8). Each class

	A	B	C
1	1	1	3
2	1	2	2
3	1	3	1
4	2	1	2
5	2	2	1
6	2	3	3
7	3	1	1
8	3	2	3
9	3	3	2

Figure 6.7 Pair-wise combinations of three factors that have three levels each

5. A class family is a class and all of the classes that inherit from that class.

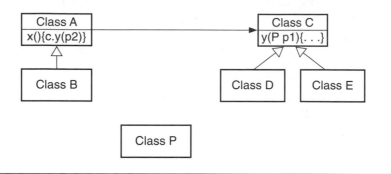

Figure 6.8 A general example of applying OATS

has a state transition diagram associated with it. The details are not important. The number of states that we are assuming each class has is shown in Figure 6.9.

The major activity in this technique is to map the problem of testing the interaction of two inheritance hierarchies with respect to a parameter object. To identify test cases using orthogonal arrays, observe the following five steps:

Step 1: Identify all factors. The sending hierarchy is one factor. The receiving hierarchy is a second factor. There is also a factor associated with each parameter position in the message. There is an additional factor associated with each class factor—namely, the states associated with instances of the class. This experiment (see Figure 6.8) has six factors: the class A hierarchy, the class P hierarchy, and the class C hierarchy and factors for the states associated with each class hierarchy.

Step 2: Determine levels for each factor. The levels for each factor are determined by considering the set of possible values.

Class	Number of States
A	1
B	2

Figure 6.9 The number of states associated with classes in the general OATS example

■ One factor has one level: the parameter class family only has one member: P.

■ Two factors have a maximum of two levels; the sending class family has two members: A and B; the maximum number of states for a class in the P family is two.

■ Three factors have a maximum of three levels: the receiving family has three members, and the maximum number of states for a class in the A family and in the C family is three.

Step 3: Locate a standard orthogonal array that fits the problem. Given our need for six factors of, at most, three levels, we turn to the tables of precomputed arrays called **standard arrays** [Phadke89]. The notation $2^1 \times 3^7$ for L_{18} (see Figure 6.16) indicates that the array addresses one factor with two levels and seven factors with three levels. L_{18} is the smallest standard array that will fit the problem. A standard array can be larger than a problem, but not smaller.[6]

Step 4: Establish a mapping from each factor onto the integers in the array so that the standard array can be interpreted. Standard array entries are integer values. We analyze each factor in the following list.

■ For the sender class family there are two classes, A and B, so the first column in L_{18} can be used to represent this data (Figure 6.10). We adopt an encoding in which a value of 1 in the first column of the array corresponds to the A class and a value of 2 corresponds to the B class.

■ Class A has two states and class B has three states. When there is a difference in the number of levels, we can use a column that matches or exceeds the maximum. The second column in L_{18} has a maximum of three, which will fit this data. The interpretation of the values in the second column depends on the values in the first column. For a value of 2 (class B) in the first column, we are representing the states of class B in

Domain Value	Array Value
A	1
B	2

Figure 6.10 Class A hierarchy

---

6. Use a larger array if the number of levels is likely to change in the future—for example, if more subclasses might be added to a receiving class family. Using a larger array allows for future expansion of test cases when levels are added.

Domain Value	Array Value
A, state 1	1
A, state 2	2
A, state 1	3
B, state 1	1
B, state 2	2
B, state 3	3

Figure 6.11 States for class A hierarchy

the second column. If the value in the first column is 1, then the second column represents the states of class A. In Figure 6.11, the state values for class B directly correspond to the integer values in the column. Since class A only has two states, how do we interpret a 3 in the second column when there is a value of 1 (class A) in the first column? We interpret it as though it were either 1 or 2. When a value in the column does not properly correspond to values in other columns, then we interpret it as some other domain value that is repeated. In this case, as denoted in the table, 3 in the array will correspond to state 1. The interpretation can be arbitrary or based on an observation that an instance of A is more likely to be in state "1" or there is a higher risk associated with being in state "1."

■ The third column in L_{18} represents the parameter hierarchy that only has one class, P. Any value in the third column represents P (Figure 6.12).

■ The fourth column represents the states of P, of which there are two (Figure 6.13). However, the column has values 1, 2, and 3. An array value of 1 corresponds to state 1, a value of 2 corresponds to state 2 of the P class, and a value of 3 will repeat state 2 of class P.

■ The fifth column represents the class C hierarchy, which has three members. There is a direct correspondence between classes and the integer values in the array. The interpretation is shown in Figure 6.14.

■ The sixth column represents the states of the C, D, and E classes (Figure 6.15). Since C has only 2 states, the array value of 3 will correspond to a value of 2. For classes D and E, there is a direct correspondence between states and array values.

Note: the last two columns of L_{18} are not used.

Domain Value	Array Value
P	1
P	2
P	3

Figure 6.12 States for the class P hierarchy

Domain Value	Array Value
P, state 1	1
P, state 2	2
P, state 3	3

Figure 6.13 States for class P hierarchy

Domain Value	Array Value
C	1
D	2
E	3

Figure 6.14 The C Class hierarchy

Domain Value	Array Value
C, state 1	1
C, state 2	2
C, state 2	3
D, state 1	1
D, state 2	2
D, state 3	3
E, state 1	1
E, state 2	2
E, state 3	3

Figure 6.15 States for class P hierarchy

Test Case	A	A_{state}	P	P_{state}	C	C_{state}		
	1	2	3	4	5	6	7	8
1	1	1	1	1	1	1	1	1
2	1	1	2	2	2	2	2	2
3	1	1	3	3	3	3	3	3
4	1	2	1	1	2	2	3	3
5	1	2	2	2	3	3	1	1
6	1	2	3	3	1	1	2	2
7	1	3	1	2	1	3	2	3
8	1	3	2	3	2	1	3	1
9	1	3	3	1	3	2	1	2
10	2	1	1	3	3	2	2	1
11	2	1	2	1	1	3	3	2
12	2	1	3	2	2	1	1	3
13	2	2	1	2	3	1	3	2
14	2	2	2	3	1	2	1	3
15	2	2	3	1	2	3	2	1
16	2	3	1	3	2	3	1	2
17	2	3	2	1	3	1	2	3
18	2	3	3	2	1	2	3	1

Figure 6.16 The standard orthogonal array L_{18} (2^1 x 3^7)

Step 5: Construct test cases based on the mapping and the rows in the table. Each row in the orthogonal array, Figure 6.16, specifies one specific test case. The orthogonal array is interpreted back into test cases by decoding the level numbers for a row in the array back to the individual lists for each factor. Thus, for example, the 10th row of L_{18} is interpreted as test case number 10 in which an instance of class B in state 1 is to send the message by passing an instance of class P in state 3 to an instance of class E in state 2. The last two values in the row are ignored since we did not use those factors.

Adequacy Criteria for OATS

One of the useful things about OATS is the ability to vary how completely the software under test is covered. Here are some possible levels that can be used:

■ *Exhaustive*—All possible combinations of all factors are considered. Lots of confidence, lots of expense.

■ *Minimal*—Only the interactions between the base classes from each hierarchy are tested. Little confidence from few test cases.

■ *Random*—The tester haphazardly selects cases from several of the classes. Confidence level unclear, number of test cases arbitrary. Not a statistically random sample.

■ *Representative*—A uniform sample that ensures that every class is tested to some level. Confidence level is the same across classes; number of test cases is minimized.

■ *Weighted Representative*—Adds cases to the representative approach based on relative importance or risk associated with the class. This is the approach we have illustrated in this section. At any point where the matrix has more levels than the actual problem does, the tester has the opportunity to generate additional tests for priority levels of factors.

Once all the test cases have been run, look at the results to see if failure can be associated with one or more specific factor levels—for example, perhaps most of the test cases associated with instances of class A, state 2 fail. This information is useful for developers to track down bugs, and it is useful for testers to indicate that additional test cases might be warranted.

Another Example

Now let us return to the MoveableSprite::collideInto() example from page 227. A MoveableSprite object may be passed to any Sprite object when it is sent the collideInto() message. In the present design, the Sprite class family includes MoveableSprite, StationarySprite, Puck, Paddle, Brick, Wall, RightWall, Left-Wall, Floor, and Ceiling.

We make the following analysis and observations:

1. Classes Sprite, MoveableSprite, StationarySprite, and Wall are abstract classes. We will talk about how to test abstract classes in the next chapter, but for now, they will not be a part of the OATS scenario.

2. Only Puck and Paddle are derived from MoveableSprite, so only MoveableSprite, Puck, and Paddle can receive the collideInto() message. However, all the classes derived from Sprite can receive the collideWith() message.

3. Each of the objects passed as a parameter is in a specific state. The objects may behave differently in different states. An instance of MoveableSprite may be moving or not. If it is moving, then it is moving in a specific direction. From a state perspective, the directions can be grouped into states named DueNorth, DueSouth, DueEast, DueWest,

NorthEast, NorthWest, SouthEast, and SouthWest. Note that an instance of Paddle can only move DueEast and DueWest.

4. In this case, the sender object and the parameter object are the same, so there are only two class family columns and two state of classes columns.

The possible values for each attribute of the test case are shown in Figure 6.17.

If we tested all possible combinations, the number of possible tests is 2 x 9 x 8 x 9 = 1296. Some of these can be eliminated because nonmoveable sprites do not have the direction states. The total now appears to be 2 x 9 x 2 x 9 + 2 x 9 x 6 x 1, = 432 test cases—still quite a few. By using OATS, we can further reduce the number of test cases and still be effective. For example, these are the selected combinations from Figure 6.17:

1. Paddle, DueEast, Puck, SouthEast
2. Paddle, DueEast, Puck, NorthEast
3. Paddle, DueEast, Puck, NorthWest
4. Paddle, DueEast, Puck, DueWest
5. Puck, DueEast, Puck, DueWest

Sender Class	Sender State	Receiver Class	Receiver State
Puck	DueNorth	Puck	DueNorth
Paddle	DueSouth	Paddle	DueSouth
	DueEast	Brick	DueEast
	DueWest	Wall	DueWest
	NorthEast	RightWall	NorthEast
	NorthWest	LeftWall	NorthWest
	SouthEast	Ceiling	SouthEast
	SouthWest	Floor	SouthWest
	NotMoving		NotMoving

Figure 6.17 Test attribute values

```
class Stack<class T>{
    Stack<T>();
    void Push(const T &object);
    T Pop();
    bool isEmpty();
};
```

Figure 6.18 A C++ class template for Stack

OATS would allow case #4 to be eliminated because in #3 Paddle is tested while moving DueEast; in #5 Puck is tested moving DueWest; in #3 Paddle is tested colliding with Puck. The complete OATS analysis would reduce considerably the number of tests required.

Another Application of OATS

Consider the need to test a collection class such as Stack, in which the class is implemented as a C++ template (see Figure 6.18).

The developer's intention is for template parameter T to be replaced by any class when Stack is instantiated. Obviously, we cannot test the Stack class definition with all possible substitutions. The Stack, like any collection class, does not invoke any methods on the objects that it contains. Therefore, the interface implemented by the parameter class does not matter.

To test the template code, we would select a stratified sample of classes from all of the classes that are available including vendor libraries, language libraries, and application code. Depending on the exact programming language used and other factors, the categories in the stratification will include the amount of memory used by each instance, the number of associations, and whether the objects placed in a collection are persistent. Then we would select a subset of this set of classes each time a collection class needs to be tested. This second sampling can be guided by OATS.

For more complex templates, sets of possible substitutes for each parameter are created. Then OATS creates tests that involve combinations of parameter substitutions. These tests provide the maximum search for interactions among the parameters with the minimum number of tests.

Testing Off-the-Shelf Components

Increasingly, functionality is added to an application by purchasing "chunks" of software referred to as *components*.[7] The quality of these components varies tremendously from one vendor to another. Until standardized measures are adopted or the marketplace forces improved quality, you should plan to do an acceptance test on any newly acquired component.

---

7. Chapter 10 will cover topics about components, but this is a natural place to talk about them.

An acceptance test should put the component into the context in which it will be used. The test cases should thoroughly investigate the limits of the specification.[8] Creating the specification document will not be a wasted effort because developers will need it in order to properly use the component.

We like to begin an acceptance test with extreme, even incorrect, values—for example, running the mouse back and forth across the desk to generate a large number of *mouse move* events. A defective component may be overwhelmed by the large number of events and crash. Other stress tests include holding down a "repeat" key or making multiple menu selections before the program can respond and gray out certain selections on a menu. This is as much a test of the component manufacturer's attention to detail as it is a test of the software. If there are many failures here, you have to suspect that the quality is fairly poor.

If we continue beyond that set of tests, the testing of this component proceeds along the lines of any class. Even if the component is constructed from several classes, there is usually a main class that presents the component to the user. The tests are based on that class.

A Case Study in Component Acceptance Testing

Let's consider a commercially available Grid user-interface component and examine how we would test it before using it in an application.[9] Figure 6.19 presents the test plan for the Grid component. Figure 6.20 presents a **life-cycle scenario**, which is a description of one specific use of the component that can be used to build certain types of test cases.

A grid JavaBean displays information in row and column format. It allows users to select, manipulate, and store information presented. The product we will consider contains 4 interface definitions (implemented as abstract classes in C++) and 10 public class definitions. Additional classes are nested within these public classes. Of the 10 public classes, two—GridMain and GridBigAdapter—are the classes that developers use to integrate the component into their application. The documentation comprises standard JavaDoc HTML pages. These contain comments placed by the class developers, but nothing about the "component." Each method is presented in the form int compareTo(java.lang.Object anotherObject).

The compareTo() method returns a value of type int and requires one parameter, anotherObject, which is of type Object. There is no information about any constraints on anotherObject nor any indication of the range for the return value, even though our analysis discovered that it can only take on three different values.

---

8. Create a formal specification if one does not exist.

9. We use an actual product, but we have changed the name to avoid legal hassles.

Testing Off-the-Shelf Components ■ 239

Component Test Plan

Component Name Grid	**Tracking Number** CT-007
Developer(s) Anon.	**Tester(s)** John D. McGregor

Objectives for This Component

This component is intended for use in the user interface of the applications being built in the company. It is part of a purchased library from the NoTest Software Company.

Guided Inspection Requirements

The product is already completed and no design documentation comes with the library. No guided inspection is possible.

Building and Retaining Test Suites

The test suites shall be prepared in accordance with project standards. A GridTester class shall contain the test driver. In that class, operations shall be provided to execute functional, structural, and interaction test cases. Reporting shall be in conformance with project standards. The test class will be available to developers as interaction tests in their application.

Specification-based Test Cases

Construct pre- and postconditions for each method in the documented API. Execute test cases for every clause of each postcondition of every method. Test cases can be found in the GridTester class.

Implementation-based Test Cases

Only the binary is available. No implementation-based testing is possible.

Interaction Test Cases

Follow the use scenarios such as the one in Figure 6.20 to determine the objects in a typical application with which Grid will interact. Build and execute tests so that Grid interacts with these objects. Tests are stored in GridTester.

State-based Test Cases

The documentation does not provide a state diagram to use. Substitute scenarios in which a life cycle of uses is defined. A sample scenario is shown in Figure 6.20. These tests may be combinations of other specification-based tests.

Figure 6.19 A component test plan for the component Grid

The Grid component presents a list of system attributes. The three-column display shows the attribute name, the current value, and the default value. The user selects the **Screen Color** attribute and edits the current value. The user then selects the **Save** action from the File menu to store the information in the Grid.

Figure 6.20 A life-cycle scenario

GridMain has over one hundred methods. Many of them are simple accessor methods, but a large number are modifier methods that set specific attributes in the object. While testing could be a large job, a component will provide a large amount of functionality and, therefore, conducting a thorough test at one time will save much effort for the many developers whose objects will interact with the component.

An acceptance test combines elements of a class test and an interaction test. Therefore, we are interested in the patterns of interaction of this component with the rest of the system as well as the specification of the individual methods on the interface of the component. This component follows a standard Java user-interface design pattern. It uses an Adapter class to support the creation of the Listener objects needed to capture various types of events. An interaction test of this component should follow that pattern to achieve an effective interaction test.

First, let's analyze. Grid is primarily a collection class. It holds and displays data and has very little interaction with the objects that it holds. The major interactions that it has are with the event producers. The interaction that it has with its contents is to display them, store or retrieve them, and forward events on to them. Another type of interaction is when one object requests that a grid provide the object stored in a specific cell. Is the requesting object handed a clone? A reference? Does this action prevent the grid from being garbage collected?

A few simple interactions that the grid is intended to have include the following:

1. A mouse button click occurs in a certain cell of the grid.

2. A mouse button release occurs in a certain cell of the grid.

3. A mouse button is double clicked in a certain cell of the grid.

A test harness should be created that consists of a specialized Adapter that listens for these events and at least logs when the event has happened and has been handled. The tests should automatically create events for a variety of actions and pass the events to the grid. The resulting behavior of the grid should be evaluated.

A more complete interaction test would examine the complete life cycle of a grid. Create a few life-cycle scenarios that briefly describe typical uses of the component under test, as shown in Figure 6.20. The test harness would instantiate Grid with a variety of data types from the current application in the cells. The test harness should stimulate the grid to read its contents from storage and display it. The tester should perform a series of mouse actions. Another object should request and hold the contents of at least one cell in the table. The test harness should stimulate the grid to save the data and finally destroy the grid. Validating the test requires that the tester observe the visual behavior of the grid as the events are created, and check that the garbage collector can remove the grid while an object holds a reference to one of the content objects.

Tip

Use the basic logic of the manufacturer's sample programs as the basis for individual test cases. We use our standard test driver and then build test cases by beginning with the basic code from sample programs.

Incidentally, we found several problems during our acceptance test. These were submitted as bugs to the component company and were subsequently fixed in later releases.

Protocol Testing

As an object interacts with other objects, it will receive multiple messages. These messages must be sequenced in accordance with the specification. Protocol testing investigates whether the implementation of a class satisfies its specification. The various protocols that an object participates in can be inferred from the pre- and postconditions for individual operations defined in its class. Identifying sequences of method invocations by combining a method whose postcondition enables the precondition of another method defines a protocol. It is much easier to see these sequences from the state diagram for a class than deriving them from written pre- and postconditions.

The interaction test suite includes tests of each protocol. This is basically a special form of life-cycle testing. Each protocol represents a life cycle for objects from the class under test in combination with instances of other classes. Each protocol corresponds to a sequence of states beginning with initial states of the two objects (as denoted on the state diagrams of the two classes), a sequence of states for each object, and ending with the terminal states (again, denoted on the state diagrams). A test case takes the two objects through one complete sequence of methods.

Consider the Timer class and its state diagram given in Figure 2.19. A protocol can be found by tracing through that state diagram. One protocol would be to create the object then sending one or more attach(...) messages followed by the enable() message, the disable() message, and finally, the delete() message. This provides a life-cycle test case. This provides an effective test of the object in the ways that it will interact with its client objects.

Test Patterns

Test patterns are design patterns for test software. Design patterns [GHJV94] capture and reuse design knowledge that has gained widespread application in the object-oriented software development community. Each pattern is a specific configuration of interactions among a set of objects that form some cluster in the overall design. The pattern description explains the context within which the pattern should be considered, provides a set of forces that guide a trade-off analysis, and explains how to construct the objects. We use the same format for the pattern description as the design community, but we can place more specific meaning on certain sections of the description.

We have been successful with the concept of relating a test pattern to a particular design pattern. When a developer uses a specific design pattern to structure a portion of the system, a tester (who may be another developer) then knows which test pattern to use to structure the test code.

The Grid component is based on the Listener design pattern, which is related to the more general Observer design pattern to incorporate event handling into its GUI. In the next section, we will explain the associated test pattern.

Listener Test Pattern

Intent

There is a need to test the interactions among the Listener, ActionListener, and TargetObject objects that are participating in the Listener design pattern (Figure 6.21). The interactions need to be examined to ensure that:

- each interaction correctly sets the state of each participating object
- each interaction is complete in that all objects that should be affected are
- each interaction is consistent with the specification of the participating objects

A Listener object is passed to an object that receives events. A Listener is only "interested" in a certain set of event objects. The ActionListener object forwards to a registered Listener only those events for which the Listener is registered. Each Listener is associated with some instance of TargetObject. When the Listener receives an event, it performs some action on its target object. That action was defined as a method in the class Listener.

Context

The Listener design pattern has been heavily used in Java, but equivalent event-handling patterns are used in all object-oriented languages. The pattern is particularly used in the context of the user interface. Most Java programs contain a large number of instances of the Listener pattern. Very little original code is

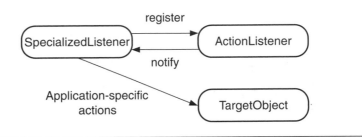

Figure 6.21 Conceptual interactions in the Listener pattern

written in a Listener class. Developers usually define the original code using the anonymous class mechanism. This makes it more difficult to test the mechanism in isolation.

Forces

There are several forces that constrain the design of the test classes:

■ Modifying the production software to accommodate testing requires that additional tests be run after the production software is returned to its original state. Therefore, we prefer not to modify the application in order to test it.

■ The test class must know when events are received by the Listener object. This may be accomplished by having the test class produce the events, or by having the test class register for the same events as the Listener class being tested.

■ Participating objects have already been class tested. Therefore, the accessor and modifier methods of the individual objects will be trusted and used during this test.

■ The small size of each Listener subclass and the large number of Listener classes used in an application requires that the tests be easily created and ported to a new Listener class.

Solution

A TestListener class creates an environment in which the interactions between objects in the Listener design pattern are exercised and observed. The Test-Listener object instantiates the pattern. A TestListener object can generate any of the events for which a Listener object can register.

There is essentially one type of test case. An event is generated by the Test-Listener object and sent to the ActionListener object. If the ActionListener object is working correctly, the event is forwarded to all of the registered Listener objects. The Listeners invoke specific actions on their TargetObjects. The

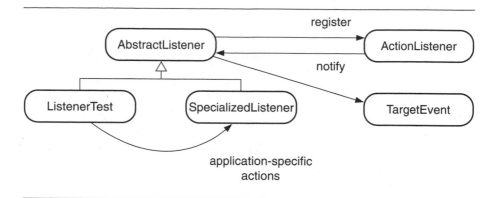

Figure 6.22 Conceptual interactions in the Listener pattern extended for testing.

TestListener object registers with the ActionListener so that it receives the event at basically the same time as the Listener object being tested. The ListenerTest object then checks the TargetObject to determine whether the expected changes have occurred there.

Design

An instance of the TestListener class, after inheriting from the AbstractListener class, can register with the ActionListener object. It will then receive a notification of a specific event and will know to activate tests on the SpecializedListener object, Figure 6.22.

Specific Example

The pattern can be applied to the *Brickles* TimerObserver class and those associated classes, Figure 6.23.

Resulting Context

The production classes participating in the Listener pattern have been tested relative to their interaction with each other. A series of test classes and test cases have been created that can be reused, with slight modifications, for a variety of types of events. By using the pattern approach, new events and new listeners can be tested cheaply.

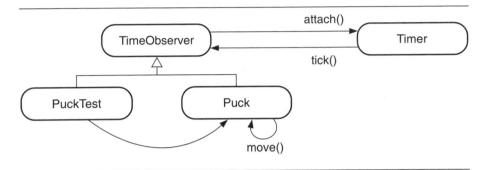

Figure 6.23 An instantiation of the Listener pattern extended for testing timer observers in *Brickles*

Testing Exceptions

An exception provides an alternative route for returning from a method that does not necessarily move to the next statement after the method is invoked. Exceptions are powerful in two respects:

- The exceptional return value is an object and can be arbitrarily complex.

- The points at which an exception is thrown varies based on the depth of the aggregation hierarchy.

Most interface designers use exceptions to handle error conditions that can arise during processing. Exceptions provide an alternative to return codes and in some situations can reduce the amount of code needed to process return codes. However, exceptions are also useful for processing exceptional conditions that arise during processing that are not really associated with errors. Our design for *Brickles* uses exceptions to terminate play of the game when either the puck supply is exhausted or the last brick is broken. Figure 6.24 shows how exceptions and return codes can be used in C++ to handle a problem reading from an input stream.

While the prototype for readInt(int) documents that only exceptions of the class ReadError (and its derived classes) will be thrown, C++ does not *require* a function (or member function) to list the types of exceptions it can throw. This presents a problem for testing (and probably for developing as well!) in that postconditions may not be tested completely. There is always a possibility that an unexpected perhaps system-level exception could be thrown within the context of a function's execution. Consequently, it is a good practice in C++ development to use exceptions to fully specify any interface that uses exceptions.

```
// Return code
enum Status {OK,FILE_CLOSED,BAD_DATA};
Status readInt(int &data);
    // Reads an integer value from the standard input stream,
    // stores it in data, and returns OK. If an integer value
    // could not be read, then an indication of the problem is
    // returned.
...
void main() {
    int count;
    ...
    switch (readInt(count)) {
    case OK:    process(count); break;
    case FILE_CLOSED:
                // Take some recovery or termination action...
                ... break;
    case BAD_DATA:
                // Take some recovery or termination action...
                ... break;
    }
    ...
}
```

```
// Exceptions
class ReadError {};
class FileClosedReadError: public ReadError {};
class BadDataReadError: public ReadError {};

void readInt(int &data) throw (ReadError);
    // Reads an integer value from the standard input stream
    // and stores it in data. If the read fails, then one of
    // the exceptions FileClosedReadError or BadDataReadError
    // is thrown.

void main() {
    int count;
    ...
    try {
        readInt(count);
        process(count);
    }
    catch (FileClosedReadError) {
        // Take some recovery or termination action...
        ...
    }
    catch (BadDataReadError) {
        // Take some recovery or termination action...
        ...
    }
}
```

Figure 6.24 Code structure for return code and exception methods of error handling

"Testing exceptions" provides two different perspectives. First, at the class-testing level the focus is on whether each of the methods in that class does in fact throw the exceptions that it claims to in the appropriate circumstance. This will be handled as a normal part of class testing since each potential throw should be a postcondition clause. The PuckSupply class would have tests that determine that the OutOfPucks exception is thrown when the puck supply has been exhausted. The coverage criteria requires that a class throws every exception contained in the specifications of the methods. There would be at least one test case per exception.

The test driver establishes the conditions in the object under test that will result in an exceptional event. The driver provides a try block inside which a stimulus invokes the method that throws the specific exception. The exception is caught by the test driver and verifies that it was the correct exception. Since exceptions are objects and belong to classes, the catch statements can use the typing system to verify that the exception is of the correct type.

Second, during integration, interaction testing will determine whether these exceptions that are being thrown at the correct time are being caught at the correct place. This is a test of the interaction between the originating object that initiates the sequence of method invocations that result and catch the exception, and the throwing object that reaches an exceptional state and throws the exception. For example, in the *Brickles* game, when the OutOf-Pucks exception is thrown, is it caught? Is it caught in the correct place? The originating object is several levels of aggregation removed from the PuckSupply object that actually throws the exception.

The test driver, in this case, instantiates the originating object. The originating object is responsible for creating those levels below it in the aggregation hierarchy. The test driver stimulates the originating object to create all of the levels and to place the originating object into a state in which the lower-level object will throw the exception. The coverage criteria for this level of testing is to be certain that every exception thrown is caught in the correct location.

Both of these points of view can be tested very early in development. During the guided inspection of the system-level design model, every user-defined exception that is instantiated should be traced to an object that will catch the exception using the sequence diagram for the scenario that throws the exception.

Testing Interactions at the System Level

At some point, components become so complex that it is easier to test them in the context of the application itself instead of in the environment provided by a test driver. Some parts of the system might not be modeled by a single class. For example, the user interface provided by most application programs is not a single instance of some class, but a community of objects that supports input and output. The interactions that can be tested at the system level are only those that can also be verified at the system level. That means that we can see the direct results of the tests, and it also means that there must be a direct relationship between the user interface and the ability to view test results.

Summary

In an object-oriented system the interactions between objects provide the main structure of the program. By testing specifically for problems between objects as they are integrated into larger and more complex objects, problems involving checking preconditions and the sufficiency of objects returned as the result of a message are discovered early. There are many factors that influence each interaction. Statistical sampling techniques such as OATS provide a means of selecting an effective subset of combinations of these factors to investigate using test cases.

The design of test software is influenced by the design of the software it is intended to test. In an object-oriented software development environment, the design of the production software is guided by a set of standard patterns. By discovering and documenting the standard ways in which test objects interact with each other and with the software under test, less experienced testers can benefit from the knowledge of more experienced testers. The result is test software that is of a better quality and is more reusable.

Exercises

6-1. Design a test suite for the exceptions defined in the *Brickles* design documents.

6-2. Construct test inputs for the `Velocity::setSpeed` method.

6-3. Construct a test plan for a commercially available component. How would the plan be different if the component is a domain-specific component versus a user-interface control?

6-4. Select a design pattern used in a project on which you are currently working. Find other projects on which it has been used. Examine those projects' test code. Generalize this code to create a test pattern.

Testing Class
Hierarchies

☞ **Need to know what must be retested in code that is inherited? See Hierarchical, Incremental Testing on page 253.**

☞ **Want to encapsulate the test cases for a specific class using PACT? See Organizing Testing Software on page 262.**

☞ **Want to know what testing is possible if the class is abstract? See Testing Abstract Classes on page 263.**

Chapter 7

Inheritance is a powerful mechanism for interface and code reuse. In this chapter we describe approaches for the execution-based testing of classes in an inheritance hierarchy. We show how to test a subclass given that its superclass has been tested using the techniques in Chapter 5 and Chapter 6. We consider many aspects of subclass testing, including adequate testing of subclasses, reuse of test cases for a class in testing subclasses of that class, and implementation of test drivers for subclasses. We also cover testing abstract classes. We provide examples of the techniques in both C++ and Java.

We begin the chapter with a brief review of inheritance and a discussion of assumptions we make about how inheritance should be used. Then we analyze the inheritance relationship from a testing perspective to identify what needs to be tested in a subclass. We describe parallel architecture for class testing (PACT), which is a way to organize Tester classes in an inheritance hierarchy.

Inheritance in Object-Oriented Development

Inheritance provides a mechanism for reuse. Inheritance, as a mechanism for *code* reuse, was probably a significant factor in making object-oriented programming attractive in the 1980s and early 1990s. However, good object-oriented design calls for inheritance to be used in a very disciplined way—that is, in accordance with the substitution principle (see Substitution Principle on page 33). Under that discipline, inheritance is a mechanism for *interface* reuse instead of code reuse.[1] In our discussions in this chapter, we assume inheritance is used only in accordance with the substitution principle. Under that assumption, the set of test cases identified for a class is valid for a subclass of that class. Additional test cases usually apply to a subclass. With careful analysis of the incremental changes that define a subclass in terms of its superclass, testers can sometimes avoid execution testing of some parts of a subclass because the test cases that apply to the parent just exercise the same code that was inherited intact in the subclass.

During analysis and design, inheritance relationships between classes can be recognized in the following two general ways:

- As a *specialization* of some class that has already been identified
- As a *generalization* of one or more classes that have already been identified

Inheritance relationships can be identified at just about any time during an iterative, incremental development effort. In particular, the specialization relationship can be applied even fairly late in an effort without a large impact on most other program components. This flexibility is one of the big advantages to using inheritance and one of the strengths of object-oriented technologies.

It is also a strength of the technology that code for execution-based testing of classes in a hierarchy can be reused. We will show how test plans and test drivers for a derived class can be derived from the tests for its base class.

Subclass Test Requirements

Implementing classes is more straightforward when done from the top of the hierarchy down. In the same way, testing classes in an inheritance hierarchy is generally more straightforward when approached from the top down. In testing first at the top of a hierarchy, we can address the common interface and code and then specialize the test driver code for each subclass. Implementing inheritance hierarchies from the bottom up can require significant refactoring of common code into a new superclass. The same thing can happen to test

---

1. In our experience, code reuse frequently falls out of interface reuse.

drivers. To keep our discussion simpler, we will assume that the classes in an inheritance hierarchy are to be tested top down. First, we will focus on testing a subclass of a class that has already been tested.

Consider that we would like to test a class D that is a subclass of another class C. Assume C has already been tested adequately by the execution of test cases by a test driver. What do we need to test in D?

Since D inherits at least part of its specification and also part of its implementation from C, it seems reasonable to assume that some of the test software for C can be reused in testing D. That is indeed the case. Consider, for example, the degenerate case in which D inherits from C and makes no changes at all. Thus, D is equivalent to C in its specification and implementation. Class D need not be tested at all if we are willing to assume that the compiler correctly processes the code. Under such an assumption, if C passes all its test cases, then so must D.

In the more general case in which D contains incremental changes from C, the effort needed to test D adequately can be reduced by reusing test cases and parts of the test driver for C. We will show how we can extend the testing done for C in a straightforward way to test D.

Refinement Possibilities

As supported by Java and C++, inheritance permits only a small number of incremental changes in deriving a class D from a class C. We can define a new derived class D that differs from C in only four general ways:

1. Add one or more new operations in the interface of D and possibly a new method in D to implement each new operation.[2]

2. Change the specification or implementation of an operation declared by C in one or two ways:

   a. Change in D the specification for an operation declared in C.

   b. Override in D a method[3] in C that implements an operation inherited by D.

   Note that either or both of these can apply. It is common to override a method in a subclass. It is also possible to change a specification for an operation without directly changing the method that implements the operation in a subclass.[4]

---

2. A new operation might be abstract (*pure virtual* in C++ terminology), deferring implementation to subclasses.

3. We assume if the class is implemented in C++, then such operations are declared *virtual* in the base class. Failure to use a virtual member function violates the substitution principle.

4. For example, the implementation might be based on a Template Method pattern [GHJV94].

3. Add into D one or more new instance variables to implement more states and/or attributes.

4. Change the class invariant in D.

While inheritance can be used for many reasons, we will assume that inheritance is used only in accordance with the substitution principle. This is a reasonable assumption because many of the benefits of object-oriented programming arise from polymorphism. The substitution principle ensures that objects bound to an interface behave as expected, thereby resulting in more reliable and readable code. We also assume that the principle of information hiding is followed so that any data in an object is not public. If data is indeed public, then we will augment our discussion with an assumption that reads and writes to public data correspond to implicit *get* and *set* operations, respectively.

Since D inherits part of its specification from C, then all the specification-based test cases used in testing C can be used in testing D. The substitution principle ensures that all the test cases still apply. We need new, additional specification-based test cases for new operations, perhaps additional specification-based test cases for operations whose preconditions have been weakened or postconditions have been strengthened, and implementation-based test cases to test new methods. If the class invariant has been refined in the subclass, then we will need to add test cases to address the refinements.

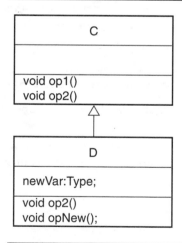

Subclass D adds a new instance variable (newVar) and a new operation (opNew()). D overrides the method for op2() defined in C because the operation has a new specification and/or a new implementation.

Figure 7.1 Refinement possibilities in an inheritance relationship between two classes

Hierarchical, Incremental Testing

The incremental changes between class C and its derived class D can be used to guide the identification of what needs to be tested in D. Consider the incremental changes from a testing perspective. Since D is a subtype of C, then all the specification-based test cases for C also apply to D. Many of the implementation-based and interaction-based test cases also apply. We use the term **inherited test cases** to refer to the test cases for a subclass that were identified for testing its base class. We can determine which inherited test cases apply to testing a subclass through a straightforward analysis. As part of that same analysis, we can determine which inherited test cases do not have to be executed in testing the subclass. We repeat here the list of incremental changes given in the previous section and examine each from the testing perspective.

1. Add one or more new operations in the interface of D and possibly a new method in D to implement each new operation.

   A new operation introduces new functionality and new code to test. A new operation does not directly affect existing, inherited operations or methods. We need to add specification-based test cases for each new operation. We need to add implementation-based and interaction-based test cases in order to comply with coverage criteria in the test plan if the operation is not abstract and has an implementation.

2. Change the specification or implementation of an operation declared by C in one or two ways:

   a. Change in D the specification for an operation declared in C.

      We need to add new specification-based test cases for the operation. Additional test cases provide new inputs that meet any weakened preconditions and check outputs for the new expected results that result from any strengthened postconditions. The test cases for this operation defined for C still apply, but must be re-run. In addition, we need to add strengthened postcondition requirements to the output for each of the test cases used to test this operation in class C.

   b. Override in D a method in C that implements an operation inherited by D.

      We can reuse all the inherited specification-based test cases for the method. Since there is new code to test, we will need to review each of the implementation-based test cases and interaction-based test cases, revising and adding to them as needed to meet the test criteria for coverage.

3. Add into D one or more new instance variables to implement more states and/or attributes.

A new variable is added most likely in connection with new operations and/or code in overriding methods, and testing will be handled in connection with them. If a new variable is not used in any method, then we do not have to make any changes.

4. Change the class invariant in D.

Class invariants amount to additional postconditions for every test case. We prefer to view them as implied postconditions and to write test cases without explicit references to invariant constraints. Test case output is subject to invariant constraints—that is, "*and* the class invariant holds" is implicit in every test case output. Thus, if a class invariant changes, then we need to rerun all inherited test cases to verify that the new invariant holds.

We do not need to add specification-based test cases for operations that are unchanged from base class to derived class. The test cases can be reused *as is*. We do not need to run any of these test cases if the operations they test have not changed in any way—that is, in specification or in implementation. We do, however, need to rerun any test cases for an operation if its method has changed indirectly because it uses an operation that itself has changed. We also might need additional implementation-based test cases for such methods.

We refer to applying the above analysis and its results as **hierarchical incremental testing** (HIT). We can use the analysis to determine for a subclass what test cases need to be added, what inherited test cases need to be run, and what inherited test cases do not need to be run. Determining which test cases do not need to be run is a bit tricky. In practice, it is usually easier and more reliable to just rerun all test cases. However, it pays to determine which test cases can be reused.

Figure 7.2 summarizes the analysis associated with HIT. We classify each operation defined for a derived class D in the first column as *new*, *refined*, and *unchanged*. The second column specifies whether that change affects specification-based testing. The third column specifies whether that change affects implementation-based testing. The table adds a dimension of *public* and *private*. Private features of a class do not affect the public interface.

A *No* entry in the table indicates that the incremental change (for the row containing the entry) has no incremental effect on the test suite—that is, the test cases for the superclass are still valid for the subclass. A *Yes* entry indicates that test cases must be added to address that incremental change. A *Maybe* entry indicates that a tester must examine the code in the implementation to determine if more test cases are needed to achieve some level of coverage. As a short example, consider the Timer class in the design of *Brickles* that represents the passing of time as a sequence of discrete "ticks." Each timer event is processed by a Timer instance that notifies other objects in the match. Those objects, in turn, process another timer tick. This aspect of the design is based on the *Observer* pattern [GHJV94]. A Timer instance occupies the role of sub-

	Incremental Change	Affect Class Specification?	Affect Class Implementation?
new operation	public	Yes	Maybe, if the new method affects, directly or indirectly, inherited variables
	private	No	Yes
refined operation/ overridden method	public	Yes	Maybe
	private	No	Yes
new variable	public (constant)*	Yes	Yes
	private	No	Yes
unchanged operation	public	No	Maybe, if the method uses, directly or indirectly, an operation on itself that is changed
	private	No	Yes

*We assume that any public variable is declared **const** (**final**). We discourage using any variables in a class interface, preferring accessor operations instead.

Figure 7.2 Summary of refinements and effects in hierarchical incremental testing (HIT)

ject, and other objects in a *Brickles* match assume the role of observers. If we implement the design as shown in Figure 7.3 based on existing, tested classes Subject and Observer prescribed by the *Observer* pattern, then we can identify from Figure 7.2 what needs to be tested in class Timer. Specifically, the specifi-

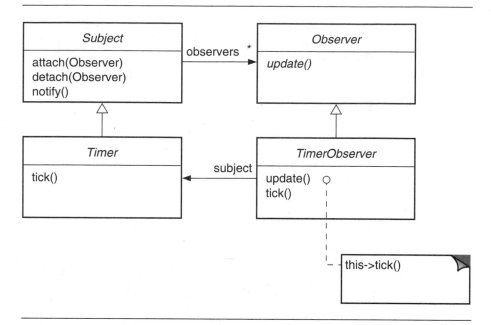

Figure 7.3 Class diagram for Timer and TimerObserver

cations of attach(), detach(), and notify() do not need to be tested further because their specifications have not changed from what was defined in Subject. No new implementation-based test cases are needed either because the code (not shown) reveals that there has been no changes to the execution flow in these methods—that is, these methods do not use any of the new code in Timer or there is no new interactions with other objects. We do need to add specification-based test cases for the new operation tick(), which processes a timer event, and implementation-based test cases for the method that implements it. With respect to testing TimerObserver, HIT shows we need to test the overridden update() operation by adding specification-based test cases because the specification of the operation changes in the subclass (it specifies possible state changes in a concrete subclass). Since the operation is abstract in Observer, the *Maybe* in the HIT table translates to a need to add implementation-based test cases as well.

Let us now examine hierarchical incremental testing from the context of a test plan—that is, from the perspective of identifying test cases. Then we will examine it from a more detailed level. We will use as an example the inheritance hierarchy rooted at Sprite in *Brickles* (see Figure 7.4). A *sprite* is an abstraction that represents any object that can appear on a playfield in an arcade game. The name has historic significance in the domain of arcade games

[Hens96]. Some attributes associated with a sprite are a *bitmap* that renders a visual image, a *size* that describes the width and height of the bitmap, a *location* on a playfield, and a *bounding rectangle* that is the smallest rectangular area of the playfield that contains the sprite's image (if it is on a playfield[5]).

A *movable sprite* is a sprite that can change position in a playfield. Associated with a movable sprite is the velocity at which it is currently moving. A *velocity* represents a direction and a distance traveled (in playfield units) in a unit of time. In our model, a *puck* and a *paddle* are both concrete kinds of movable sprites.

A *stationary sprite* is a sprite whose position is fixed as long as it is on the playfield. In our model, a *brick* is an example of a stationary sprite. Since we have only one kind of stationary sprite in *Brickles*, we have—probably shortsightedly—elected not to represent stationary sprites by an abstract class in the current increment. Thus, class Brick inherits directly from Sprite in our model.

Specifications for some of the operations in these classes in the Sprite hierarchy are given in Figure 7.5.

Specification-Based Test Cases

Under hierarchical, incremental testing, changes in a subclass's specification from the specification of its base class determine what needs to be tested. Test requirements are summarized in the column labeled *Affect Class Specification?* in Figure 7.2. While our discussion will be based on the relatively informal specifications given in Figure 7.5, the techniques apply to any form of specification, including Object Constraint Language (OCL) and state transition diagrams.

Let us focus first on the class MovableSprite, assuming test cases have been identified and implemented for class Sprite (see Figure 7.6).[6] MovableSprite adds some new operations and attributes to model motion in a playfield and also overrides some methods. Among the new operations in class Movable-Sprite are move(), which updates a movable sprite's position in a playfield; set-Velocity(const Velocity &), which changes the velocity at which a movable sprite is moving; isMoving() const, which inspects whether a movable sprite is currently in a moving state; and collideInto(Sprite &), which modifies the state of a movable sprite to reflect a collision with some other sprite in the playfield. Among the overridden methods are the constructor. Most of the operations declared by Sprite are inherited unchanged.

---

5. Consider, for example a puck in play and a puck not yet put into play. The former is on a playfield, the latter is not.

6. We'll address the problem of testing an abstract class, such as Sprite, later in this chapter.

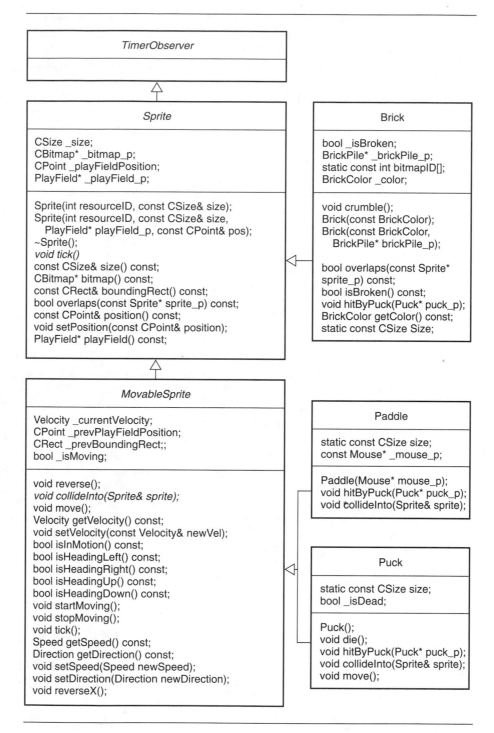

Figure 7.4 A class model for the Sprite inheritance hierarchy

Sprite
:   either on a playfield or not on any playfield

Sprite(int resourceID, const CSize& size):

pre: *resourceID* identifies the bitmap and *size* correctly reflects the height and width of the bitmap

post: the new instance has an image but is not positioned on any playfield

Sprite(int resourceID, const CSize& size, PlayField* playField_p, const CPoint& pos):

pre: *resourceID* identifies the bitmap, *size* correctly reflects the height and width of the bitmap, *playField_p* is not null, and *pos* is a valid playfield position

post: the new instance has an image and displays on the playfield at the given position

---

MovableSprite
either on a playfield or not on any playfield; either moving or not moving

MovableSprite(int resourceID, const CSize& size)

pre: *resourceID* identifies the bitmap and *size* correctly reflects the height and width of the bitmap

post: the new instance has an image, is not positioned on any playfield, and is not moving

void setVelocity(const Velocity& newVel)

pre: none

post: the receiver has velocity *newVel*

void move():

pre: none

post: if not in the moving state then do nothing else move to a position determined by the current position and the current velocity. If a collision occurs in the process with another sprite *S*, collideInto(*S*).

void collideInto(Sprite& sprite):

pre: none

post: updates own state and that of sprite to reflect a collision in which the receiver has collided into *sprite*

Puck
either on a playfield or not on any playfield; either moving or not moving; either in play or not in play

void move():

pre: none

post: if not in play or not moving then do nothing else move to a position determined by the current position and the current velocity. If a collision occurs in the process with another sprite *S*, collideInto(*S*).

void collideInto(Sprite &sprite)

pre: updates own state to change direction of travel and updates state of *sprite* to reflect being hit by a puck

---

Figure 7.5 An informal specification for some parts of the Sprite class hierarchy

Component Test Plan

Component Name Sprite	**Tracking Number** TBS
Developer(s) Dave Sykes	**Tester(s)** Dave Sykes

Objectives for This Component

This class represents the abstraction of every object that can appear in a playfield in an arcade game. Its primary purpose is to establish a protocol for all the various subclasses of sprites.

Guided Inspection Requirements

As this is a critical component; 100% of its code shall be inspected.

Building and Retaining Test Suites

The test suites shall be prepared in accordance with project standards. A SpriteTester class shall contain the test driver. In that class, operations shall be provided to execute functional, structural, and interaction test cases. Reporting shall conform to project standards.

Specification-based Test Cases

Execute test cases for each combination of precondition and postcondition of every method. Also check that the class invariant holds as part of each test case. Execute test cases that cover every transition in the state representation.

Implementation-based Test Cases

Execute test cases that cover every line of code in each nonabstract method.

Interaction Test Cases

None.

State-based Test Cases

None in addition to those cases covered in specification-based test cases.

Figure 7.6 A component test plan for class Velocity

The implementation of MovableSprite uses the following two new variables to store the velocity attribute and indicate whether the sprite is moving:

- ■ _currentVelocity, which is an instance of class Velocity used to store the current velocity.

- ■ _isMoving, which indicates whether the movable sprite is currently in motion. When this variable is *false*, move() has no effect.

What do we need to do to adequately test MovableSprite given that Sprite has already been tested? The subclass's code is based on the code tested in the superclass. From the class model (Figure 7.4) and the specifications for the operations shown in Figure 7.5, we can identify the following based on the HIT information in Figure 7.2:

- ■ The changed invariant demands that all the test cases defined for Sprite should be run for MovableSprite and the new invariant checked.

- ■ The new operations in MovableSprite need to have specification-based test cases generated as well as implementation-based test cases generated. We will want to check interactions among many of the new operations—for example, setting the velocity and then moving a movable sprite a few times to ensure it has adopted the specified velocity, or changing the velocity and verifying that the heading (*up, down, left,* or *right*) is correct.

- ■ The operations in Sprite for which methods have not been overridden in MovableSprite need no additional test cases.

Implementation-Based Test Cases

The column labeled *Affect Class Implementation?* in Figure 7.2 specifies what needs to be tested with respect to implementation. If an entry contains *Maybe*, then a tester must examine the code to determine whether additional test cases are required. In the case of MovableSprite, quite a few methods have been added to implement the operations concerned with movement. Methods for operations associated with a position in the playfield have not been overridden. The method tick() is overridden so that it causes a movable sprite to change position in the playfield based on its current velocity.

Based on the information in Figure 7.2, we can determine the following about implementation-based testing of MovableSprite:

- ■ No new test cases are needed for size(), bitmap(), boundingRect(), overlaps(), position(), setPosition(), or playField(). After examining the code for these methods and determining that there are no interactions among them with tick(), we conclude these test cases do not need to be rerun.

- ■ Implementation-based test cases are needed for all the new methods such as reverse(), move(), and so on.

∎ Implementation-based test cases are needed for the implementation of the abstract method tick().

We also need interaction test cases associated with checking the correct implementation of startMoving() and stopMoving() and the effect of the state change on other operations such as tick() and reverse().

Organizing Testing Software

The relationship between test requirements for a subclass, such as Movable-Sprite, and the test requirements for a base class supports an inheritance relationship between Tester classes that we described in Chapter 5. In other words, we can develop a test driver for a subclass D by deriving its Tester class from the Tester class for C, D's superclass. Figure 7.7 shows the structure, which we refer to as the parallel architecture for class testing (PACT) [McGr97]. The structure determined by PACT for the Sprite class hierarchy is shown in Figure 7.8.

Using PACT reduces the effort needed to test a new subclass. The organization of test case methods and test script methods we described in the previous two chapters facilitates the testing of subclasses by letting us invoke them in Tester subclasses. If an operation is refined in a subclass, then the corresponding tester methods can be reused in the subclass and refined as necessary to reflect new preconditions, postconditions, and/or implementation. Test case methods and test script methods for new operations can be added in the subclass Tester. PACT presents a clean organization and is easy to implement.

At the root of the PACT hierarchy is the abstract class Tester that we described in Chapter 5. Each subclass of Tester must provide implementations

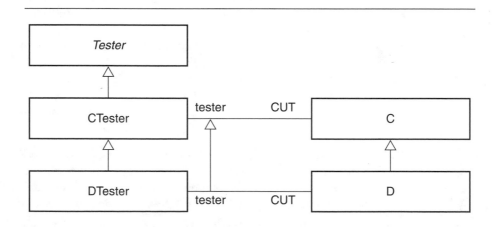

Figure 7.7 Parallel architecture for class testing (PACT)

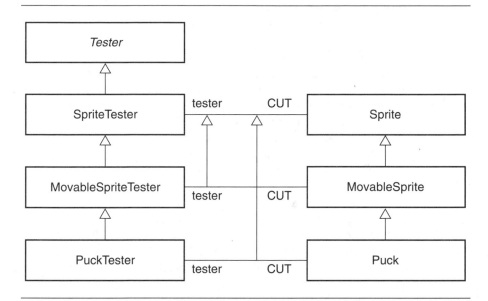

Figure 7.8 PACT structure for the Sprite hierarchy

for the abstract operations and could override methods for any of the other operations. Each subclass has the same basic organization presented in Chapter 5: test case methods, a method corresponding to each constructor to create an object under test, and a method to create an object under test in some specified state. These classes are straightforward to implement once the test cases have been identified.

Testing Abstract Classes

We usually expect the root class of an inheritance hierarchy—and even some of its direct descendents—to be abstract. In this section, we discuss possible ways of testing abstract classes, such as Sprite and MovableSprite. Execution-based testing of classes requires that an instance of the class be constructed. Most object-oriented programming languages, including C++ and Java, support syntax for identifying abstract classes. Language semantics generally preclude instances of abstract classes from being created. This presents a problem for testing because we cannot create the instances we need. We have identified some different approaches to testing abstract classes. Each has strengths and drawbacks. We present these approaches in the context of testing the Sprite abstract class.

One approach to testing an abstract class, such as Sprite, is shown in Figure 7.9. Under this approach, a concrete subclass of Sprite is defined solely for the purpose of testing. In the figure, we name this class ConcreteSprite. The implementation of ConcreteSprite defines a stub for each abstract operation of Sprite. If one or more of the methods in Sprite is a template method using one of Sprite's abstract operations, then that abstract method must be stubbed appropriately—so that it effectively appears to meet the postconditions for the operation it stubs. In some instances, this is not difficult to accomplish. For some complex operations, writing a satisfactory stub can require substantial effort. Once a concrete subclass has been implemented, the object-UnderTest() factory method of the Tester class—for example, SpriteTester—creates an instance of the concrete subclass.

One disadvantage to this approach is that the implementation of abstract methods cannot be propagated easily to abstract subclasses without using multiple (repeated) inheritance. Consider, for example, what is now necessary for testing the abstract class MovableSprite, which is a subclass of the abstract class Sprite illustrated in Figure 7.10. Ideally, the ConcreteMovableSprite class could reuse the stubs implemented in ConcreteSprite. However, this reuse is not immediate unless ConcreteMovableSprite inherits from both Movable-Sprite and ConcreteSprite. While multiple inheritance is available in C++, it is not in most object-oriented programming languages nor is its use for this purpose encouraged.

A second approach to testing an abstract class is to test it as part of testing the first concrete descendent. In the context of testing Sprite, this would be done in testing, say, Puck. This approach eliminates the need to develop extra classes for testing purposes at a cost of increased complexity in testing this con-

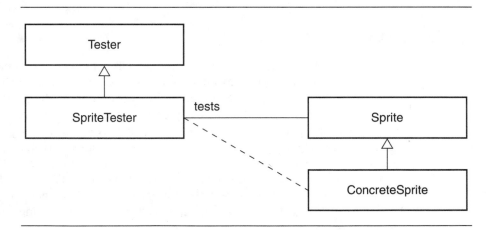

Figure 7.9 One approach for the execution-based testing of an abstract class

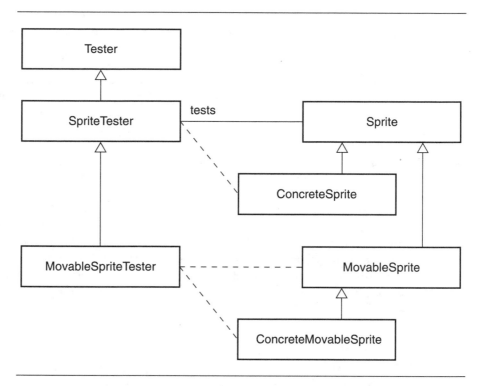

Figure 7.10 Another approach for the execution-based testing of an abstract class

crete class. In writing the Tester class for a concrete class such as Puck, we need to take care to implement a Tester class for each ancestor, thereby providing each with the appropriate and correct test case and test script methods. This is straightforward to do in practice. Careful review of the code in the Tester classes for the abstract classes can reduce the effort needed to get the concrete subclass Tester class implemented correctly. If the concrete subclass passes all its test cases, then the assumption is that the ancestor classes pass their test cases. This assumption is not always valid. For example, a concrete subclass might override a method defined in one of the abstract classes. In that case, another concrete subclass that does no such override must be used to test that method.

Neither of these approaches is completely satisfactory. We have investigated a third approach based on the direct implementation of a concrete version of an abstract class for testing purposes. In other words, we have tried to find a way to write source code for a class so that it can easily be compiled as an abstract or a concrete class. However, neither an approach based on *editor inheritance* nor one based on conditional compilation[7] has produced good results because the resulting code is complex and hard to read, thus it's susceptible to error.

A good alternative is to test an abstract class using guided inspection instead of execution-based testing. Reviews are acceptable because a typical abstract class provides little or no implementation for the abstract operations. In our experience, public interfaces for abstract classes tend to stabilize fairly quickly. The concrete operations are primarily inspectors or simple modifiers that can easily be tested by inspection. Constructors and destructors are more complicated to test by inspection only—for example, the constructor for the Sprite class involves finding a bitmap image associated with a resource ID.

We still prefer to do execution-based testing of concrete classes because it supports easier regression testing. PACT offers advantages for testing families of classes, so we still want to develop Tester classes for abstract classes. In our practice, we prefer the second approach we discussed—that is, testing abstract classes with the first concrete subclass to be tested. This approach is straightforward and requires relatively little additional coding effort for implementing testers. We still have the advantage of easily performing regression testing.

Summary

It is widely accepted that the inheritance relationship provides a powerful analysis and design tool. It provides a very powerful testing tool as long as inheritance is applied during design in accordance with the substitution principle. An inheritance relation holds for test suites. Test suites for subclasses can be derived from the test suite for their parent classes. Based on an analysis of the changes, we can decide what test cases need to be added, what test cases need to be rerun, what test cases need to be modified, and what test cases do not need to be run at all. PACT provides a very useful way of organizing test drivers for class testing.

---

7. Editor inheritance refers to the cloning of code by copying existing source code and then editing the copy to add, remove, or change its function. In this case, we copy the code for the abstract class to a separate file, then implement any abstract operations to make the class concrete. Of course, the main drawback of editor inheritance is that any change to the original source code is not propagated automatically to the cloned source code.

To work around this drawback, we can use conditional compilation based on, for example, C++ preprocessor directives `#if defined(TEST)` and `#elif` and `#endif,` to put the code for abstract and concrete versions of the same class in the same source file. Using conditional compilation makes code very difficult to read and maintain.

Exercises

7-1. Hierarchical, incremental testing (HIT) approaches testing with an idea that, with a little analysis, we can avoid retesting code that has already been tested. Select classes from an inheritance hierarchy on your project and perform a HIT analysis. Estimate the effort to implement enough test cases to fully test all classes in the hierarchy and compare that estimate with your HIT analysis effort.

7-2. Write a test driver for an abstract class with a small number of operations. Evaluate the effort needed to test the class using the three approaches described in the last part of this chapter.

7-3. Implement a PACT hierarchy of Tester classes for the classes in an inheritance hierarchy to which you have access. Modify the abstract class Tester described in Chapter 5 to be useful in your test environment. Enhancements can include measuring memory allocation, collecting timing information, and doing more sophisticated logging of results.

Testing
Distributed Objects

Need to define standards for specifying distributed systems? See Specifying Distributed Objects on page 287.

Interested in a new definition of "path" especially for distributed systems? See Path Testing in Distributed Systems on page 275.

Need to develop tests that explore the temporal characteristics of a program? See Temporal Logic on page 288.

Want to explore testing an Internet application? See The Ultimate Distributed System—The Internet on page 303.

Chapter 8

Few systems these days are designed to execute on a single processor in a single process. In an attempt to gain flexibility and extensibility, many systems are designed in pieces that are sufficiently independent that can reside in a separate process from the others. The term *distributed* means systems with a client/server architecture in which the client and server pieces are designed to be in separate processes. Today's systems are much more varied than the client/server systems of the eighties in which the server was always a database server and the clients simply queried or modified the data. Appplications often begin with one component of the application being downloaded to run on a customer's computer. Information is streamed back to an application server, which in turn works with a database component to fulfill a transaction.

In this chapter we will add to our repertoire of testing techniques to include tests that are targeted at new types of defects specifically related to concurrent, distributed software. Basically we will consider the following two types of faults.

■ Concurrent threads of execution must coordinate their accesses to shared data values. Failure to synchronize these accesses can lead to incorrect data values being present in memory even though each thread is correctly computing its result.

■ A specific node in a distributed system can fail to perform correctly even if every other processor is working properly. A network link between nodes can also fail while the remainder of the system continues to function. This results in a system failure.

The *Brickles* example, as we have been using it thus far, is not distributed and not useful in this context. We will use examples from the Java version of *Brickles* that is multithreaded and that uses an applet running in a Web browser as its interface.

Basic Concepts

The basic unit that we will deal with in this chapter is a **thread**. A thread is an independent context of execution within an operating system process. It has its own program counter and local data. A thread is the smallest unit of execution that can be scheduled. Most modern operating systems allow a single process to group multiple threads into a related set that shares some properties and keeps certain others private. A single thread is a sequence of computations and is the simplest testing situation. Techniques discussed in earlier chapters have "covered" the various entry points into and the paths through a single thread of computation. The techniques have accounted for alternative paths through the logic including the dynamic substitution of one piece of code for another.

The basic complication introduced by having multiple threads arises when they share information or access data stores that are available to more than one thread. For concurrency to be of value, there should be as few dependencies between threads as possible. Dependencies imply that the order in which computations in the two threads occur matters. Since each thread is independently scheduled by the operating system, the developer must provide some mechanism to **synchronize** the threads so that the correct order is followed.

Object-oriented languages provide some natural means of synchronization by hiding attributes behind interfaces and, in some cases, making threads correspond to objects. This means that synchronization is visible in the object interface (such as the synchronize keyword in Java) and that messaging is a key element in synchronization. In this environment, class testing does not detect many, if any, synchronization defects. It is only when a set of objects interact that the real opportunity to detect synchronization defects occurs.

The case study that we have been using was originally written sequentially and the C++ version that can be downloaded from the Web is a sequential version. The Java version does introduce concurrency. Essentially, the Movable-Piece objects are autonomous from the other computations in the game. They are in the sense that the Timer object maintains a separate thread and sends the tick() message to every MovablePiece object that is registered with it. The synchronization problem that must be examined is whether it is possible for the Timer thread to retain control of the processor and send the tick() message to a single object several times before the thread that manages the display can compute a collision, change the location of the object that was moved, and update the display.

Computational Models

Sequential processing of program statements is the "default" model of computation. In this section we will discuss some other models and briefly talk about the testing implications of each.

Concurrent

The concurrent model of computation introduces a logical notion of multiple things happening at the same time. Physically it may or may not be possible for two things to happen at the exact same time, but a design must be constructed to assume that things are happening at the same time. The introduction of light-weight threads into recent operating systems have made this model easy to realize.

Testing for concurrency defects should focus on those points at which two threads interact. Methods should receive the typical testing described in Chapter 5 before being exercised in an interaction setting. The interaction tests, which we began talking about in Chapter 6, should provide opportunity for two or more clients to request the same service. But more about this later in the chapter (see Path Testing in Distributed Systems, on page 275).

Parallel

The parallel model of computation uses a set of physical processors to achieve true physically concurrent computing. As many computations as processors may proceed at exactly the same time. There are various definitions of this term but a "parallel computer" is usually taken to be one in which these multiple processors share a common high-speed data bus and are thought to be in the same "box." The National Oceanic and Atmospheric Administration (NOAA) uses a computer with over two thousand processors to compute forecasts from vast quantities of measurements from around the world. We will not discuss the issues associated with this model.

Networked

In this model, physical concurrency is achieved by linking together separate boxes with communication devices that operate at a slower speed than the internal data bus. This is a model we will consider because it is applicable to such heavily used systems as the Internet. One of the testing problems associated with networked computing is the difficulty in synchronizing the many independent machines that comprise a networked system. This can make it difficult to determine how thoroughly an implementation has been tested because the times at which events occurred are measured in terms of each local clock. Without getting into the details of networking and Web communication, we will discuss some techniques for testing systems that incorporate a Web component.

Distributed

Distributed systems use multiple processes to support a flexible architecture in which the number of participating objects can change. Although the objects of a system can be distributed across multiple processes on the same machine, they are usually distributed across multiple physical computers. These distributed components must be able to locate the other components with which they must interact. An object variously named the "Naming Service" or registry or some other name is known to all the components. In some cases a configuration file lists the machines that are authorized to participate in the system. These and other pieces constitute what we will refer to as the infrastructure of the distributed system. This infrastructure may be standardized and reusable across a number of systems with little or no modification. We will consider a number of issues related to testing these distributed components and systems.

Basic Differences

We want to consider some of the basic differences between sequential systems and these other models particularly from a testing perspective.

Nondeterminism

It is very difficult to exactly replicate a test run when the software contains multiple concurrent threads. The exact ordering is determined by the scheduler of the operating system. Changes in programs not associated with the system under test can affect the order in which threads of the system under test are executed. This means that if a failure is encountered, the defect is isolated and repaired and the test is repeated, we can't be certain that the defect is removed just because the error does not reoccur during a specific run.

This leads us to use one of the following techniques:

■ **Conduct more thorough testing at the class level.** The design review of a class that produces distributed objects should investigate whether there is an appropriate provision for synchronization in the design for the class. The dynamic class testing should determine whether the synchronization is working correctly in a controlled test environment.

■ **Execute a large number of test cases while attempting to record the order in which events occur.** This provides a higher probability that all possible orderings have been executed. The problems we are attempting to detect result from sequences of actions. If all possible sequences of these actions have been executed, the defects will have to be found.

■ **Specify a standard test environment.** Begin with as clean a machine as possible including as few connections to networks, modems, or other shared devices as possible. Identify those applications that must run for the platform to be viable. Add a basic set of applications that would be running on the typical machine. Each test case should provide a description of any modifications made to this standard environment. This includes the order in which processes are started. Including a debugger in the standard environment allows the tester to verify the order in which threads are created, executed, and deleted. The larger the environment and the more it can be shared and networked, the more difficult it is to maintain consistency within that environment. Wherever possible there should be a testing lab in which machines are isolated (at least for the initial testing phases) from the rest of the corporate net and dedicated to the test process.

Additional Infrastructure

Many of the distributed object systems rely on an infrastructure provided by a third-party vendor. Over time, successive versions of this infrastructure will be released. A regression test suite should be created that tests the compatibility between the application and the infrastructure.

A second issue here is the reconfiguration of the system. Some infrastructures are self modifying and reconfigure themselves when the system reconfigures itself. Essentially a specific input data set can cause a different path to be executed because the previous path no longer exists. An analysis of the infrastructure should provide a set of standard configurations for the infrastructure and tests should be executed for each different one.

Partial Failures

A distributed system can find that a portion of its code cannot execute because of hardware or software failures on one of the machines hosting the system. An application running on a single machine does not experience this type of failure: it is either running or not. The possibility of partial failure leads us to include tests in which failures are simulated by removing or disabling network connections or by shutting down a node in the network. This can be implemented in the previously mentioned test lab.

Time-Outs

Networked systems avoid deadlock by setting timers when a request is sent to another system. If no response is received within a specified time, the request is abandoned. The system may be deadlocked or one of the machines in the network may simply be very busy and may be taking longer to respond than what is allowed by the timer. The software must be able to perform the correct behavior in the case when the request is answered and when it is not, even though that behavior may be very different in the two situations. Tests must be run with a variety of loading configurations on the machines in the network.

Dynamic Nature of the Structure

A distributed system is often built with the capability of changing its configuration, for example, where specific requests are directed dynamically, depending on the load on the various machines. Systems are also designed to allow a variable number of machines to participate in the system. Tests need to be replicated with a variety of configurations. If there are a set number of configurations, it may be possible to test them all. Otherwise, a technique such as orthogonal array testing system (OATS) can be used to select a specific set of tests and configurations.

Threads

We have already introduced the concept of a thread as a unit of computation that can be scheduled. During design, the principal trade-off concerns the number of threads. Increasing the number of threads can simplify certain algorithms and techniques but increases the risk of sequencing problems. Reducing the number of threads reduces sequencing problems but makes the software more rigid and often more inefficient.

Synchronization

When two or more threads must access the same memory location, a mechanism is needed to prevent the two threads from interfering with each other. Two threads may try to execute a method that modifies a data value at the same time. Some languages, such as Java, provide a language keyword that automatically adds the mechanism to prevent this simultaneous access. Others, such as C++, require explicit structures that each individual developer must construct.

Synchronization can be easier in an object-oriented language because the mechanism can be localized on the modifier method for the common data attribute. The actual data is protected from direct access by more than a single specific method.

Specifying the Need for Synchronization

In design documents, synchronization can be specified in the guard clauses of the UML state diagram. In Java, the keyword **synchronize** is used on the signature of a method to specify the need for a synchronization mechanism. C++ has no keywords for specifying synchronization; however, the synchronization mechanisms are designed as classes. The creation of an instance of a monitor object, for instance, indicates the location at which synchronization is needed.

Testing That the Need Is Met

Even though the language automatically provides the mechanism, the developer may have misplaced the specification for synchronization. During class testing, a test harness should create multiple thread-based test objects. Each of these fires a request against the object under test (OUT).

Path Testing in Distributed Systems

Path testing is a well established technique for selecting test cases. A path is a set of logically contiguous statements that is executed when a specific input set is used, such as the following:

```
S1;
if(cond1) S2
else S3
```

There are the paths S_1, S_2 and S_1, S_3. Other control structures introduce new paths and may result in an indeterminate number of paths or, worse still, an infinite number of paths.

Coverage is measured by computing the percentage of paths that have been exercised by a test case. Executing 100% of the paths in a program provides complete code coverage although it may not detect defects related to the computation environment. Of course, this is difficult to achieve when there are an infinite number of paths. Alternatives include only measuring the branches out of selection statements, or `if` and `case` statements that have been covered. This does not cover the combinations of a branch from one control structure to another.

Another definition for a path is to link the place where a variable is given a value (a *def*) with all those places where the variable is used (a *use*). Covering all def-use pairs constitutes complete path coverage. Other types of significant attributes of the code can be used to define a "path." For example, branch testing, as previously mentioned, is defining paths that are based on the decision statements in the program.

For distributed systems, Richard Carver and K. C. Tai [CaTa98] have identified a definition of a path that results in effective coverage. First, we provide a couple of definitions:

> **SYN-event:** A SYN-event is any action that involves the synchronization of two threads. The spawning of one thread by another is one example of a SYN-event.

> **SYN-sequence:** SYN-sequence is a sequence of SYN-events that will occur in a specified order. This is one type of path through the program code.

The idea is to design test cases that correspond to SYN-sequences. For example, when a program begins execution, a single thread is operating. When it spawns a second thread, that is a SYN-event. In the simple case, each thread carries out simple computations. Eventually, the two threads join and the program terminates. This is a single SYN-sequence since any single input data set causes both threads to execute. The basic or "main" thread does not count in the number of paths since it executes regardless of the data set.

Figure 8.1 illustrates the interactions between several objects. The Brickles-View object is the main thread of the program. It creates the second thread that is devoted to the Timer. The Puck and Paddle objects are controlled on the main thread. The `tick()` message from the Timer object to the Puck and Paddle objects are points of synchronization and thus SYN-events. The SYN-sequences of interest run from the creation of the Timer to its destruction. In this case there are an infinite number of SYN-paths because the Timer simply keeps sending `tick()` messages until it is destroyed. The create, destroy, and start and stop messages are SYN-events. Analysis of these events leads to the following SYN-paths that should be executed by test cases:

1. create the timer, it runs until the game is over, the timer is destroyed

2. create the timer, it runs for a while, it is stopped, it is started, the game is over, the timer is destroyed

3. create the timer, it runs for a while, it is stopped, the user destroys the game, and the timer is destroyed

4. create the timer, it runs for a while, it is stopped, it is started, the timer is stopped and started three times, the game is over, the timer is destroyed

Our experience and research has shown that this technique of SYN-paths identifies defects that are related mainly to synchronization defects. Use of this analysis technique does not replace the need to use conventional path testing techniques to find defects unrelated to synchronization errors.

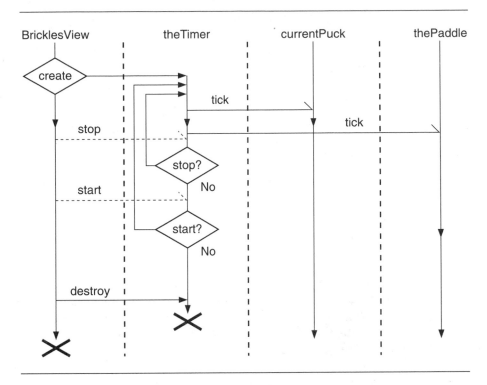

Figure 8.1 An activity diagram of multiple threads

Now that we have looked at an example, let's analyze the types of events in an object-oriented language that might qualify as SYN-events.

- Creation and destruction of an object that represents a thread.

- Creation and destruction of an object that encapsulates a thread.

- Sending of a message from an object on one thread to an object on another thread.

- One object controls another by putting it to sleep or waking it up.

The tester should trace paths from one of these events to another. Even if there are multiple paths through control statements from one SYN-event to the other, only one path needs to be covered to give SYN-path coverage. Exactly where these events occur depends partially on where the threads are located.

An object that has its own thread should receive thorough testing as a class (with all of its aggregated attributes) before being interacted with other objects. In Figure 8.2, we show selected portions of the TimerTester. In particular we include a few test cases. The Timer instance had been working in the context of the completed game for a short time when it was class tested. A

Objects on Threads and Threads in Objects

There are only a few basic models for threads in object-oriented programs. An object has its own personal thread or it is visited by the active thread as necessary. Usually most programs will have examples of each approach. The Timer class from the Java implementation of *Brickles* is an example of the object owning its own thread. All of the other objects share the "main" thread. An object that owns a thread also indicates when it can be interrupted by other threads. In either design, there must be a mechanism that prevents multiple threads from operating in the same modifier method at the same time.

problem was found that allowed the timer to start but it never stopped! The pause() method set a Boolean attribute so that no further ticks were sent out, but the thread was not halted so it continued to use system resources. This was only found when the absence of ticks was tested rather than their presence.

In the code in Figure 8.2, the test object registers with the timer to receive the tick() message. This is possible because the TimerTester class implements the TimeObservable interface. A test case like this one can be easily constructed because the test object receives the event or message directly rather than having to create a surrogate object that receives the message and then informs the test object.

Thread Models

The "motto" of Java is "Write Once Run Anywhere." The reality is "Write Once Run Anywhere after Testing Everywhere." A particular example is the differences in behavior of Java threads among operating systems. The test suite of any Java program that creates threads should include tests on multiple operating systems chosen for its different behavior. Using a Windows version, Sun Unix and Mac OS give a cross section; however, variants of Unix and even different models of workstations with different options installed may give different results.

Running the applet version of *Brickles* on a Windows machine and a Sun workstation results in different behaviors, some correct and some not. The thread for the Timer does not necessarily release control of the processor to allow the display to be updated.

```
public class TimerTester extends Tester implements TimeObservable{

protected boolean testScript2(){
  if(newCUT()){
      boolean result = testCase2();
      logTestResult("Script2",result &&   classInvariant());
      ((Timer)disposeOUT).pause();
      disposeOUT;
      return result;
  }else{
        OUT=null;
        return false;
  }
}

 protected boolean testCase2(){
   Timer OUT = (Timer) getOUT();
   OUT.start();
   for (int i = 0; i < 100000; i++{
       for (j = 0; j < 100000; j++{}
   }
   return tickReceived;
}
```

Figure 8.2 Selected TimerTester code

Design for Testability #2

After our discussion about testing threads, you should notice that Timer implements the TimeObservable interface.

Design Rule: In Java, with single inheritance, the root of every inheritance hierarchy should be an interface.

This allows the test harness, which must inherit from a tester parent class to also implement the interface. This is often useful as in the case for TimerTester, which needs to register itself with the OUT. This is the Java equivalent of the long time C++ design rule that the base class for any hierarchy should be abstract.

Design for Testability #3

It is not obvious from the code used in `TimerTester`, but the `Timer` class is very difficult to test. This is due to the following statement:

```
OUT = new Timer(new BricklesView());
```

The parameter to the constructor, BricklesView, requires most of the classes in the application: `BricklesGame`, `ArcadeGamePiece`, `StationaryObject`, `MovableObject`, `Puck`, `Paddle`, and `Brick`. These classes must be in the compiler's path before it can be constructed even though the reason those classes are aggregated into `BricklesView` has nothing to do with the actions of the time.

Design Rule: Wherever possible define a default constructor that can be used during unit testing without requiring dependencies on a large number of other classes. The default constructor need not be public.

In some cases, creating a default constructor in the class to be tested is a good design decision. In some cases it is not. With `Timer`, this was not possible because the `Timer` implementation assumes it has a reference to a `BricklesView` object and aborts its main loop when that reference is null. Since this object is a parameter to the only constructor, it is a reasonable precondition that the reference is not null.

Life-Cycle Testing

We have discussed using life-cycle testing in Chapter 6, and we will continue the discussion in Chapter 9, as a technique that is applicable at various levels of development. We need to first determine what life cycle to use and then develop test cases based on it. For a distributed system, this life cycle may be measured by the lifetime of the infrastructure components instantiated to support the system.

The test plan for the system should include a test run starting from nothing instantiated, followed by bringing the system up, executing a series of actions, and then bringing the system completely down. The following three important checks should be made to determine if this system test has succeeded:

- Did each of the actions carried out by the system complete successfully?

- Were all resources allocated by the system released after the system was terminated?

- Can the system successfully be restarted? (Or has the infrastructure stored a state that makes it impossible to restart?)

Life-Cycle Testing

A life-cycle approach to testing implies that a series of test cases will be selected so that whatever is being tested is exercised from its creation to its destruction. Typically, there are many paths through the complete life cycle. The test plan should select representative paths to provide maximum coverage. For a class, life-cycle testing means choosing a series of tests that construct an instance of the class, use it through a series of messages, and then destroy the object. An effective life-cycle test should validate more than just correct answers. It should also validate that the item being tested interacts correctly with its environment. For a class, checking that after destruction all acquired resources have been released is a useful validation. Also checking that other elements with which the tested piece interacted are in correct states is a good idea. For example, when a server crashes, the "Naming Service" for a CORBA object request broker (ORB) might be corrupted and revert to a default setup.

Models of Distribution

We now want to discuss testing programs that use some of the standard infrastructures for distributed systems.

Basic Client/Server Model

The client/server model in which multiple clients all have access to the server is the simplest model of distribution. The server is a single process and an indefinite number of client processes can request service from the server. This model has a single point of failure since all of the clients interact with the same server. This model gives a basic idea of a few of the testing issues for distributed systems, but a few systems raise issues that are more difficult than this model.

Testing implications:

1. Can the server deliver correct results to the correct client in the face of a steady load of a moderate number of requests simultaneously over an extended period of time? The server may occasionally send the answer to a request to the incorrect client. This set of tests can be modified to reflect the profile of expected requests in which the number fluctuates with some business cycle.

2. Can the server correctly handle a rapidly increasing load? The server may quickly degrade as the load increases, or it may abort. The test set should present a large number of test cases at increasing arrival rates.

Standard Models of Distribution

The simple client/server model has been generalized to allow the single point of failure of the client/server model to be eliminated. Multiple servers can provide the same service and a client can select which server to use. The early implementations of these models were error prone even in the hands of highly qualified developers because of the primitive pipe and socket structures that had to be manipulated. With the advent of object-oriented techniques, models were developed that abstracted away the networking details and reduced the number of errors. We will not go back and talk about testing the more primitive implementations. We will remain at the object level and assume that a commercial infrastructure is available to hide the communication details.

We will provide just a brief introduction to each of three standard models and then discuss how each supports or facilitates testing systems written using the model. Later, we will discuss the basic infrastructure for Internet applications.

CORBA

The Common Object Request Broker Architecture (CORBA) has been developed by the Object Management Group (OMG) as a standard architecture for distributed object systems. The central element in this architecture is an object request broker (ORB) that one object uses to communicate with other objects in the system. The standard infrastructure provided by a CORBA-compliant system provides services that allow one object to find other objects based on objects being requested, location, or load. The infrastructure also provides services needed to connect two objects written in different languages or objects that are executing on different types of machines. A number of vendors provide products that form the infrastructure for this model. This "standard architecture" does not totally specify an implementation so the software provided by different vendors have competitive differences such as faster throughput and a smaller footprint. CORBA is sufficiently mature so that many of these products have experienced many releases and can be considered "trusted." The CORBA standard is based on the following set of assumptions:

- The machines being linked by the infrastructure may have different operating systems and different memory layout.

- The components that comprise the distributed system may be written in different languages.

- The infrastructure may change its configuration based on the distribution of the objects and the types of machines in the network.

CORBA has the advantage in terms of flexibility. We will focus on this technology in the following examples although the techniques can be applied to the other models with slight modifications.

Testing implications:

■ Does the system work correctly regardless of the configuration of the infrastructure? Test plans should provide test cases that result in the expected variety of configurations of the infrastructure being tested.

■ Can the test cases be made more reusable by building them based on the services of the standard infrastructure? The infrastructure design is sufficiently mature so that the structure of the test cases should be very stable and the implementation should be mature. The test cases should be designed to use the infrastructure as much as possible.

■ Does a specific new release of the infrastructure integrate effectively with existing applications? There should be a regression test suite and test harness that allows new releases of the infrastructure to be tested prior to it being integrated into products.

DCOM

The Distributed Component Object Model (DCOM) is a standard developed and promoted by Microsoft. This infrastructure is freely distributed with the Windows operating system, thus making its cost a clear advantage. The DCOM "standard" is described in terms of standard interfaces containing specific methods rather than architectural generalities. Each standard interface provides a specific set of services. A single component may implement the services of several interfaces or several components may each implement the services of the same interface but in different ways.

The DCOM infrastructure supports the initial connection between components but not as an ongoing part of the application. This reduces the layers through which messages must flow and increases the throughput. However, the standard is largely limited to Intel-compatible machines. This eliminates the need for any type of translation or interfacing services at a cost of the types of systems that can be included in the system. DCOM is a low-level technique that requires an understanding of low-level details and requires the developer to make a number of detailed decisions correctly. Some tools are emerging that automate some of the implementation process and reduce the number of errors.

Testing implications:

■ Did the developer correctly align the required unique identifiers at various places in the various components? Test cases should be written to utilize all the various components to ensure that all needed connections can be made.

■ Does each component implement the required interfaces? Test cases again should utilize all of the available components to ensure that all services are available and perform the expected functions.

■ Do the implementations of the standard interfaces provide the correct behavior? This implies there should be a set of tests defined for each standard interface. That set of tests can be applied to each server that implements the corresponding interface.

RMI

The Remote Method Invocation (RMI) package in Java provides a simplified distributed environment that assumes that no matter what machines or what type of machines are connected, they will all be running a Java virtual machine. This homogeneous environment has a structure that is similar to CORBA but is simpler due to the less flexible assumptions. A registry object is provided and all objects participating in the distributed system must know which port the registry listens to for messages.

The latest version of RMI uses the Internet Inter-Orb Protocol (IIOP) to allow RMI objects and CORBA objects to work together. But more about this in the following general model.

Testing implications:

■ Which CORBA test patterns can be used in RMI-based systems? Test cases may be structured the same as many CORBA test cases.

Comparisons and Implications

These three models emphasize the prominent role of interfaces in object-oriented systems in general and distributed systems in particular. Distributed objects advertise services by listing their interfaces with the naming service of the infrastructure. The implication is that functional tests can be organized by interfaces. In particular, in DCOM applications, many classes may implement the same interface and the reuse of the tests for a specific interface will be high.

Distributed object systems are based on a relatively small number of standards. Each model that we have discussed has a more or less formal standard, at least to the extent of standard design patterns. Tests based on these standards have the potential to be reused many times on a single project and across projects in a development organization.

A Generic Distributed-Component Model

As we present testing techniques for distributed components, we will generalize about the architecture and infrastructure for the system. Our specific examples will come from CORBA. We have even abandoned the terms "client" and "server" because they tend to have very rigid architectural connotations for some people. In a distributed object system, any provider of service will almost invariably also be requesting service from some other object.

Basic Architecture

In Figure 8.3 we illustrate the basic architecture of a distributed system. The major action occurs when the **service requester** sends a message to the **service provider**. That is certainly the intent of each test case. The request is first sent to the surrogate object that is local to the requester so the requester does not handle any of the distribution semantics. The surrogate contacts the communication infrastructure and passes on the request. The communication infrastructure may actually have to instantiate the service provider, but it eventually obtains a reference to the provider from an **object locator** service and passes along the request. The request may be channeled through a **requester surrogate** so that the provider is also protected from the details of distribution. The return, if any, follows the route back.

At this level basically all three models are the same, although DCOM would return the result directly to the requester. As we discuss the components of the architecture, remember that an object can be, and often is, both a requester and a provider.

Requester

The **requester** participates in the distributed system as a stimulus. As such, its behaviors have been previously tested using the class testing techniques that we have already discussed with one exception: timing. If the requester sends any asynchronous messages (one-way messages in CORBA), the test cases must investigate the effect of the length of the time it takes to receive a reply. That is, when an asynchronous message is sent, the sender immediately proceeds to other business. The implementation of the sender may be written to expect an

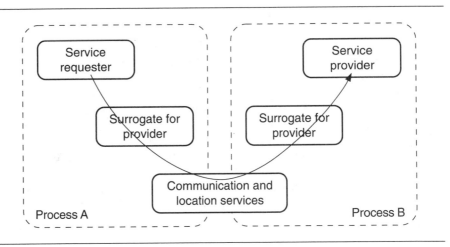

Figure 8.3 Generic architecture

answer to the message within a certain amount of computation, but the implementation may not be properly written to wait for that answer if it is not received in the expected time. Test cases should be written to test this interaction under various load conditions, thereby introducing different amounts of latency (delay) in the communication.

The requester also participates in the interaction tests once the provider has been class tested using the specialized techniques discussed in the next section. The focus of these tests is the protocol between the requester and providers. Remember from Chapter 6 that the protocol describes the complete set of messages sent between two objects to accomplish an identifiable task. This is a separate phase of testing because there are often multiple providers of the same service. The protocol test suite and the individual test cases can be reused every time a new provider for a given protocol is added to inventory. The protocol test suite provides a life-cycle approach to testing the interactions.

Provider

The provider is the central figure in a distributed interaction. It performs behaviors and, in some cases, returns information to the requester. The complete interface of the provider can be tested using the basic class testing techniques discussed previously. Those behaviors that are expected to be invoked by other distributed objects will require specialized testing that we will describe in the next section.

The provider is registered with the infrastructure along with information about the services that it provides. In some cases, the provider may not be an object waiting actively in memory for a request to be received. It is first instantiated, and then the request is forwarded to it. This can be the source of timing differences. Any provider that can be dynamically instantiated upon request should be exercised using test cases starting both from instantiated and noninstantiated scenarios.

Stubs and Skeletons

A **stub** is the surrogate for the provider in the requester process. A **skeleton** is the surrogate on the requester side. The stub keeps the requester from knowing about the semantics of the infrastructure. Some implementations of these infrastructures are intelligent enough to reconfigure themselves depending on whether the two objects are actually in the same process, in different processes on the same machine, or on different machines with different architectures.

As it reconfigures itself, the infrastructure will add or remove stubs and skeletons or other method calls. This changes the path through which a request must travel. Interaction test suites should be designed to execute a set of tests over the path corresponding to each possible configuration.

Local and Remote Interfaces

The interface of a distributed object is often divided into local and remote interfaces. The remote interface is the specification of those services that may be requested by an object that is outside of the process in which the provider is located. Those behaviors specified in the local interface can only be accessed by objects in the same process.

The local interface can be tested using the usual class testing techniques that we have already discussed. The remote interface can be tested by local test harnesses as an initial step but additional testing requiring a specialized environment is still needed.

Specifying Distributed Objects

Interface Definition Language

The specification for service providers is usually written in an interface definition language (IDL). Since they are only for specification, the IDLs are simpler than a programming language. The IDL specification provides several pieces of information that are useful for testing purposes:

- **signature**—The main portion of the IDL specification is the usual signature for a method. This includes the name of the method, the types of each of the parameters, and the type of the return object, if any. The standard techniques for sampling values for each of these parameters should be followed in constructing test cases.

- **one-way**—This designation signals an asynchronous message. Testing messages with this attribute requires that the test be conducted over a complete life cycle. There is the possibility that the requester will need the requested information before the provider sends it. There is also the possibility that the message will result in an exception being thrown by the provider. Tests should specifically investigate whether such exceptions are caught in the correct object.

- **in, out**—This attribute of a parameter defines whether the requester is to provide this information or whether it should expect the parameter to be modified by the provider. The tests of a method that specifies an out parameter must locate the returned object (because most object-oriented languages do not handle this case gracefully) and must verify that it has the correct state.

Traditional Pre- and Postconditions and Invariants

We have already presented techniques for building tests from traditional pre- and postconditions, so we will not repeat them here. Distributed components should be designed not to know their location relative to other components; however, the components do have to know about an expanded set of possible errors. The postconditions are expanded to include exceptions for scenarios such as a service that isn't available from the specified provider, a provider that doesn't respond in time, and a requester that provides an invalid address. As with any postcondition, each clause, such as an invalid address, should be covered by a specific test case.

Implicit Tests

Any method that sends a request to invoke a method on a provider may receive a "Provider not found" exception from the infrastructure. Developers are seldom patient enough to write this out as a possible postcondition of every method that causes such an exception to be generated. It is usually the case that there is a set of exceptions that many of the methods in a class may provoke. This is just one example of what we refer to as **implicit specifications**. These should be matched by implicit test cases. For a distributed system, some appropriate implicit test cases would include the following:

- Test that a requester can handle a "Provider not found" exception.
- Test that a requester can handle a "Provider busy" time-out exception.
- Test that a requester can handle a null provider reference (obviously any null pointer is a problem, but some infrastructures invalidate a pointer after some amount of inactivity).
- Test that a requester can handle a null "out" parameter.

These test cases should be made as general as possible so that it is easy to apply them to each method that fits the implicit specification. The tests should be included in a test checklist for the type of class being constructed.

For each "domain" there is a different list. User-interface objects will have implicit specifications about events and displaying. These should be captured in lists as part of the project test strategy and delivered to the developers and integration testers.

Temporal Logic

Time is one of the critical issues in distributed systems, but it is not handled well with most specification techniques. We have found that interval temporal logic is useful in expressing temporal relationships. The operators of temporal logic allow concepts of time ordering to be expressed and reasoned about. Interval temporal logic allows concepts about time periods, as opposed to specific points in time, to be expressed. For example, the before(a,b) states that in the time period before event b happened, condition a was true.

The time periods about which we are reasoning must be appropriate to the problem at hand. Two distinctly different time periods are used in computer-based systems. One is real calendar time that is represented in domain objects. This is usually in the form of dates. The second type of time period is execution time. In object-oriented systems, this is often related to the lifetime of an object. This will be where we focus most of our discussion.

Temporal logic operators have been used implicitly for a long time. The always operator is an implicit part of every class invariant. Remember that the class invariant is a statement of those properties that are *always* true. The precondition is implicitly a before condition.

A few of the temporal operators that we have found useful include the following:

- before(a, b) a is true before event b occurs
- until(a, b) a is true until event b occurs
- after(a, b) a is true after event b occurs

An interval temporal operator applies for some period of time. Therefore, a test that seeks to verify that the implementation satisfies such a requirement must cover this interval. So how do you test something like the invariant

$$always(x >= 0)$$

We handle this by repeatedly testing the validity of the invariant statement during all of our class tests. Always is interpreted as anytime that there is an instance object alive. Part of the behavioral specification for Timer objects might state the following:

> *After it is started, the* Timer *instance sends* tick() *messages to every registered listener until it is stopped.*

It is fairly easy to test this at the class level, but it does require special handling. In the case of Timer, the test harness should inherit from TimeObservable so that it can be registered with the Timer instance. The test harness would do the following:

- Register itself with the Timer instance.
- Check that no tick() messages are being received.
- Send the start() message to the Timer instance.
- Check that tick() messages are being received.
- Send the stop() message to the Timer instance.
- Verify that no tick() messages are being received.

This basic test case should be repeated for a variety of time intervals between the various messages. A StopWatchTimer would be used to tell the test harness when to move to the next step.

To test that a temporal constraint is not violated, you can use two approaches. The first is to encapsulate the object on which the constraint is written. Then any access to the state about which the constraint applies can be monitored. After the access, the validity of the constraint is checked. The disadvantage of this is the possibility of altering the operation of the object by the instrumentation. We will consider this in the next section.

The second approach, as previously illustrated with Timer objects, is to sample over the interval about which the constraint is written. The intervals over which we normally sample would be the following:

■ an interval in which a beginning time and an ending time are specified

■ from instance creation until a specified time

■ from a specified time until object destruction

Note that when we say a "specified time," it is usually specified as the occurrence of a specific event. The specified time is just whenever that event occurs.

Class and Object Invariants

We would like to make a distinction here between the class and object invariants that parallels our earlier distinction between class objects and instance objects. There can be a "class invariant" that corresponds to the class object and an "instance invariant" that corresponds to the instance objects. Basically, an invariant is any statement that should always be true when the subject of the invariant is in a steady state. We can also have system invariants. For example, the Singleton design pattern requires that there should only ever be at most one instance of the class. The class invariant would be

```
number of instances < = 1
```

The instance invariant would be related to the semantics of the domain. The instance object has no idea about the number of instances that can be created and its invariant shouldn't address that issue.

Please note that this is not accepted terminology in the industry, but hopefully it will make you think about the precise expression of invariants.

Temporal Test Patterns

In this section we will present three test patterns written in an informal style for the sake of space.

When a postcondition or a semantic description includes constraints written using temporal logic, new test conditions must be satisfied. In general, temporal constraints impose time requirements on the testing process. As a result, the parallel architecture for component testing (PACT) objects that exercise these tests will need to maintain their own threads of control so that they can independently act over an interval of time. In most cases those intervals are not based on clock time (although in a real-time system they might be), but rather the interval is from some event such as a method that has been completing until some event occurs. The PACT object will have to spawn observer objects to monitor the OUT.

The following are three of the operators that were previously defined and descriptions of how we have been successful in testing them.

Eventually(p)

Eventually, the postcondition of b.x(), p, will be true, but the temporal constraint is part of the postcondition of a.y(). It states a condition that will become true sometime in the future. The "future" is relative to the lifetime of a.y(). Anything that happens after a.y() terminates is in a's future.

Testing this condition obviously requires delaying the decision as to whether p is satisfied. The test must be conducted in the future of a.y(). In this situation, the PACT object for a is placed in a context that will last as long as the context for b. The PACT object has a separate thread. Periodically the a PACT object wakes up and sends messages to b to determine whether b.x() has completed execution. When it is determined that b.x() has occurred, the PACT

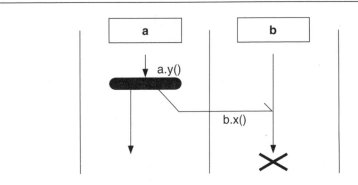

Figure 8.4 Eventually(b.x())

object logs the fact and uses the results from the other portions of the postcondition of a.y() to determine whether the entire postcondition is satisfied. It then logs that result as well.

The PACT object continues to interrogate the b object until either b.x() occurs and p can be evaluated or b is deleted. If it is still checking when b is deleted, the PACT object logs a failure.

Until(p,q)

Until b.x(), b is in a state s_1. This is stated as until(s_1, b.x()). To validate that this constraint holds, we need to test from the point that this assertion remains active until the b.x() event occurs. The PACT object is "fired off" at the moment the constraint becomes effective. It then periodically wakes up and checks the condition.

In the case of until, we need to determine that the condition "b is in s_1" is true every instant in time "until" the occurrence of the specified event. With eventually, we only evaluate the truth value of the condition once, after the event occurs, but with until we must continuously evaluate the condition "until" the specified event. If it evaluates to true every time until the terminal event, then the constraint is satisfied.

We obviously can't check the truth value continuously or no other work would get done in the system! If we check only at the time that the event occurs, we can't be certain what value the constraint had previous to that time, and the constraint doesn't say what should happen after the event has happened. The PACT object tester has to check previous to the event occurring. Checking once is hardly sufficient. Basically, we set the interval when the PACT object is created. The shorter the interval, the more certain the evaluation.

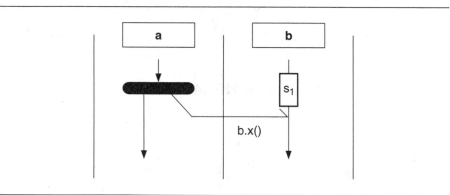

Figure 8.5 Until(b.x(),s_1)

Always (p)

The always temporal operator is the most heavily used of the operators because every class invariant is essentially an always constraint. The always constraint says that at any point in the b swimlane, the logical constraint statement p is true.

Always as a class invariant refers to a time interval that corresponds to the lifetime of each instance of the class. As we stated about until, we cannot test continuously. We compromise by sampling periodically and evaluating the truth value at each time. In Chapter 5, we talked about testing for the class invariant at the end of each test case. This is the sampling technique we use as a default: test with each test method invocation. The potential problem is that a test case may cause several methods to be invoked. This is why we even call the invariant evaluation method multiple times in a test case method if the test case directly invokes multiple methods on the OUT.

Each temporal operator imposes different testing conditions, but each time the operator is used it follows the same basic pattern. The basic principles we have presented here should provide a basis for you to create your own test patterns.

A Test Environment

Class Testing

Class testing of distributed components often requires a special environment such as the one illustrated in Figure 8.7. The purpose of this environment is to provide a means of trapping messages to the OUT so that issues such as the timing of messages can be analyzed and changes of state can be logged.

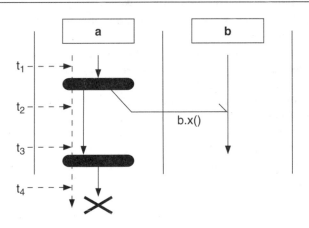

Figure 8.6 The always temporal operator

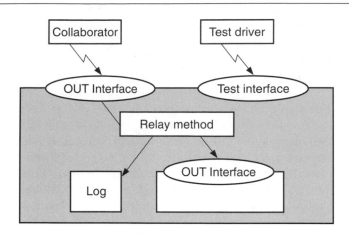

Figure 8.7 Class testing wrapper

This wrapper is an object that simply encapsulates the OUT. We have used various types of implementations to automatically extract the interface of the OUT and copy it into the wrapper. The wrapper object can be injected into a larger system context and behaves just as the OUT as far as the larger system is concerned. The wrapper has fairly standard implementations of each of the OUT interface methods. Each method does whatever logging is wanted and then forwards the message on to the real implementation in the OUT. The return path will return control to the wrapper. At that time, the method will validate the state in the OUT, log the results, and return the object returned from the OUT.

This approach invades the larger system and is not considered to be testing that context. The objective is testing only the OUT.

This approach is also useful for testing the reordering of asynchronous messages. The wrapper object can simply receive and hold $message_1$ until $message_2$ is received. It can then forward $message_2$ prior to forwarding $message_1$.

One value of this approach is that it allows complex computations from other parts of the system that would be difficult to provide from a test harness, and allows them to be utilized in testing a class. The wrapper can be built automatically except for the implementation of the OUT methods in the wrapper, but even these use functionality in the wrapper class for logging, checking, and other functionality.

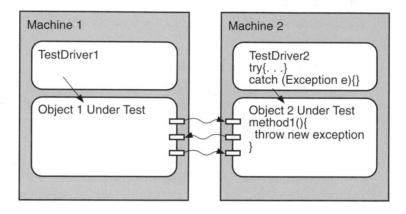

Figure 8.8 An interaction test

Interaction Testing

Testing the interaction between two objects that are distributed in separate processes from each other uses a configuration such as the one shown in Figure 8.8. As we have previously discussed in Chapter 6, testing a complete protocol is one important aspect of interaction testing. In a distributed system, one of the testing questions that must be addressed is whether messages are really received in that order, even if they are sent in the sequence described by the protocol.

In the testing environment shown in Figure 8.8, the presence of a distributed test architecture allows many operations to be done locally. That is, when test driver$_1$ initiates a test, it informs test driver$_2$ which test has been executed. Test driver$_2$ can then verify, on machine$_2$, that the portion of the test running on machine$_2$ has been successfully completed. It then informs test driver$_1$. This greatly reduces the amount of information that must flow from one machine to another and speeds up the testing process.

Test Cases

Much work has been done to make distributed system infrastructures as abstract as possible so that users have little to worry about with respect to the distribution semantics. Each vendor works to make its product conform to the standard it is addressing. These two factors make it possible to have a set of model-specific and then application-specific test cases.

Model-specific Tests

Each standard model results in its own set of design patterns. This in turn results in a set of test patterns.

Tests for the Basic Client/Server Model

We have already described a couple of types of tests for the client/server model; however, the basic client/server model has a number of variations. In the following test pattern, the design pattern under test is a widely used variant named *distributed callbacks*.

Problem: The synchronous messaging between two objects is modified to be asynchronous messaging by adding a Callback object. The client constructs a Callback object and sends it a request and the address of a server. The Callback object submits the request to the server synchronously. When an answer is received, the Callback object forwards the answer to the Client object.

Context: The code for the design under test is being used because the designer wants to be able to do other work while this message is being answered. Potentially, the original thread will complete its work before the answer is ready.

Forces: Functional tests may pass when executed once, but race conditions can lead to inconsistent results so repeating the same tests may obtain different results. Numerous factors affect the visibility of failures due to race conditions.

Solution: Construct test suites that execute each test case multiple times. The test suite should adjust factors to make race conditions more visible. The system should be set back to its original state after each test. The tests should include the following (see Figure 8.10):

- A test in which the server returns the expected result almost immediately.

- A test in which the client is deleted before the callback fires.

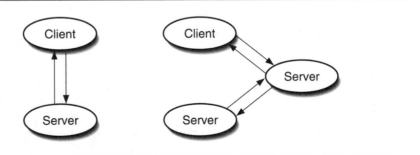

Figure 8.9 Adding callbacks to a client/server pattern

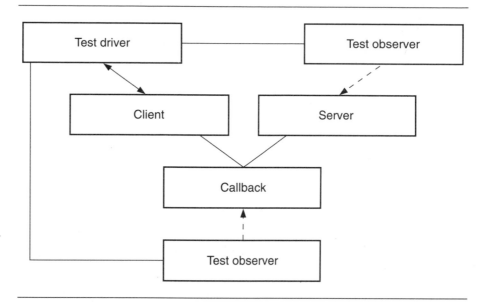

Figure 8.10 Testing the distributed callback pattern

- ■ A test in which the server fires an exception.
- ■ A test in which the server is deleted before returning a value.

Tests for the Generic Distribution Model

Now let's return to the generic distributed architecture and consider some tests. To organize this we have completed test plans for the Provider and the Requester objects, as shown in Figure 8.11 and Figure 8.12. These are not specific to the semantics of each, but they do address the general function of each component.

Testing Every Assumption

The different models of distribution make very different assumptions about the type of application or the deployment environment. These should be the focus of tests. Some of these should be done during the Guided Inspection phase while others will have to wait for an executable.

Component Test Plan

Component Name Provider	Tracking Number TBS
Developer(s) Dave Sykes	Tester(s) John D. McGregor

Objectives for This Component

This component is intended for use in a distributed system that follows a standard model of distribution. The provider provides behaviors to other objects in response to requests. The provider has a specified set of services that it provides.

Guided Inspection Requirements

A guided inspection of the design model for a distributed system should check that the provider's set of services is complete with respect to its role as a domain object in the analysis model. The provider's specification must make public those services that are consistent with the needs of the requester objects. The signatures of methods must be correct with respect to the domain model.

Building and Retaining Test Suites

The test suites shall be prepared in accordance with project standards. A `ProviderTester` class shall contain the test driver. That class will inherit from the `GenericModelTester` class that is specific to the distribution model being used. Every provider that provides a certain protocol can use the same test cases so these should be grouped into a separate object and aggregated into the `ProviderTester`.

Specification-based Test Cases

Every provider provides a set of services based on the model of distribution. Test cases based on these services are in the `GenericModelTester` class. Test cases based on the application-specific services should have test cases in `ProviderTester`.

Implementation-based Test Cases

The test cases should meet the usual path and code coverage criteria.

Interaction Test Cases

The provider should be interacted with a representative sample of the requester objects that will request services. Each major protocol should be tested with at least one requester that participates in the protocol.

State-based Test Cases

The provider may be in one of several states when a requester makes its request and may receive requests from multiple providers at the same time. The provider should be taken through its complete life cycle using all of the protocols necessary.

Figure 8.11 A component test plan for the provider

Component Test Plan

Component Name Requester	Tracking Number TBS
Developer(s) Dave Sykes	Tester(s) John D. McGregor

Objectives for This Component

The requester has the role, in a distributed system, of initiating actions by requesting services from provider objects. It manages the information that is returned from the provider in response to a request.

Guided Inspection Requirements

A guided inspection of the design model for a distributed system should check that the requester has access to the complete set of services that it needs. If the requester uses multiple providers, the inspection should be certain that the various providers provide consistent results for the same service. The inspection should ensure that each requester method uses the correct service at the correct time.

Building and Retaining Test Suites

The test suites shall be prepared in accordance with project standards. A `RequesterTester` class shall contain the test driver. In that class, operations shall be provided to execute functional, structural, and interaction test cases. Reporting shall be in conformance with project standards. The test class will be available to application developers as interaction tests in their application.

Specification-based Test Cases

Construct pre- and postconditions for each method in the documented API. Execute test cases for every clause of each postcondition of every method.

Implementation-based Test Cases

The test cases should meet the usual coverage criteria. Use the techniques from Chapter 5 and Chapter 6 to select and construct tests.

Interaction Test Cases

The main interaction tests will be with the providers that the requester uses. The focus should be on complete protocols between the requester and each of its providers. Artificial delays should be inserted to study the effects of timing.

State-based Test Cases

Requesters will have a set of states related to being distributed, such as being connected to the infrastructure and disconnecting as well. A complete test suite will exercise these states as well as the states related to the semantics of the application.

Figure 8.12 A component test plan for the requester

Language Dependence Issues

The RMI model assumes that the part of the system for which it is being used is completely written in Java. CORBA makes no assumptions about the languages of even two interacting requesters and providers. Specific tests should be designed where two components written in different languages interface even through the infrastructure. The code of the infrastructure is tested and will handle the transfer correctly; however, the application code may not be correct. Depending on the infrastructure, the programmers have some degree of control (hence the possibility of mistakes exists) and must manually be certain that the data types used in the two classes are compatible. The documentation for the infrastructure may do a less than perfect job of explaining what is possible. We recently experienced errors when passing an array between a Java requester and a C++ provider due to incorrect documentation. Test cases not only detected a failure, but they also provided a pointer to the cause of the problem.

During guided inspection, the inspectors should determine that the correct mappings are being used. CORBA, for example, uses a set of types that are very compatible with most C++ types. The variation between CORBA types and Java types is much greater. Java also does not directly provide support for "out" parameters. The inspection should determine that return objects are being handled properly.

Platform Independence Issues

Basically, all of the models of distribution are independent of the platform on which they run, although DCOM is used primarily on Intel-compatible platforms at this time. However, the bigger issue of deployment environment remains critical. Implicit requirements about the size of available memory or processor speed can still cause the software to work differently on one specific machine from another.

One technique we have found useful is to provide deployment tests with a product release. Each user can then run these tests after installation to determine whether the application is operating correctly. We will discuss this in more detail in Chapter 9.

Infrastructure Tests

The infrastructure delivered from a vendor is "trusted" code that will not be subjected to detailed testing. There are situations beyond the control of the vendor that can corrupt the infrastructure. For example, the stubs and skeletons needed in a CORBA implementation are produced automatically by a compiler for the IDL specification. Often developers will edit these default implementations. This is no longer trusted code. There should be tests that will at least exercise all of the modified code.

Compatibility Tests

When a new version of the infrastructure is released, compatibility tests should be run to determine if modifications in the application are required. This is usually done by a designated group on a project. This is the same type of testing needed for new versions of frameworks or even tools.

Testing the Recovery of Failures

One of the critical differences in a distributed system is the possibility of partial failures of the system due to the breakdown of one of the machines hosting the system. As a part of the deployment testing effort, the following type of test case should be built using the distributed test harness illustrated in Figure 8.8. A system configuration should be constructed in which there is a "main" machine on which the locator portion of the infrastructure is running (this may not be possible for all types of systems), and for which a server is instantiated on a specific machine. Once the server has registered with the infrastructure, the test driver on the machine containing the server should display a dialog box on that machine that requests that the tester remove the network cable from the machine. Once the user selects OK on the dialog box, this test driver would send a message to the main test driver. The main test driver would then initiate a sequence in which the application would attempt to contact the server that is now unavailable. The ability to recognize that the server is not available and to handle it gracefully is one of the implicit requirements we discussed in Implicit Tests, on page 288. The correctness of the implementation relies on the experience of the individual developer as opposed to detailed specifications.

Dynamic Modification of Infrastructure

CORBA infrastructure implementations provide the means by which it can be modified during program execution. One vendor, for example, provides the ability to add or remove "filters" from the pathway between requester and provider during execution. These modifications change the configuration of the system and can change the timing and execution path. Since these modifications usually occur in specific situations, tests should be constructed that exercise each possible configuration given the dynamic components that are available.

Logic-Specific Test Cases

The types of logic defects that can occur in a distributed system are not that different from a sequential system with a couple of exceptions.

Different Sequences of Events

With asynchronous messages between processes, events may occur in a variety of sequences. A requester may send several requests in a short period of time and not wait for any of them to complete. The order in which these requests return can vary considerably from one execution to another. If the design assumption is that it makes no difference in what order the replies are received, the testing obligation is to test as many of the combinations as possible. The statistical sampling techniques discussed in Chapter 6 can be used to determine the minimum number of possible tests.

Requested Object Unavailable

Many systems allow users to enter the names of providers or other resources. Users may misspell names, omit a portion of the name, or request a resource that once was available but no longer exists. This is certainly a common occurrence with Internet browsers. It is slightly different from the previous case in which the object is registered but not available due to machine failure. In the partial failure case the infrastructure returns a null pointer, whereas with this case the infrastructure may throw an exception. This type of fault and the test cases to detect it only make sense in the event that the provider's identification is acquired dynamically. The testing objective here is to determine whether the exception is caught in an appropriate location in the requester, and whether the application is able to abort the operation gracefully and give the user another chance to give the address of the provider or some other appropriate response.

Test Case Summary

Use the test suite giving the following coverages:

1. every method of each standard interface
2. every SYN-path,
3. every logical control path

Apply the test suite repeatedly using variations in the following factors:

1. load of applications running on the same systems
2. load of user input into the overall system
3. connections between machines
4. configurations of the infrastructure

The Ultimate Distributed System—The Internet

The Internet represents a very large and dynamic distributed system. Servers are added to and removed from this network continuously. Applications that live in this environment must be able to operate in the presence of partial failures in the form of missing systems or nonexistent addresses on machines. Some of these systems form basic business environments for the company running the Web site. These e-commerce systems have specific and stringent requirements for reliability and security. In this section we will consider the issues specific to this type of environment. It will not be a complete overview, but we will provide an outline of how these systems should be tested.

The "Web pages" that are displayed in the browser include both data, in the form of marked up text using HTML or XML, and behaviors, in the form of scripted functions using languages such as JavaScript. These pages often allow input from the user, perform computations, and format and present output. The browser is an extensible application that can sense when the data that it has been provided requires an additional application in order to handle it properly. These "plug-in" modules add functionality dynamically so that the browser is a changing execution environment.

So what does testing a Web page mean? It means testing that the intended display is presented to the user; that input is accepted and forwarded to a waiting application correctly; and that all actions are performed as intended. The display can fail in terms of the following:

- incorrect fonts being displayed

- mismatch of coordinates so that a figure is not visible

- the wrong language is used or different languages are used for different sections of text

- a mismatch between the platform configuration and the browser display attributes

There are pieces of code embedded into the display file as well as separate script files. Browsers can directly execute code written in languages such as Java. The Java version of *Brickles* runs as an applet in a browser. The browser and the standard plug-ins are "trusted" code. The testing objective is the content of the display data plus embedded and external script files. Failures include the following:

- incorrect or insufficient permissions to execute code in a specific file

- an inability to create a file when necessary

- the usual failures associated with any function such as computing the wrong answer

- inability to locate resources during execution, such as missing bitmaps

Several pieces of code may be added to the browser by a single page. This may include the Acroread PDF file viewer, a RealPlayer video player, and even the Visigenics CORBA ORB. Once loaded by a page, the code may remain loaded while other pages are loaded and other plug-ins are added. It is impossible to test all possible combinations of programs for interactions. However, it is possible to construct tests that result in different combinations of code being loaded into the browser environment. You should analyze the source listing for each of your pages and construct paths through the pages that lead to different combinations of plug-ins being loaded.

GUI versus API Testing

Earlier we discussed the differences between testing an application from the GUI or from its API. The API level is chosen less often in this situation because functions embedded in a Web page are so visually oriented that it takes less effort to simply use the GUI. The display text can be parsed and validated as syntactically correct. Then sufficient tests are constructed that execute the script code to achieve levels of coverage similar to that of a programming language.

Web Servers

The browser and Web pages sometimes work in conjunction with an application server, as shown in Figure 8.13, to invoke other applications. These servers are generic software applications available from vendors; therefore, after an

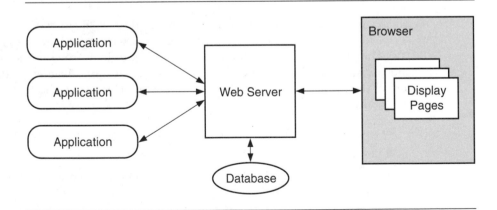

Figure 8.13 Web server architecture

acceptance test, they will be "trusted" code. The server incorporates a database that stores both the content of the pages and the data produced by users of the system.

These systems automate certain aspects of customer service. A page might accept input into a customer order form, create a client record, invoke applications that automatically generate an account number and password, and then e-mail the account information to the customer.

These systems are designed to be very modular. The application programs can be changed with no modifications to the Web server and only minor changes to the Web pages. The Web pages are changed by simply changing the data, which is often stored in XML format.

Testing these systems involves two facets. First, do the scripts do what they are intended to do? There have been many versions of the browsers and their scripting languages in a very short time. As a result, unless you are deploying browsers into a managed environment in which everyone runs the same version, the tests should be run on the different combinations of the browser version and the script language version. Frames and tables are examples of features that have varied radically from one environment to another and have resulted in very different display results. Many developers include alternative paths depending on whether the browser supports frames or not. There should be test cases to cover these different possibilities.

Second, is the current data correct and in the form expected by the applications and Web pages? Testing this aspect requires scenarios in which the various data displays of the Web site are combined with the types of data that the user would enter. This analysis follows the same process as described in Using Scenarios to Construct Test Cases on page 317 in Chapter 9. The data types for each entry are analyzed, equivalence classes are defined, and values are sampled from each class.

Life-Cycle Testing of Internet Applications

Life-cycle testing, in this context, means testing across a set of user transactions. These should be selected to utilize the complete set of back-end applications. The life-cycle perspective will typically span several different platforms including the user's system, the Web site, and the supplier applications. For example, with an e-commerce system, we would begin with the presentation of material to the user. Is it presented accurately? Many of the pages are constructed using XML trees of information. It is possible for the program to incorrectly associate descriptions and prices. After presentation comes the acceptance of a customer order. This involves the Web page to receive and handle events and data, and it involves the database to manipulate inventory and to record the order. The application must allow the user to modify the order by adding or deleting items. Other applications are used to order the goods from suppliers so that they search for new orders, bundle all the items for each supplier, and interact electronically with the supplier applications. The test suite should identify multiple interlocking life cycles based on the actors for the system. The client actor has a life cycle of creating an order while the supplier actor has a life cycle of creating a different type of order.

There are significant interaction testing activities in two dimensions in this example. First, complete systems written by different teams must interact. The Web site software itself also integrates several different technologies. The example system probably includes HTML, JavaScript, XML, and Java technologies. There are issues about the compatibility of data types as well as the timing of events and limiting their effects.

One of the most important tests for a Web application is to construct test cases that stress the Web site. There are tools that make it easy to clone Web pages and invoke multiple operations on the server. The stress test should be designed to accurately reproduce the expected profile of use. There should also be tests of the server's capability to limit the number of connections in a controlled manner (display a message) rather than in a catastrophic manner (server crashes).

Perhaps the most important function of a Web page is to recognize that a request it has made has not been fulfilled. Browsers set timers to monitor every connection that must be made to another resource such as other pages and servers. Since the browser is "trusted" code, we are not testing whether the failure to obtain a resource will be recognized. We are testing whether the scripts in the page handle that failure appropriately.

What Haven't We Said?

The important areas of performance and security have not been covered. There is a growing number of tools devoted to those topics because of their implications for e-commerce. As the second major wave of e-commerce sites are deployed these areas will be a particular focus. Research is being conducted and some sophisticated models are being developed that described performance characteristics. Maybe we can cover this in the next edition.

Summary

Distributed objects are first of all objects and need much of the same type of testing as other objects. One of the principal differences between distributed and nondistributed systems is the importance of timing. Timing is influenced by the sequence of statements in a method, the scheduling algorithms of the operating system, and the number of objects and their relationships. An initial question is whether the design sufficiently expresses the timing assumptions made by the design. The main testing question is whether the implementation is sufficiently flexible to operate correctly in the face of all legitimate orderings of execution. We have discussed temporal logic as a means of being expressive, and some instrumentation that allows us to investigate the effects of various sequences.

Exercises

8-1. Examine the distribution infrastructure being used in your project. Determine the conditions under which the infrastructure changes its structure, and the way the paths of request change. Identify a set of initial test case conditions that would cover all possible configurations.

8-2. Construct a test suite for a concurrent application by identifying the places at which SYN-events occur and defining SYN-sequences to do test cases.

8-3. Study any software that you have developed using design patterns and select one of the patterns to study or read a design pattern description. How did you or would you test the software developed using the design pattern? Write the description in the test pattern style.

8-4. Identify a Web site to be tested. Based on the application on the Web site, describe a set of actions that represent a typical session, from start to finish, that a visitor might participate in on the site. Include as many of the data input pages as possible. Write test scenarios that cover all of these possibilities.

Testing Systems

Chapter **9**

We have reached the point in the development process in which the word **testing** is used in its popular sense. But even this meaning has changed. *System testing* usually refers to the testing of a completed application to determine that it provides all of the behaviors required of the application. We will consider a somewhat broader definition that encompasses completed increments that provide some degree of end-user functionality. We have already discussed this level of testing in Chapter 4 for the case when code has not yet been written. In this chapter we assume that executable code is available.

This level of testing has been seen as "throwing it over the wall" to an unrelated group after the development is completed. However, in an incremental development effort, system testing usually refers to successive rounds of testing end-user functionality with extensive feedback and interaction between the development staff and the test team. The test plan and the development plan must coordinate this interaction.

The words "system" and "application" are used as synonyms by some and distinct concepts by others. When used as distinct concepts, **system** refers to a "complete" environment including the program being developed, that is, the **application**, and the operating environment including the operating system, virtual machines, Web browsers, and hardware. We will not make the distinction. We will use the two terms synonymously to mean the complete environment.

Originally we said that testing was a search for defects. Well, that was the truth, but not the whole truth. The focus for testing at this point in the development process shifts from a search for defects that lead to program failures (although some will still be found) to a search for defects that are variances between the actual operation of the system and the requirements for the system. Remember that we took this same viewpoint back in Chapter 4 when we tested the system-level analysis and design models. At that time we investigated whether the analysis and design models were a complete, consistent, and correct solution to the problem stated in the requirements. This early round of validation reduces the number of "variance-from-requirements" defects found during the "end-of-development" round of testing.

This testing phase may be a multilevel activity. For software that will be executed on a processor embedded within special purpose hardware, you should first test the software on a simulator of some type before looking at the actual hardware. The scope of the "system" will also change as development progresses. Eventually "system" test can be applied to the integration of several embedded applications into a single system. For example, many modern automobiles have a number of controllers located in assemblies such as the sunroof or the automatic windows. These controllers communicate with each other in some cases and receive data from sensors in places where there are no controllers.

There are several other types of testing that occur at this point in the development process. These are related directly or indirectly to the requirements. Performance, security, load, and deployment testing activities are all speciality tests conducted under certain circumstances. We will consider these activities in the context of object-oriented systems in this chapter.

Many development contracts call for an **acceptance test** that is performed by the customer prior to the development activity that's officially ending. This testing is carried out in the deployment environment at the customer site. The customer performs the test and determines whether the product is performing satisfactorily from her point of view. Acceptance testing is a special kind of system testing.

In this chapter we will continue the work from Chapter 4, only now we will assume that code is available. We will consider strategies for selecting the most effective test cases, and we will consider the effect of different testing strategies on the growth of the reliability of the system. But first we must plan.

Defining the System Test Plan

The system test plan is a more formal and more comprehensive document than the component test plans we have been using. In many cases it will be reviewed by the customers. In Figure 3.14 we listed the sections in the IEEE test plan format. We are not going to discuss every section, but we will cover some of the sections and we will complete some of the sections for the *Brickles* application. We will touch on a couple of the items here, and then, in the following sections, we will expand on the more important ones. In Figure 9.1 we provide an abbreviated system test plan for *Brickles* using the format that we have used in previous chapters.

Features Tested and Not Tested

Some amount of validation testing is performed as each increment is delivered. Rather than having sections on which features are tested, we have a schedule that is a copy of the project's increment plan combined with dates by which each increment will be tested. This increment plan is usually defined in terms of use cases and so is the test plan.

For *Brickles* we created a plan that called for three increments, as shown in Figure 3.2. First we developed the basic infrastructure, the "Move Paddle" and "Lose Puck" use cases. The second increment contained the "Break Brick" and "Win/Lose" use cases. The third increment provided the "Pause" use case. The test plan schedules a system validation at the end of each increment.

Test Suspension Criteria and Resumption Requirements

Since system testers are neither debuggers nor developers, if the system being tested contains too many defects, testing may need to be suspended before all planned tests have been run. Typically we would begin with tests of one of the use cases scheduled for the current increment and then move on to the next use case. If we run a test against a use case and it fails, then we move to tests for the next use case. Testing is suspended if there is no use case for which we can successfully complete a test. Testing is resumed when sufficient development effort has been expended to cause a significant percentage of the use cases to pass tests.

System Test Plan

Application Name Brickles	Tracking Number TBS
Developer(s) D Sykes and JD McGregor	Tester(s) D Sykes and JD McGregor

Objectives for This Application

The objective of this application is to provide a game that the user enjoys. That means that the game must move sufficiently fast to keep the player's interest. It must be accurate. When the puck hits a brick, it should break. When the player moves the mouse, the paddle should move.

Guided Inspection Requirements

The earliest inspections will inspect the game framework. The guided inspection test cases should consider several board games and whether the classes are capable of representing those games. Later inspections should consider the details of how each use of the game can be accomplished.

Building and Retaining Test Suites

The guided inspection test scenarios follow the structure of the use case model. As each use case is modified, the associated test cases are modified. Each of the test scenarios will be specialized to produce specific test cases for the executable system test process. Changes to use cases are propagated to the test scenarios and on to the test cases.

Specification-based Test Cases

Specification tests are the tests based on the use case model. These are derived from the test scenarios as previously discussed.

Implementation-based Test Cases

Although system tests are usually considered to be requirements based, we can construct implementation-based tests in which the paths are between the externally visible units such as DLLs or jar files.

Interaction Test Cases

At the system level, interactions occur with the operating environment. For the Java applet version of *Brickles*, one important interaction test is to cover the applet with another window and then uncover it.

State-based Test Cases

The state model for the system is shown in Figure 9.2. The machine is sufficiently simple so that all paths could be covered.

Figure 9.1 A system test plan for *Brickles*

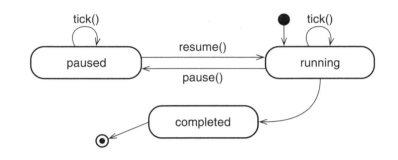

Figure 9.2 A *Brickles* state diagram

Complementary Strategies for Selecting Test Cases

There are two possible avenues for selecting test cases for the system. One approach is to think about the types of defects that a product might contain and write test cases to find them. A second approach is to determine how the system will be used and build test cases that take it through its paces. In the following sections we will describe each technique and discuss how we use them together for an effective test strategy. Ultimately, we use the second approach to determine how many test cases to apply to each use case and then use the first approach to guide the selection of the test cases for maximum defect-finding power.

Use Profile

A traditional system test approach is to construct an **operational profile**. The profile is a listing of the relative frequency with which each end-user function in the system is used. For example, in *Brickles*, the player uses the mouse and moves it from side to side as the most frequent operation. Selecting a help feature or pausing play by depressing a mouse button are very infrequent operations.

This approach is also used in the computation of the reliability of a piece of software. Reliability is a measure of how long a software system operates without failure in a specific operational environment. The operational profile is one technique for specifying the operational environment. However, it is difficult to specify the operational profile until the system has been deployed for some time.

We defined a **use profile** in Chapter 4 as an accurate estimate of the operational profile. The use profile uses the **priority** of an operation rather than the **frequency.** It is possible to estimate the priority of a use case more accurately than it is to estimate the frequency of specific operations that may be used by several different types of users. We can estimate the priority of a use case by considering estimates of both frequency and criticality for each individual actor and then combining these for individual use cases. The use profile is built from the actor and use case diagrams.

ODC

Orthogonal Defect Classification (ODC) is a technique developed at IBM for capturing information about the type of faults that are present in a software system under development. This technique is useful for collecting and analyzing test information to direct a process improvement effort; however, our intent is to use the standard classifications developed by the creators of ODC as a basis for selecting test cases (see Orthogonal Defect Classification as a Test Case Selector on page 125).

Figure 9.3 lists the six categories of causes of failures identified in the ODC technique. Our interest is to be certain that we have built test cases that will allow each of these triggers to occur. Some of the categories, such as *Startup* and *Normal Mode*, are actually hard to avoid. However, the *Exception* category reminds us to cover every system-level exception just as we tried every exception at the component level. The word *Recovery* in that category also reminds us that the expected result of catching an exception should be clearly specified. It is not always possible to continue operations in the face of some exceptions; however, others are routinely encountered, such as "File Not Found." Any good program should be able to handle these.

The *Hardware* and *Software Configuration* categories are less obvious but very important areas for testing. For personal computers, software memory, for example, can be a major issue because there may not be a provision for virtual memory, or at least one that is sufficient. We have had clients who were very proud of the up-to-date development environment that every one of their developers had been given. Unfortunately some of their customers did not have that same environment and the program failed because the developer

---

Work Volume/Stress

Normal Mode

Recovery/Exception

Startup/Restart

Hardware Configuration

Software Configuration

Figure 9.3 ODC system-level failure triggers

never encountered the situation in which insufficient memory was available to the program. The code failed to catch and handle out-of-memory exceptions.

The system test plan should include the use of a range of machines that have a variety of hardware devices. The sidebar System Configuration provides just one example of the interactions that can happen among software and hardware drivers. Likewise, software configurations can cause problems. Many programs have been thwarted by the order of libraries in a search path. While this is not a program defect, it is a defect in the installation process or the program documentation.

System Configuration

We developed a version of a tic-tac-toe game using the CORBA object request broker (ORB) that comes in the Java Developer's Kit (JDK). The naming service that comes with the JDK runs as a separate process that servers register with and clients query to locate the servers. We created a release of the game and tested it. The game was installed on a laptop that contained a combination modem/networking card. The game started, but did not appear to accept output. The process was left running while we went away to do something else. When we returned, the game was ready for a player to select a square. Selecting a square froze the game again. When the laptop was plugged into the network and the game was started, it ran at reasonable speed. Subsequent tests showed that the naming service object changed behavior with every state of the modem/networking card and was different on machines that had no network card at all.

There are many elements that go into the configuration of a system. Often these seem unrelated but later defects are traced to interactions between these elements. Different versions of the operating system, including foreign releases that are different from the domestic ones, font and language metrics, and even the environment variables can affect the execution of a system. Orthogonal array test designs can be used to reduce the number of combinations of factors that must be tested.

Use Cases as Sources of Test Cases

To test for conformance to requirements, we want to construct the test cases from the use cases that specify requirements. As we previously noted, we need to determine how many test cases to use from each use case and then build the test cases themselves. Although we discussed this in Chapter 4, we will provide additional details here.

Constructing Use Profiles

The construction of a use profile begins with the actors from the use case diagram. The actor profile in Figure 9.4 is for the player actor in the *Brickles* game. When there is a single actor, that profile should match the frequency field in the use cases. The interesting, and useful, case is when there are several actors. Seldom will all of these actors use the system in exactly the same way. The frequency field in the use case is a composite of the frequency values in the individual actor profiles.

In Figure 9.5, the frequency in *Use Case #1* would be some type of average of the frequencies provided in the profiles of actors A and B. You might wish to weigh the frequency of actor A more heavily than that of actor B. The frequency field for each of the use cases is constructed from these actor profiles.

This technique is a very useful one for systems that have never been deployed. It is more accurate to estimate how each actor will use the system than to guess what the aggregate of individual uses will be. After deployment the use case frequencies can be updated based on actual data and used for regression testing.

Name: Player	**Abstract:** No
Description: The Player controls the game	
Skill level: Average	

Actor's Use Profile

Use Case Name	Frequency
Win	Medium
Lose	Medium
Move Puck	High
Pause Game	Low

Figure 9.4 An actor profile

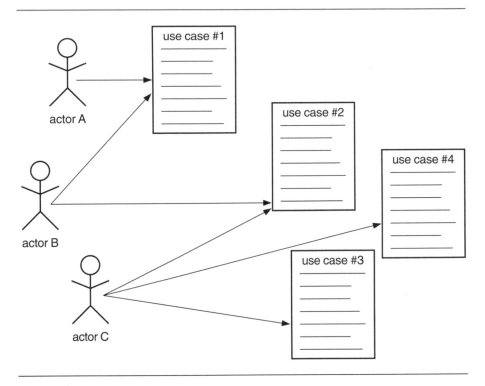

Figure 9.5 Actor to use case mapping

Using Scenarios to Construct Test Cases

A use case typically contains multiple scenarios that could be converted to test cases. The use case section labeled *The system responds by* is the normal case and is the first source of test cases. There will be data attributes that should be analyzed in the same way as any parameter to a method. The Boundary Conditions sidebar on page 180 provides one type of analysis that can be used. Here we take a few lines to give the details of a table-driven approach.

The process for identifying specific values from the variables mentioned in a use case has four steps:

1. Identify all of the values that would be supplied by the actors contained in the use case model.

2. Identify equivalence classes of values for each input data type.

3. Construct tables that list combinations of values from the various equivalence classes.

4. Construct test cases that combine a single permutation of values with the necessary environmental constraints.

Variable Name	Object Type	Equivalence Classes
Name	String	1. Name that exceeds the maximum length of the string
		2. Name that exactly matches the maximum length
		3. Complete name with remaining space
		4. Blank name
Person	Personnel	1. Newly created
		2. Preexisting
Authorization	Security Code	1. Authorized for local access only
		2. Authorized for system-wide access

Figure 9.6 Input value specifications for a personnel system

Since there are not enough inputs to our continuing example to make for an adequate example, we will consider a few variables from the personnel system example first introduced in Chapter 3. There are three variables mentioned in the use cases for that system. Each person has a name, an indication of whether the person is new to the system or has been existing, and a level of security authorization. Figure 9.6 shows the equivalence classes for these three variables. Figure 9.7 contains a column for each variable. Down the column are values from different equivalence classes for the variable. Each row of the table specifies a test.

The use case section *Alternative Courses of Action* is one of the most frequently used sections. These are less frequent but still normal cases. Also the *Extends* section provides successful cases in which the system achieves the use indicated in the main scenario and performs additional behaviors as well. These

Name	Person	Authorization
Complete name with remaining space	Preexisting	Authorized for local access only
Complete name with remaining space	Newly created	Authorized for local access only
...		

Figure 9.7 Input data permutations for a personnel system

scenarios receive relatively less testing attention in the extending use case than in the original use case.

The *Exceptions* section provides those scenarios in which the use described in the normal cases cannot be achieved. These cases will be covered for the full system test; however, they will not be covered in regression test suites unless life-critical or safety-critical issues are involved.

The number of test cases that are created will depend on the contents of the frequency attribute of each use case. One technique for estimating the appropriate number is to take the number of distinct inputs and the number of equivalence classes for each input type and multiply them to get the maximum number of permutations:

$$E_1 * E_2 * E_3 * ... * E_n$$

in which E_i is the number of equivalence classes for the ith input. This gives the maximum number of test cases that could be created using this approach.

The number that will actually be created can then be limited either by the importance of the use case or by the amount of resources available. A small pilot effort or historical data can be used to determine the amount of resources required for a typical use case. Given the total number of use cases, an estimate can be made of the total effort that would be required for the full project.

The Expected Results Section of a Test Case

One of the most difficult things about testing complex systems is being able to determine the expected results from a test run. Telecommunication systems, scientific systems such as spacecraft control software, and information systems for multinational corporations are examples of systems for which test data and test results are expensive to construct. For each of the test cases derived from scenarios in the previous section, there must be a description of the results expected from the system during the test.

On a recent project we began to construct scenarios and derive test cases from them. It was only when we were ready to evaluate the test results that it became obvious that the development staff and their management had no idea what the exact system behavior should be for each of the scenarios!

A couple of techniques are useful to reduce the amount of effort required to develop expected results. The first is to construct the results incrementally just as the test cases are constructed incrementally. In this approach the test cases are written to cover some subset of a use of the system, perhaps only the data entry portion. Then, in succeeding cases the scope is broadened to cover the complete use. As the cases are broadened, the test results are extended.

This can be expanded to include iterative development of test cases. In this mode we begin by writing small test cases and gradually increase in size and complexity until the tests are realistic in terms of the production environment. In a database system, we might begin with a database containing fifty records and gradually increase until we have several thousand. The results expected at each new level must include any interactions that will occur because of the new cases. For example, in a database the presence of one record may inhibit the selection of another record that was selected in the previous test.

The second technique is to develop **grand tour test cases** in which the result of one test case produces the data that is input to the next test case. In this approach each test moves the test data through an entire life cycle. The resulting state of the database is then used as the input for the next test. This technique is particularly useful for life-cycle testing after low-level testing has found most of the failure-causing defects. By sequencing the test cases properly, the state after a successful execution of test case 1 establishes the database expected as the input to test case 2. The obvious problem with this approach is that a failure of test case 1 leaves the database in an unexpected state and we either cannot run test case 2 or at least must fix the database before we do.

Brickles

In Chapter 4 we began the system-level testing of *Brickles* by conducting a guided inspection. In preparation for that we prioritized the use cases using the frequency and criticality measures from the use cases. Figure 4.23 shows the results of that analysis. By the time the first increment is ready for code-based testing, we should reexamine this analysis to determine whether there are reasons to change the ratings for individual use cases. We will continue to use the ratings that were computed in Chapter 4.

With such a simple set of inputs there are few input parameters to analyze. Figure 9.8 shows the results of the analysis and adds additional factors such as the operating system version.

Figure 9.9 gives a subset of the permutations of those variables. Each row provides a test scenario. We will use the set of rows for a single Java operational environment, such as the Appletviewer, as the test suite for the C++ version.

In the first row, if zero pucks are lost, the expected end result would be that the game is won. However, in *Brickles*, if there is no movement of the paddle, all pucks should be lost (eventually). This is referred to as an **infeasible test case**. That is, it is a test case that is generated by some algorithm, but it is not possible. There is another infeasible case in which only three pucks are lost and there is no movement.

There is another variable that affects the operation of the game and the portion of the paddle on which the puck hits. A different computation is performed depending on whether the puck hits the paddle on the left, center, or right portion of the paddle. However, the analysis of the sequence of hits on the paddle produces a very large number of possibilities. The tester might choose to informally explore this dimension by having some hits occur in each of the regions. We will add it to the table because we are about to use an orthogonal array testing system (OATS) to reduce the number of tests needed to cover the problem.

Variable Name	Object Type	Equivalence Classes
Number of pucks lost	Integer	zero, all, some
Paddle movement	Mouse move event	no movement, slow movement just in time to bounce puck, fast movement and wait for puck
Portion of paddle hit	Enumerated type	left third, right third, and center
Operational environment (Java version only)	Enumerated type	Appletviewer, Netscape Navigator, Internet Explorer
Operating system	Enumerated type	Windows 95/98, Windows NT, Windows 2000, Unix, Linux

Figure 9.8 Input value specifications for *Brickles*

Number of Pucks Lost	Paddle Movement	Portion of Paddle Hit	Operational Environment
0	no movement	left	Appletviewer
0	no movement	central	Appletviewer
0	no movement	right	Appletviewer
0	fast	left	Appletviewer
0	slow	left	Appletviewer
3	no movement	right	Appletviewer
3	fast	central	Appletviewer
3	slow	central	Appletviewer
all	no movement	right	Appletviewer
all	fast	right	Appletviewer
all	slow	right	Appletviewer
3	no movement	left	Netscape
3	fast	left	Netscape
3	slow	left	Netscape
...	...	...	...

Figure 9.9 Input data permutations for *Brickles*

$$L_9\,(3^4)$$

	1	2	3	4
1	1	1	1	1
2	1	2	2	2
3	1	3	3	3
4	2	1	2	3
5	2	2	3	1
6	2	3	1	2
7	3	1	3	2
8	3	2	1	3
9	3	3	2	1

Figure 9.10 Array for an OATS test design

Our table of permutations, shown in Figure 9.9, has four factors.[1] Each factor happens to have three levels. Figure 9.10 provides the standard orthogonal array that fits the problem. Figure 9.11 shows the same array with problem-specific values substituted for the integers. These nine cases assume that each of the factors is independent of the others. Cases 1 and 4 are infeasible because if there is no movement then all the pucks will be lost. There is a dependency between these two factors, but it is not a perfect correlation. By changing the number to all, we can still use the test cases to cover some of the permutations.

Test Case	Number of Pucks Lost	Paddle Movement	Where Paddle Hit	Platform
1	all	no	left	Appletviewer
2	0	fast	center	Netscape
3	0	slow	right	IE
4	3 all	no	center	IE
5	3	fast	right	Appletviewer
6	3	slow	left	Netscape
7	all	no	right	Netscape
8	all	fast	left	IE
9	all	slow	center	Appletviewer

Figure 9.11 Mapping of equivalence class values onto array

---

1. See the earlier discussion of OATS in Orthogonal Array Testing on page 228 if you have forgotten the terminology.

Fewer and fewer software development projects build a complete system from the raw products of a programming language and a comprehensive set of requirements. Many are "remodeling" projects in which a portion of an existing system is replaced with updated, often expanded, functionality. Commercial-off-the-shelf (COTS) software is used when possible to provide portions of the functionality of a system, whether it's completely new or renovated.

For example, one project we are working on as we write this is the incorporation of a voice-recognition engine; another is using a spreadsheet component comprised of several classes; and yet another is using a commercial application server as the middle layer in a three-tiered architecture. So does this, and should it, affect the test cases we use and the levels of coverage we require?

Any product that is purchased from a vendor to be included in a product or to be used to help produce a product should be subjected to an acceptance test by project personnel. Components that are purchased as a library from a vendor and components that come included in a product such as a development environment should be tested. We will discuss this in Chapter 10.

For projects that focus on a portion of a development effort, such as the renovation of a piece of legacy software, the basic testing phases remain but the relative importance of the phases shift. We have participated in a number of these projects over the years. Our experience has shown that each project should develop a test plan that clearly defines the amount of testing to be conducted at each phase. The amount is determined by the quality of the product being renovated, the depth of the renovation, and the quality demanded by the domain.

Legacy Projects

For legacy projects, in which a portion of the existing functionality is being replaced with new code, two types of testing are emphasized. First, guided inspection is conducted to ensure the quality of the interfaces that are designed to isolate the new portion of the system from the remaining legacy code. These interfaces are intended to represent at least the functionality that existed previously in the code that is being replaced. The interfaces to the legacy are complete if they provide all of the behaviors needed by the extension software to be able to implement their behavior. The interfaces are consistent if a behavior in the legacy code is accessed through a single entry point in the interfaces. The interfaces are correct if they accurately transmit the behavior of the legacy code.

The second type of testing that is emphasized is integration testing. This focuses attention on the points at which the new code actually interacts with the legacy code. Depending on how the modifications are implemented, you may find issues of compatibility among even primitive data types if the languages are different across the interfaces.

Protocols between the legacy and extended code should be identified, documented, and tested. This includes the usual messages going back and forth, and the exceptions that each throws that are caught by the other. To digress for a moment, a widely used design pattern, Facade, formalizes the protocol into an object. We use this approach so that if more of the legacy system is later converted to objects, the protocol objects will be thrown away and a new set will be created at the new interface between legacy and object code.

For both levels, the issues are relatively the same:

1. consistency of ranges of values used as parameters across legacy boundaries in both directions
2. consistency of new and existing state machines
3. completeness of the interfaces
4. correctness of the new computations

The system test plan should identify the interfaces being created in the project and should plan for extensive testing of those interfaces.

Testing Multiple Representations

Few systems these days are written in a single, compiled language with a single data representation. More likely, they are a composite of compiled servers, perhaps written in C++, and interpreted clients, perhaps written in Java, whose screen presentation is dynamically computed as the representation is pulled from a database. The customer data is structured in a relational architecture and must be repackaged to reflect the object-oriented architecture of the computational logic.

Several features of these systems are important from a testing perspective:

1. interactions between two data models
2. interactions between pieces written in different languages
3. interactions between static and dynamic portions of the program

The first step in addressing these features is a thorough unit test process. Each piece of the system, especially the dynamic pieces, should be exercised in its native language. The second step is to test the interactions across language and representation boundaries. The focus of these tests should be boundaries on the data types for parameters that are passed between code written in different languages.[2] We implemented the tic-tac-toe game in Java using a variation of our game framework. It included a strategy component that determined the

---

2. This same situation will arise when one data type is converted to another. This type of testing should be conducted to ensure that conversions are working correctly.

next move a computer player would make. We implemented the strategy piece in C++ and used an interface between Java and C++ to return the results to the main Java program. Our initial testing found defects such as data-word alignment issues that resulted from misunderstanding the type mapping between languages.

Test the interfaces between two languages to determine that a complete object is transferred. First, be certain that each connection in either direction is exercised. Second, validate the test results by examining the transformed objects in detail to ensure that nothing is missing or misrepresented. Measure coverage by covering all of the primitive types of each language. Testing here is primarily implementation-based.

One example of testing the dynamic aspects of a system involves the mapping from one type of representation to another. For an XML-based system, the first step is to use a validating parser to determine that the XML itself is of the correct form. The portion of the program logic that manipulates the XML description is then tested under the assumption that the description is correct. This validation of input data by a validating XML parser is conceptually the same as the use of a direct SQL query facility to validate the results of tests in a system based on a relational database or the object viewer for an object-oriented database. That is, first determine that the inputs are correct and then address the correctness of the outputs.

Another example of mixing system types is the fairly common approach of using a relational database as the back end to a system that has an object-oriented front end. The interface between the two models provides an opportunity for incorrect mapping as data coming from the relational side is grouped into objects. The test suite should include validation of the newly created objects.

Tip

Exercise all of the interfaces between two data representations by identifying existing test cases that together map a representative of each equivalence class. Verify (1) that the mapping from one representation to another happens correctly, (2) that everything is mapped in each direction (completeness), and (3) that each element is mapped the same all the time (consistency).

What Needs to Be Tested?

Testing against Functional Requirements

Checking functional requirements is the traditional "system testing" activity and is one that we have already covered. It is based on the derivation of test cases from use cases.

Testing for Qualitative System Attributes

Project charters and advertising literature often present qualitative claims that go unsubstantiated. A mature software development organization wants techniques for validating all system "requirements," including claims that are intended to make a product distinctive. In this section we address testing a system to validate qualitative claims.

There are two types of claims that a development organization may make about their products. The first type is a claim of interest only to the development organization. For example, "the code will be reusable." The second type of claim is one that is of interest to the users of the system. For example, the system will be more comprehensive than others on the market currently. Clearly not all of these claims can be subjected to validation through testing.

Most of these claims are best tested by examining the design rather than executing the code. The Guided Inspection technique in Chapter 4 provides a method for examining these types of system-level attributes.

Technique Summary—Validating Qualitative Claims

1. Translate each qualitative claim into measurable attributes that covary with the qualitative attribute or that define the qualitative attribute.
2. Design test cases that can detect the presence or absence of these measurable attributes.
3. Execute the test cases and analyze the results.
4. Aggregate these results to determine if a specific claim is justified.

One type of claim that can be validated by executing code is performance-based claims. Component manufacturers may make claims that their database performance remains acceptable under a rapid increase in the number of transactions. To substantiate this claim, the system testers perform a load test as follows:

1. Quantify the terms "acceptable performance" and "rapid increase." Acceptable performance would be quantified by a number of transactions per second given a record size of 1024 bytes. Rapid increase

would be quantified by defining the shape of the increase curve, "a quadratic increase over a 10 minute period."

2. The testers would create new data or capture and groom historical data for use in the tests. A test frame capable of delivering the maximum number of transactions per second would be developed. The frame would include instrumentation that would assist in collecting service times.

3. The tests would be run. Test results and timing data would be collected.

4. The test group would make a pass/fail determination for that claim.

Clearly this type of testing will not be used on every project, but it is an important aspect of a complete validation program.

Testing the System Deployment

Testing the deployment mechanism for your application is not necessarily new, but it takes on added importance for configurable systems and those that require dynamic interaction with the environment. Deployment testing is intended to ensure that the packaging used for the system provides adequate setup steps and delivers a product in working condition. The most expensive part of this process is handling the installation of options.

The initial test case is a full, complete installation. This might seem to be a sufficient test all by itself; however, there are usually interactions between options. If certain options are not installed, libraries or drivers may be needed for other options, but they are not copied to the installation directories. An interaction matrix (see Chapter 6) can be used to record the dependencies between options. Test cases can then be designed that attempt to install one option but not the other. The expected result, if the two options are not interdependent, should be normal operation of the system. There can be many possible combinations, particularly if the different types of platforms on which the system will be installed are considered. This is a canonical situation for applying OATS, but we will not do a detailed example here since we have already included two examples. The factors are the options that are to be installed and which levels are installed or not installed. In the case of mode complex options the levels might be the canonical ones: typical, custom, and full installations.

Normal operation is judged by running a set of regression tests for the system. The regression set must be pruned to remove any tests that use options that were not installed.

Technique Summary—Deployment Testing

1. Identify categories of platforms on which the system will be deployed.
2. Locate at least one system of each type that has a typical environment but that has not had the system installed on it.
3. Install the system using the deployment mechanism.
4. Run a regression set of system tests and evaluate the results.

Testing after Deployment

A natural extension of deployment testing is to provide **self-test** functionality in the product. Deployment testing exercises the mechanism for deployment in a test lab environment while the self-test functionality tests the actual deployment in the customer's environment. A separate self-test component of the architecture is designed to invoke the end-user functionality of the product and to evaluate the results. This provides a user with the opportunity to run a set of tests whenever there is doubt about the "sanity" of the application.

The test suite for this type of testing is a subset of the regression test suite for the system. The test suite concentrates on those parts of the system that can be affected by changes in the environment. We consider that software "wears" over time due to changes in its interactions with its environment much as mechanical systems wear over time due to friction between components. As new versions of standard drivers and libraries are installed, the mismatches increase and the chance of failure increases as well. Each new version of a dynamic link library (DLL) brings the possibility of mismatched domains on standard interfaces or the exposure of race conditions between the library and the application. The self-test functionality must provide tests that exercise the interfaces between these products.

Testing Environment Interactions

On a recent project, the development was performed on a Windows NT platform with 256 megabytes of RAM and a 20 gigabyte hard drive. When the system was placed into beta testing, it failed on a range of systems. It crashed more dramatically under Windows 95, but it failed on several systems that had a range of configurations. There was an interaction between the size of RAM and the available space on the disk due to the swap space allocated by the operating system.

We investigated this by defining a set of test cases like the ones shown in Figure 9.12. Because the development machines were larger than many of the machines on which the system would typically be deployed, memory handling had not been properly investigated. One problem was that every window that was opened increased the need for swap space even though RAM was available

Test Case #	Disk Availability	RAM Availability	Expected Result	Actual Results
1	High Level	High Level	Normal Operation	Normal Operation
2	High Level	Low Level	Normal Operation	Normal but Slow Operation
3	Low Level	High Level	Normal Operation	Failure
4	Low Level	Low Level	Failure	Failure

Figure 9.12 Test cases for memory/disk interaction

for the entire window. This problem did not appear until we accidently executed the program with the disk nearly full so that the swap space could not be allocated. That failure caused us to create a set of test cases that investigated the failure (see More Truth below).

Technique Summary—Defining a Context

1. Describe the scope of the context, such as a single platform or distributed environment of heterogeneous machines.
2. Identify the attributes of the system that affect the operation of the system, such as the amount of memory in the platform or the other applications running concurrently.
3. Analyze each of the attributes and identify the usual equivalence classes.
4. Construct combinations of attribute values that provide good coverage of the context.

More Truth

So we lied when we said that the purpose of testing was to find failures. We came closer to telling the truth when we added that testing is also intended to determine whether the system satisfies its requirements. Now, some more truth. Testing can also provide information to support the repair effort after a failure. The test cases in Figure 9.12 were constructed to systematically investigate the root cause of a failure. By sending this table back to the developers, the testers speed the diagnostic process.

Test the application in a variety of situations that a user might create—for example, execute the application concurrently with Microsoft Word, Lotus Notes, or other application programs.

Test System Security

Testing the effects of security on an application is not special to object-oriented systems, but there are some special aspects. There are three categories of issues that could be classified as security:

1. The ability of the application to allow authorized persons access and to prevent access by unauthorized persons.

2. The ability of the code to access all of the resources that it needs to execute.

3. The ability of the application to prevent unauthorized access to other system resources not related to the application.

We will not get into issues 1 and 3, which consider holes in firewalls or the usual system account/password software.

Tip

> Try special character keys as a means of accessing operating system-level loopholes to bypass security features such as password protection. Use a free-play style of testing to try combinations of CTRL, ESC, ALT and other keys to determine whether you can escape to the level where data is available for access.

Specifically, the modularity of the executables and the dynamic aspects of the code does raise some security issues. We briefly discussed (see Testing after Deployment on page 328) situations in which an application is deployed and files are copied to a number of different directories. Most will be within the directory created for the application; however, several may have to be copied to specific subdirectories under system directories. When this is done by a system administrator, the files may have permissions that are different from those used by the actual users. The application may begin operation with no problem and may even be able to be used successfully by users for certain tasks. Only certain operations may fail and, in fact, only certain operations for certain users may fail. The level of testing that should be accomplished here is to execute sufficient test cases to use at least one resource from each directory and one user from each security class.

Java now uses a permissions file that is independent of the security of the operating system. Permissions can be required for accessing any number of system or application resources. Again, inadequate permissions may not show up initially unless they are explicitly tested.

Stress Testing

Stress testing is operating a system under conditions that come close to exhausting the resources needed by the system. This may be filling RAM with objects, filling the hard drive with records, or filling internal data structures. One of our favorite tests is to rapidly move the mouse back and forth. This can cause the mouse move-events queue to overflow. If this condition is not handled properly a program will crash.

Object-oriented systems will usually be stressed by creating a large number of instances of classes. Select those classes that are likely to actually have a large number of instances in normal operation. Use random number generators or other devices to vary the values of parameters since this is a good opportunity to test constructors on a variety of classes.

Objects are often larger than you think. An object that contains a reference to a 30-second full-motion video clip has an object reference (usually 4 bytes), but the total memory required to instantiate that object includes the memory needed to hold some portion of the video clip. Object-oriented systems will often stress memory in normal operation because the developers do not pay sufficient attention to the real sizes of objects. Over the development life cycle, testing begins with a small number of objects being used during unit tests, normal operational numbers of objects during integration and system tests, and extraordinary numbers of objects later in a system test when the system has become stable under operational limits.

One of the most frequently overlooked stresses is the natural growth of information that accumulates as a system is operated. As a company uses a computerized accounting system and accumulates years of data, there is a natural tendency for users to expand their analyses. So the department head who used to budget by the seat of his pants, now asks the system to load the last five years of data. This can lead to a degradation of performance and even a system failure. This type of stress should be applied during life-cycle testing.

Life-Cycle Testing

The life cycle for a system can be rather long and therefore difficult to simulate in a testing environment. There are two types of life cycles that do make sense to test. First are domain life cycles. Second are computer application life cycles.

Domain life cycles correspond to key processes in the domain. For example, in an accounting system, you might choose to run a series of tests that cover a complete fiscal year for a specific set of accounts. This begins with initializing the accounts for the year, posting a series of transactions, and performing other operations before closing the accounts for the year. Life-cycle testing must include realistic growth in the load on the system. The schedule has to include time to manufacture test data or to write programs to convert existing data into

Technique Summary—Stress Testing

The steps in stress testing are:

- Identify the variable resources that increase the amount of work the system has to do.
- If there are relationships among these resources, develop a matrix that lists combinations of resource levels to use.
- Create test cases that use each combination.
- Execute and evaluate the results.

the appropriate format for use in the system under test. We have found that this is the most time-consuming part of the test process. Customers and domain experts can be a source of help.

The life cycle of an application begins with its installation and ends with its removal. This means that we want to test the installer program and the uninstaller program. The initial conditions are a typical machine (on which the program will be installed) that has not been used in the development of the product. Running the installer program should result in a usable application. After that, running the uninstaller should essentially return the system to its condition prior to the installation. Numbers of files on the disk and space available should be returned to their original values, otherwise the test has failed.

Problems with Real Data in Testing

When extensive past data—maybe from the operation of an earlier version of the system—is available, there is a tendency to think this is an easy way to obtain test data. The time required to analyze this data is usually underestimated. For each test case, the data must be examined to determine the expected results for test cases run against this data set. For tests that involve business rules and databases, this can be a very time-consuming task. It may be quicker to manufacture data that has specific properties than to use the real data. Test data is constructed by following these steps:

- Analyze the existing data to identify patterns.
- Construct test data that follow these patterns but for which the expected results are more easily determined.
- Design test cases that use the test data in the context of a complete life cycle.
- Execute and evaluate the results.

Performance Testing

Object-oriented systems originally had a reputation for being inherently slow. Therefore, systems for which performance was particularly critical just stayed away from the approach. A couple of things have happened to change both the perception and reality.

First, tools have improved. C++ compilers generate better code. Java virtual machines have been optimized. Much research has led to optimizations and new constructs for compilers and runtime environments. We have helped clients deploy successful systems using distributed object technologies in real-time, embedded environments.

Second, as people have become more knowledgeable in object-oriented techniques, they have become more skillful at articulating design rationales. Object-oriented systems are often slower than they have to be, in an absolute sense, because other design objectives have a higher priority. There are simply different design patterns that come into play if performance is the priority as opposed to the design in which flexibility or ease of maintenance is the priority.

"Testing" for performance is much like measuring the reliability of a piece of software. The most important aspect is defining and establishing the context within which performance will be measured. By *context* we mean a description of the environment in which the measurement will be made. The number of users logged into the system, the configuration of the machine being used, and other factors that may affect the behavior of a system should be addressed in the description. There may be multiple contexts with a different goal and different criteria in each context. A context should be meaningful to the user of the program and should include those aspects of the program that will be of value to the user.

The attributes of the system that are related to performance will vary with the type of system. In some systems, throughput of the system, measured in transactions per minute, will be the most important aspect while in others it may be the ability to react to individual events fast enough. In *Brickles*, there are two aspects of performance: the speed with which the graphics are refreshed and the speed with which a collision is detected and the display is updated.

The test cases for measuring the refresh of graphics use the heaviest load possible on the system. Each test case places the maximum number of bricks on the screen, and it calls for high levels of input. The paddle is moved back and forth very quickly. This produces the maximum number of calculations and drawing activities. The expected result during this test is no noticeable "flicker" in the graphics on the screen. The movement of the paddle image, as the mouse is moved from side to side, should be smooth and should correspond to the position of the mouse.

As discussed in the Testing Environment Interactions section on page 328, the other applications running concurrently with the tests can affect the results, particularly from a performance perspective. The context definition for the test cases should also provide a description of the state of the other applications running. The tests should be conducted using a typical load on the system.

Technique Summary—Performance Testing

1. Define the context in which the performance measure applies.
   a. Describe the state of the application to be tested.
   b. Describe the execution environment in terms of the platform being used.
   c. Describe the other applications running at the time of the tests.
2. Identify the extremes within that context.
3. Define, as the expected result, what will constitute acceptable performance.
4. Execute the tests and evaluate the results.

Testing Different Types of Systems

There are many aspects of a system that affect the way it should be tested for maximum effectiveness. We still take the view that testing is a search process. Different types of systems need to be searched in different ways and for different things. We will summarize some ideas that have been presented elsewhere in this book and provide a few new ideas as well.

Reactive Systems

Object-oriented techniques have been used heavily in building systems that are driven by the inputs of a user. One important characteristic of these systems is that there is a very large number of paths through the code. Each run is different from the last. The result is often a very complicated state machine.

One technique was illustrated in Chapter 7. The state machine can be decomposed along the lines of the inheritance relation and the "implements" relation. An interface can specify a state machine even if it is not implemented. Test cases are created from the decomposed state machines and then the test cases can be composed.

For reactive systems, it is usually possible to identify *concurrent* state machines. These often come from the inherited classes or composed objects. In particular, they come from the "listener" threads in the interface that are waiting for the user to stimulate a mouse event, keypress/release event, or other input event. These concurrent state machines can be tested separately first and then tested together.

A coverage metric that is especially useful for reactive systems is the "all events" level of coverage. This provides an input-side measure of coverage. As such it allows us to determine that the system doesn't do anything that it is not supposed to do. All events coverage for a system such as *Brickles* entails the events generated by mouse actions, events generated by the windowing system, and the operating environment. For both versions of *Brickles,* the mouse-move and button-press events are the same and the test cases can be used for all versions. A Java applet version adds events that relate to starting, stopping, and refreshing the applet. There should be test cases for each of these, as shown in Figure 9.13.

Embedded Systems

Programs that run within a piece of machinery are referred to as **embedded software**. The software is working within the constraints of limited memory and constraints (sometimes stringent) on performance. A specific set of object-oriented design patterns apply to this type of system. The development environment is also special in that a simulator is often used as the initial execution environment and the program will be compiled with one code generator and then, later, another code generator. This first raises the question of how well the simulator conforms to the real environment, and then how different the two code generators are. Certain complex compilation issues, such as template instantiation in C++, result in very different object code from two different compilers.

Event Generator	Specific Event	Expected Result
Mouse	LeftMouseButtonPress	Paddle moves inline vertically with the position of the press
Mouse	LeftMouseButtonRelease	Paddle is stationary
Mouse	RightMouseButtonPress	All movement ceases
Mouse	RightMouseButtonRelease	Movement resumes
Appletviewer	Start	Puck begins moving
Appletviewer	Stop	Puck stops moving

Figure 9.13 Events coverage test cases

When testing on two different compilers/environments, the type of testing used depends on the nature of the test cases. If the test cases are going to require extensive stubbing of other pieces of the environment, then it may be best to do a minimum amount of testing in the simulation environment and a maximum amount in the actual environment. If extensive stubbing is not needed, or perhaps if the entire system is being assembled in the simulation environment, then doing extensive testing in the simulation environment is preferred. There usually are more tools on the simulation side than the actual hardware side.

In either case, the reuse of test cases will be an important issue. The approach of writing the test cases in the language of the system implementation instead of a scripting language becomes useful at this point. The team must have language tools that work on both the simulator and the target hardware; therefore, they can apply the test cases in both environments.

Embedded systems tend to be more state driven and more safety critical than other kinds of systems. In many cases they cannot stop executing regardless of an error. This means that there is extensive recovery functionality associated with the system. This basically leads to a number of tests that inject faults into the system and evaluates whether the error recovery matches the specified behavior.

We use a technique from communication protocol testing to generate tests from the state machine for an embedded system. The technique is called an **n-way switch cover** [Chow87]. Consider the state machine shown in Figure 9.14. A very basic set of tests would cover every transition in the state machine at least once. These tests would determine whether any transitions are not provided in the implementation of the state machine. The next level of coverage would be to consider combinations of specific transitions in one of the concurrent sets of states with specific transitions in other concurrent sets.

These systems also often include a "self-test" mode like we described earlier in this chapter. Rather than thinking of this as a testing issue, we should think of it as a part of the system's behavior that should be tested in the same manner as any other behavior. A self-test capability is intended to identify portions of the system that are not working correctly. To test the self-test behavior, a tester must introduce an error in the configuration, modify file permissions, or remove a resource. Then a test case that invokes the self-test should be executed. The expected result is that the system fails.

Multitiered Systems

Multitiered and distributed systems are similar topics. A **multitiered system** is simply a distributed system with a particular architectural style. Often when this term is used, it refers to systems in which there is a pipeline-style architecture. The client has a GUI at the user's end and some amount of computational logic, an application server, or multiple layers of servers in the middle, and a

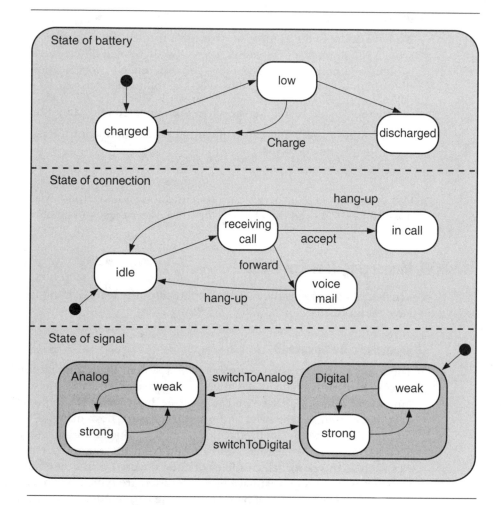

Figure 9.14 State machine for a cell phone

database on the back end. The amount of computation that can be performed at the client level varies. A client and GUI that does a minimum amount of work is referred to as a **thin client**.

These systems encompass an amazing diversity of technologies. The GUI portion of the client may be Web-based and may be written in JavaScript. The exact form of the display may be changed depending on the data being received in XML format. The GUI might contain Enterprise JavaBeans and, if so, then the middle layer is an application server.

Distributed Systems

We have addressed this topic in Chapter 8 from an infrastructure perspective. From a requirements perspective, there is only a small difference between distributed and nondistributed systems. The difference in specification is whether the system is supposed to be able to do the following:

1. Seek an alternative server when the expected one cannot be found.
2. Notify its user and pause operation while waiting for the network problem to be corrected.
3. Shut down the system.

Our point here is that the system's specification should explicitly address these possibilities. Tests can then be developed to cover these possibilities.

Measuring Test Coverage

Recall that *coverage* is the metric that indicates the level of confidence we can have in our testing.

What Is to Be Covered?

There are a large number of attributes of a system that could be used to measure coverage. Fundamentally, there are two categories of these attributes: inputs and outputs. That is, we can measure how many of the possible inputs have been used in test cases and we can measure how many of the possible outputs that a system can produce have been produced during testing.

Traditionally, coverage has been viewed from the output perspective. Metrics such as the percentage of lines of code covered or the number of alternatives out of a decision that have been exercised are typical. We have worked to cover all uses of the system based on our use case model. This approach works fine for being certain that the product does what it is supposed to do. If we can produce all of the required outputs, then the product does what it is supposed to do.

As systems have become more integrated into life-critical and mission-critical systems, expectations have increased to include "Does the system do anything it is not supposed to?" Coverage must then be measured in terms of inputs. Are there inputs that can cause catastrophic effects? Our earlier discussions about input decision tables and equivalence classes provide a basis for this. Some possible metrics include the percentage of possible events that can be generated at the interface or the percentage of values within an equivalence class that have been used.

When Is Coverage Measured?

Coverage data is collected continuously during testing. In fact, the PACT classes include specific groupings of test cases—the test suites—that are intended to achieve certain types of coverage. Each test case is selected for a reason and can be directly related to covering some aspect of the system. Since development is incremental, coverage figures are updated as additional functionality is added. For example, a use case has a main scenario and then a set of alternative paths, extensions, and exceptions. Usually these various uses will gradually be completed over the course of an increment. As test cases are added to cover the various paths through the use case, the degree of coverage increases. The test plan for the use case documents the mapping between test cases and the coverage of the use case they provide.

Coverage can change even after a product is released. In particular it can go down! When new versions of a DLL are released, additional classes may be defined in the DLL and integrated into the application dynamically. The number of possible paths is increased and, unless additional test cases are added, the coverage over the application has decreased.

When Is Coverage Used?

Our answer is "at release time." That is, coverage is part of the decision criteria for a release. We don't release until we have achieved our test coverage goals (not the promised delivery date). The system test report relates the level of coverage to the quality of the delivered product as measured by the percentage of defects found after delivery. This document is updated periodically to reflect the latest information.

ODC—Defect Impacts

We used the defect triggers defined by ODC earlier in this chapter to select test cases. Now we want to use the *defect impacts* (see Figure 9.15) to examine how well the important aspects of the system have been tested by the test cases we have selected. The defect impact categories are attributes of the system that are adversely affected by defects. As we analyze the results of a testing session, the question is whether the test set resulted in defects being identified in each of the impact areas. The system test report should list each of these categories and describe how each was evidenced in the test results.

This alternative to traditional coverage provides a means of ensuring that tests have covered those attributes that are most important to the success of the application. The difficulty is that in taking this reverse view of the world, we cannot be certain whether the program simply is not going to impact a specific area or whether our testing has not been sufficiently thorough. In Figure 9.15 we provide some additional information for the tester to consider. There is no exact algorithm to follow, but having the list in hand when writing the system test plan and evaluating coverage has proven useful for us.

ODC Defect Impact	Type of Testing Used to Detect	What to Do if No Defects That Cause This Type of Impact Are Detected
Capability	See Testing against Functional Requirements on page 326.	If no functional defects are found, reevaluate the coverage criteria for use cases. Covering exceptions and alternatives?
Usability	Since this is a general testing problem we suggest you refer to [Niels94].	Determine if all the major screens have been exercised.
Performance	See Stress Testing on page 331.	Consider if the product has been sufficiently stressed. If not, increase the load; if yes, pass.
Reliability	This impact is felt across all of the types of testing; however, negative testing will test safety.	No specific actions other than to compute the reliability based on the results of the total test suite.
Installability	See Testing the System Deployment on page 327.	If the product has not been deployed to sample systems, add those tests. If it has, then pass.
Maintainability	See Testing Models for Additional Qualities on page 151.	No specific action.
Documentation	See Guided Inspection, Chapter 4.	Determine whether the inspection has correlated user documentation and online help.
Migration/ Portability	This is a more general issue and we refer you to [Brow77].	Ensure that all reasonable targets have been included in the analysis.
Standards	See Test Cases Based on Interfaces on page 349	Identify standard interfaces. Have tests based on these interfaces been applied? If so, pass.
Integrity/ Security	See Test System Security on page 330.	If an all-directories level of security has been achieved, then pass.

Figure 9.15 ODC defect impacts

More Examples

The Java version of *Brickles* was developed on a PC and then installed on a Unix box. After installation, users reported that the game wasn't working. It went straight to the "All Pucks Gone, You Lose" message. A closer look showed that the game was working properly except that the bitmaps for the paddle and puck were not accessible. Thus the user didn't see anything and each puck dropped on the sticky floor directly! The developers fixed the problem by making the bitmaps accessible and conducted a deployment test on a clean machine to certify that the fix worked.

The tic-tac-toe distributed program uses the JavaHelp framework. When the program was created on a development machine it was not recognized that the Help system did not automatically add itself to the class path. Deployment testing found this defect during tests to cover all events including menu selections and mouse move events.

Summary

It is not so much that objects construct an application that influences how it is tested, but that the technologies encapsulate and deploy these applications. The granularity of the packaging and the dynamic nature of assembling the executable code both affect the types of tests that need to be executed.

The seemingly endless array of tests that could be run must be trimmed to the set that should be run using the functional priorities of the project, as indicated by the use profile, and the level of quality desired, as indicated by the levels of coverage proposed in the project test plan.

What we have tried to do in this chapter is to touch on several application characteristics and attributes that affect testing and to describe briefly a testing technique associated with each. Finally, we have discussed the relationship of coverage to the types of impact that defects will have on the application.

Exercises

9-1. If you have been tracking through the exercises using your own example, consider the following:

■ Write a test plan for the example using the full test plan template.

■ Select those sections in this chapter that apply to your application and write those types of tests.

■ Compare your test cases with the ODC defect impacts to determine missing areas.

9-2. Consider our running example of *Brickles*.

■ Fill in those portions of the test plan that we didn't specify.

■ Add tests to those that we have specified.

■ Compare the test suites to the ODC defect impacts to determine missing areas.

9-3. Consider the typical events that are handled by interactive systems. Write a test pattern that describes to the system tester how to build a comprehensive and effective set of tests for these events.

Components, Frameworks, and Product Lines

☞ **Need to understand the difference between testing components and objects?** See Testing Components versus Objects on page 346.

☞ **Want to understand how to create test cases from interfaces?** See Testing in a Product Line Project on page 363.

☞ **Want to understand how to test a framework?** See Framework Testing Processes on page 360.

☞ **Want to understand how testing can be organized in a software product line project?** See Testing in a Product Line Project on page 363.

Chapter **10**

Each of the topics named in the title has testing issues in its own right and we will address them in this chapter. Together they also provide power to developers and challenges to testers. The issues of ease of reuse and flexible design have been addressed in earlier chapters at the object level. In this chapter we will consider these topics once again but in a context of the development of multiple applications through component composition with a framework.

A **product line** is a series of related software applications that are developed from a common architecture that is designed to accept modifications in certain predefined ways. This is an organizational strategy that deploys development teams in a series of related application construction projects. The teams use design and implementation techniques to realize large increases in productivity and quality. The basic architecture can be realized as a type of application framework. Components are shared among the teams who populate the framework's implementation of the architecture with varying arrangements and combinations of the components.

A **framework** is a partially completed application that is designed to be modified in certain predetermined ways. This is an architecture realization strategy that uses design techniques such as design patterns and implementation techniques such as polymorphism. The object-oriented concept of a framework is designed with numerous abstract classes in strategic locations. The application developer specializes those classes that will provide the application-specific behaviors and accepts the default behaviors where appropriate. The more general component view of a framework replaces the abstract classes with interfaces that may be implemented by individual classes or more complex, even nonobject-oriented components.

Components have become the latest silver bullet for those people who could not solve all of their problems with objects. We have used the term in several places in the book without an explicit definition and you won't find one here. The term is applied to several different implementation technologies. We have been and will continue using **component** to mean a significant piece of functionality that, in our case, is supplied by a set of objects. A component implements a set of interfaces that specifies the behaviors available to the rest of the world. A component uses a packaging technology that encapsulates and hides the implementation.

Much of the discussion concerning distributed objects in Chapter 8, particularly the discussion about interfaces, applies to components. We will consider some differences between objects and components, but mainly in this chapter we will consider components in the context of frameworks and product lines.

Together these three ideas provide the technology to deliver high-quality, low-cost software applications. We will consider the interplay of the three and how the testing process can be optimized in a development environment that takes advantage of these techniques.

Component Models

One of the standard definitions for a component is given by Clemens Szyperski [Szyp98]:

> A software component is a unit of composition with contractually specified interfaces and explicit context dependencies only. A software component can be deployed independently and is subject to composition by third parties.

This addresses both the technical and market aspects of "component." Even though we will continue to use our less formal definition, we will use this definition to organize our discussion of testing components.

A component is a "chunk" of functionality hidden within some type of package but advertised through one or more interfaces. The complete specification for a component is the list of services (we will use the term *service* in place of method in the context of a component) available to users of the component. Each service is defined by a precondition and a postcondition just as we have described in earlier chapters. So creating functional test cases for a component is no different than creating them for a class except that each service is usually a larger chunk than a method and has more parameters. This, in turn, means more permutations of values. A component usually implements several interfaces and each interface may be implemented by several components.

Distributed Components

We have already discussed this topic in Chapter 8 because the infrastructure needed for component interoperability can, with only a little effort, be extended to support the distribution of components. We also discussed aspects of this topic in Chapter 9 from the "system" perspective. Here we will focus on the "component" aspect of distributed objects.

Distributed environments were the first products to provide sufficient infrastructure to separate the functionality of a unit from its ability to communicate with other units. These systems provide an extensive set of services that "glue" together components based on a set of assumptions and a set of interfaces. Some of these infrastructures support the interoperating of components that are writing in different languages, executing on machines of different architectures, or residing in a different operating environment.

The major component models include the Object Management Group's (OMG) Common Object Request Broker Architecture (CORBA) specification [OMG98], Microsoft's Distributed Common Object Model (DCOM) [Redm97], and Sun's Enterprise JavaBeans (EJB) Model [MoHa00]. We have already described CORBA and DCOM in Chapter 8 so we will focus on EJB here.

Enterprise JavaBeans Component Model

Enterprise JavaBeans are first of all Java beans. A **bean** is a cluster of one or more classes that cooperate to provide the behavior described in the bean's specification. The "bean" model relies on a developer's adherence to specific design patterns rather than requiring that every component implements a single standard interface or inherits from a common base class. The bean component model provides a standard approach to how components interact with each other and how they are comprised into applications.

The bean model adds a level of development between the design and implementation of the classes and its instantiation within an application. Each bean defines a set of properties. A property is an attribute that can take on one of a set of values. For example, a bean might select one object from a pool of available objects because that object implements a specific sorting algorithm. The values of the properties for a bean are stored in a separate properties file. Using a development tool, a developer can specialize a bean object, as opposed to a class, by giving its attributes specific values. These specialized beans should be tested to be certain the property values are behaving properly.

A bean interacts with other beans through events and standard patterns of interaction. Each type of bean specifies a set of events that it will generate and a set to which it will respond. The BeanBox [White97] is a simple bean that allows developers to instantiate and exercise their beans by sending standard events to the instance in the box and observing the response. The sidebar The BeanBox TestBox explores this further.

Enterprise JavaBeans are beans that participate in a distributed interaction with other beans using the Remote Method Invocation (RMI) protocol that was briefly described in the RMI section on page 284. These beans often also use a Web-based user interface and an application server.

Probably the most important point about beans from a testing perspective is the emphasis on patterns. Two of the most frequently used patterns in bean design are the *Listener pattern* and the *Vetoable-change pattern*. In the listener pattern, a mechanism similar to event registration and broadcast is established.

The BeanBox TestBox

The BeanBox works particularly well as a test environment for those beans that are visual. The tester can use the box to interactively cause events to be generated and then observe the result. It is also possible to specialize the BeanBox and execute a set of tests repeatedly. Even for beans that are not visual, the BeanBox can be a useful test environment with a few simple additions. A simple method is added for each event to provide a visible cue that the bean has received and reacted to the event. This works because there is a well-defined set of events that beans can respond to.

For other types of components, we have extended the BeanBox approach to what we are calling the TestBox. Each TestBox is implemented to respond to a specific set of methods that are described in an interface definition. For every interface that will be widely used, the creation of a TestBox is a worthwhile investment. We have integrated the TestBox concept with the parallel architecture for component testing (PACT) test class approach. Each test class contains test cases written to invoke methods on the TestBox.

Testing Components versus Objects

From a testing perspective, there are many similarities and a few differences between objects and components. The similarities include the following:

1. **well-defined specification**—The technologies used to encapsulate functionality into a component also support the definition of a specification. Specifications written in standard notations such as object constraint language (OCL) facilitate writing test cases. The specification for a component is an aggregation of the specifications of all of the services provided by the component. This is accompanied by an invariant that constrains the overall state of the component. The preconditions for individual services are supplemented with a specification of the "requires" interface of the component. The requires interface specifies the external behaviors that the component must have access to in order to perform correctly. See Chapter 5 for details of building tests from pre- and postconditions and invariants.

2. **dynamic plug and play**—Component technologies allow for "hot swapping" of components within an application. This is realized using the polymorphic substitution principle. The interfaces implemented by the component are the "types" that are related in a generalization hierarchy and are used to determine valid substitutions. The orthogonal array testing system (OATS) statistically guided "experiments" that test a subset of the possible configurations of components is useful in achieving thorough test coverage with the minimum number of tests. See Chapter 7 for more about sampling among polymorphically interchangeable units.

3. **standard patterns of interaction**—The design and development techniques used for components follow a pattern-oriented development approach. The use of the test patterns approach will be of benefit here. See Chapter 8 and later in this chapter for examples of test patterns.

There are some differences between components and objects. These are usually related to either the scope of the functionality or the technology used. They include the following:

1. Components are clusters of objects. Testing components has many of the elements of testing the interactions among a cluster of objects.

2. A component is larger than a single class. It is more difficult to get good code coverage using a functional approach based on the component specification.

3. A component is intended to be more autonomous than an object. The packaging for a component will usually satisfy all of its "requires" specification. That is, the component will usually be shipped with the resources, libraries, graphics, and data that it needs to work. This can present problems if resources such as dynamic link libraries (DLLs) needed by the component and packaged with it are visible and conflict with existing versions of the same DLLs used by other components. In

Testing the System Deployment on page 327 and Testing after Deployment on page 328, we talked about techniques that can be employed at the component level in the same way that they are used at the system level.

Component Test Processes

We will focus on three test processes that involve components at various points in their life cycle.

1. A component is tested as it is developed.

2. Components are tested as they are integrated into a larger aggregate.

3. A component is tested prior to being selected for use.

In each of these processes we are interested in certain features of the component that might trigger a failure.

Development-Level Component Test Process

The development process includes specifying, developing, and testing a component as an isolated entity. Some of the defect triggers include the following:

1. **Interactions**—A component will typically be an aggregate of several objects. An error in one object may cause errors to ripple through many of the objects in the component. Use the techniques in Chapter 6 to define test cases that exercise the interclass interactions between the objects within the component.

2. **Concurrency**—Most components will encapsulate multiple threads. Use the techniques discussed in Chapter 8 to test for interactions among the threads. Use PACT classes that incorporate multiple threads to simultaneously invoke methods on the component's interface.

Integration-Level Component Test Process

The integration of a set of components involves at least three special features that may trigger failures.

1. **Sequence**—The protocol previously mentioned is the sequence of messages exchanged between two components. Test cases should be constructed to cover each protocol in which the components participate. This includes throwing exceptions between components.

2. **Timing**—Race conditions can exist when two components that manage their own threads are integrated. Messages may not be sent or arrive when expected. Test cases should investigate the effects of exaggerated latencies on the interaction between two components. (It may be that your in-house network provides this as a feature.)

3. **Communication**—Components that are created in different models, such as CORBA and COM, communicate through adapters that are referred to as gateways or bridges. There are also mappings from the primitive data types in a specific programming language to the representation in the component model. Test cases should be constructed that traverse each of the communication paths in the program.

Acceptance-Level Component Test Process

When components are obtained from other commercial sources, or even freeware if you dare, they should be carefully tested to measure their quality. Although there is probably a need for a comprehensive set of tests, the following areas are particularly important:

1. Check operation at the extreme points on each service's specification. Also determine how defensive the component is by providing values outside those extreme points.

2. Check compatibility with nonstandard portions of the infrastructure. If the component is based on the CORBA infrastructure, determine that the component makes appropriate calls to connect to and use the ORB since there is not a standard API.

3. Load test the component. Simple test programs may fail to reveal a very inefficient algorithm or an abnormally large memory requirement. At least use representative amounts of data that simulate real use and, if there is time, stress the system beyond the usual limits to determine its robustness.

Test Cases Based on Interfaces

The PACT approach applies to interfaces just as it does to classes. That is, each interface should be accompanied by a test class that defines a set of functional test cases for the services listed in the interface. The test class for each implementer of the interface aggregates the test cases defined for the interface. There are two reasons why the relationship between test classes is aggregation rather than inheritance. First, many languages do not support multiple inheritance yet often multiple interfaces apply to a single class. Second, an interface does not provide an implementation, but only a specification. The test class serves as a proxy and passes through requests for tests to an instance of the interface test class.

This reuse of tests from interfaces is even more productive for "standard" interfaces. A number of international, commercial, and ad-hoc standards such as CORBA and ODBC are being used in component-based systems. Test capabilities developed against the interface of the ORB adopted by a company should be made available to the wider development community of the company. A TestBox is created for each special type of component and used in conjunction

TestBox versus Test Class

The TestBox provides an execution environment for the component under test. It provides special services that are specific to a special type of component. For example, the CORBA TestBox provides access to the object request broker (ORB) and other services. A test class is the aggregation of all the tests for a component. A TestBox uses a test class to provide test cases. A TestBox can work with many different components and their corresponding test classes.

with the test classes (see TestBox versus Test Class above). This communication of standard test cases is a service that can be provided by the quality assurance group of the company. Providing detailed tests of these standard tasks is particularly useful because many of them involve asynchronous interactions between threads.

The packaging technology for a component is used to encapsulate all of the pieces that comprise the component. DLLs and Java Archives (JAR) are two widely used packaging technologies. During the production and creation of the packages, it is important that test cases be run against the product so that every package is used at least once. This is particularly important with the dynamic JAR files and other dynamic resources such as Web pages or scripts.

The **protocol** between two components is the sequence of messages exchanged between them. This is a further constraint on the two components. Not only should a component advertise the services that it provides (through its interface) and what it requires (through its preconditions), but it should also describe the sequence in which these interactions are expected. By combining the provided and required specifications of the two components, the overall sequence is defined. One set of test cases defined from the protocols should exercise the integration of two components through the complete protocol.

Consider the interaction between two components when one controls a piece of hardware and the other interacts with the user, as in Figure 10.1. The user component wants the hardware to perform a service that will take a few seconds, but the user component does not want to block it during that period.

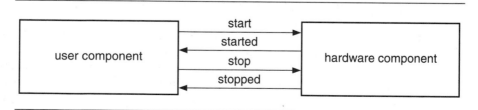

Figure 10.1 A protocol

The user might want to cancel the operation so the user component must be free to receive and process events. The user component sends an asynchronous message to the hardware component to start the action. At some point, the hardware component that services multiple clients sends an asynchronous message back that the action has been started. A similar exchange occurs when the user component wants the hardware to stop. These four messages occur as a group. A designer incorporating these components into their design need to understand this grouping for which there is no notational convention. Two of the messages are for services on one component and two are for the other component.

A component may participate in several protocols by having sets of its methods included in each protocol definition. A service provided by a component may be included in multiple protocol definitions. The component's test suite should include test cases in which the Tester class plays the role of the other component in a protocol. This means that in Java, for example, the Tester class may implement several interfaces. This allows a Tester object to pass itself as a parameter to the component under test, and then to invoke the services specified in the protocol.

Case Study—A GameBoard Component

In the Java version of the tic-tac-toe system that we developed, the game board is implemented as a Java bean called GameBoard. Among other things, this means that the game board is written to be much more general than just the user interface for a tic-tac-toe game. It is written to be configured as the game board for any game that requires a rectangular grid of positions. It also means that the "component" comprises several classes. There is a GameBoardInfo class that is a standard feature of beans and a GameBoardPosition class that abstracts the concept of each location on the board.

The GameBoard bean is designed following both standard Java and Java-Beans design patterns. The ability to select a square on the tic-tac-toe game board is implemented as a vetoable change. In this design pattern, objects register to receive notification of a change and they have the opportunity to abort, or veto, the change. If the change is not vetoed, it is made. If it is vetoed, then the change is not made. Figure 10.2 illustrates the vetoable-change algorithm.

In Figure 10.3 we provide the interface for the GameBoard bean. It includes the signature of the setMove(int) method. This method invokes the vetoable-change mechanism. The test pattern for this design pattern is described in Figure 10.4 and is implemented by the classes shown in Figure 10.5. The flow of actions in using the test pattern is shown in Figure 10.6. In Figure 10.7 we show an implementation of the vetoable-change test pattern as programmed in the setMoveTest() method. Figure 10.8 shows a test plan for the component.

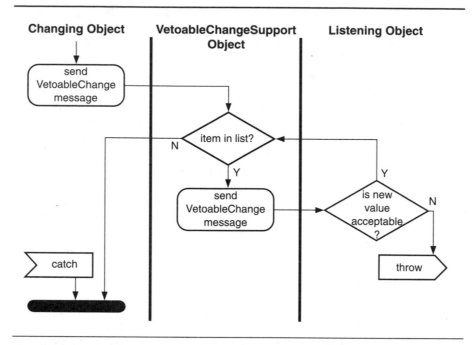

Figure 10.2 An activity diagram for a vetoable change

If there were templated methods in Java, as in C++, we could generate a test method that could be (re)used across a number of methods and across a number of classes. The method allows the tester to test each of the game positions on the tic-tac-toe game board. Since the test method is written using the Java reflective API, it can also be cut and pasted to other test classes and easily modified. The vetoable-change design pattern is used very often in JavaBeans. In fact, it is usually used multiple times within a single visible bean. The test pattern given in Figure 10.4 can be applied multiple times in the same test class.

```
public class GameBoard extends JFrame {
      public GameBoard()

      public void activateMenu()
      public void deactivateMenu()
      protected void closeWindow()
      protected void loadGame()
      protected void saveGame()
      protected void quitGame()

      public void GameBoardMouseUp(MouseEvent evt, int x, int y)

      public void setMove( int pos )
      protected void recalcPositions(int screenWidth, int screenHeight)
      public int getPlayerID()
      public void setGameBoardPositions(int[] boardState)
      protected void setPositionState(int pos, int newState)
      public void setGameStatus(int newStatus)
      public int getGameStatus()
      public void showStatus(Graphics g)

      public void paint(Graphics g)
      public void addPropertyChangeListener(PropertyChangeListener l)
      public void removePropertyChangeListener(PropertyChangeListener l)
      public void addLoadPropertyChangeListener(PropertyChangeListener l)
      public void removeLoadPropertyChangeListener(PropertyChangeListener l)
      public void addSavePropertyChangeListener(PropertyChangeListener l)
      public void removeSavePropertyChangeListener(PropertyChangeListener l)
      public void addQuitPropertyChangeListener(PropertyChangeListener l)
      public void removeQuitPropertyChangeListener(PropertyChangeListener l)
      public void addVetoableChangeListener(VetoableChangeListener l)
      public void removeVetoableChangeListener(VetoableChangeListener l)
}
```

Figure 10.3 An interface for a GameBoard bean

Problem

The designer has chosen to implement an attribute change as a vetoable change. In this design pattern, an object that aggregates an attribute that may be changed by user action maintains a list of listening objects that have requested the right to stop a change before it is made. When the attribute in question is about to be changed, the changing object traverses the list of listening objects and sends a `fireVetoableChange()` message to each listening object and usually sends the listening object the proposed new value for the attribute. If one of the listening objects wishes to veto the proposed change, the listening object throws a **Property-tyVetoException** and the change is not made. Otherwise, the change is made and then the changing object fires a **PropertyChange** message to each listening object to notify that the change has been made.

Context

The tester is designing software to test application software in which the vetoable-change pattern has been used. The pattern involves at least four different classes: the changing class, the listening classes (listening objects may come from any class), the **VetoableChangeSupport** class, and a **PropertyChangeListener** class. The pattern is intended to achieve the following goals:

1. Multiple interested parties can be easily managed.
2. Only those that are needed to make a decision are queried (the list of listeners is addressed sequentially until one vetoes the change).
3. The exception mechanism is used for the veto to simplify the application code.

The act of changing an attribute value is a three-phase algorithm:

1. A walk list notifying each registered listener in turn.
2. A registered listener decides whether to accept change.
3. A registered listener either does nothing or throws an exception vetoing the change.

Forces

- *Number of interested parties*—If there is only ever one party interested in whether a change is made, a direct relationship is used rather than the vetoable change.
- *Reuse of the test software*—The vetoable-change pattern may be applied many times in a single component. The test software must be easily applied to each of these instances.
- *Adapting to different implementations*—As with any pattern, many implementations are possible. The test pattern should be implemented to be as adaptable as possible. The use of reflective techniques can make the tests independent of specific method names or even parameter lists.

Figure 10.4 A vetoable-change test pattern

Solution

The solution defines a set of tests based on the structure of the design pattern. In Figure 10.2, the activity diagram for the pattern provides the following paths for coverage:

1. Having no object veto the change and determine that it completed successfully. Variations are formed by changing the number of listeners that have registered.
2. Having an object veto the change and then check that it was not done. There are three variations on this case. Begin with at least three objects in the list: (A) the first object is the one that vetoes the change; (B) an inner object (neither the first nor the last in the list) is the one that vetoes; or (C) the last object vetoes the change.
3. No object has registered to be notified of the change.

To support these test cases, the PACT class registers to receive the change notification. Its interface contains the methods needed to receive the notification of the pending change and the notification of the actual change. The first line of code *highlighted* in Figure 10.7 shows the creation of the test listener. The second line of code *highlighted* in Figure 10.7 illustrates the registration by the test listener object. Individual test cases will accept or reject the proposed change as appropriate for that test. In each of the first two paths, the test case should validate that the change was completely carried out (or not at all).

Example

The vetoable-change pattern was used to implement the setmove() method. The complete test code can be found in the download from the Web site. Figure 10.7 provides a portion of that code.

Resulting Forces

After applying the vetoable-change test pattern, the forces have been modified, as follows:

- *Number of interested parties*—A standard set of test cases have been designed that vary the number of interested parties. This force is resolved.
- *Reuse of test software*—A PropertyChangeTestListener class has been designed that is independent of the object under test (OUT). It can be reused with any other application of this test pattern. The GameBoardTester class is specific, although it uses reflection so that some of its actions are independent of the OUT. This force is partially resolved.
- *Adaptability of test software*—The use of reflection and the use of individual methods for each test case facilitates the adaptability of the test software as the OUT changes. There is a direct relationship between class changes and test case changes. This force has been partially resolved.

Figure 10.4 A vetoable-change test pattern *(Continued)*

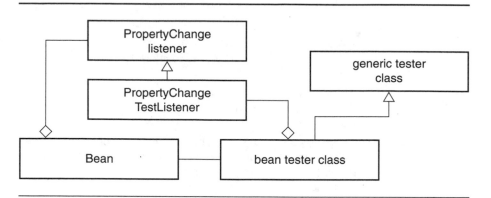

Figure 10.5 A class diagram for a vetoable-change test pattern

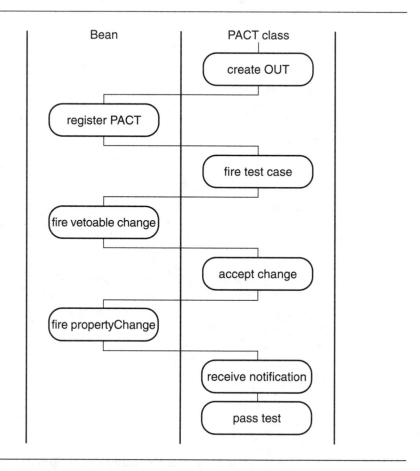

Figure 10.6 An activity diagram for the vetoable-change pattern

```
protected boolean setMoveTest(int pos) {
  boolean results;
  try {
      PropertyChangeTestListener propertyChangeTest
        = new PropertyChangeTestListener();
      ((GameBoard)OUT).addPropertyChangeListener(
          propertyChangeTest);
    Class parameterTypes[] =   { Integer.TYPE };
    Object parameters[] = { new Integer(pos) };
    invokePrivateMethod(
        OUT, // object to invoke method on
        "GameBoard", // object type
        "setMove", // method name
        parameterTypes,
        parameters
        );
    logTestResult( "setMove: invokePrivateMethod( setMove )",
                   true );
    boolean result1 =
        propertyChangeTest.isPropertyChangeReceived();
    logTestResult( "setMove: isPropertyChangeReceived()",
        result1 );
    if ( result1 ) {
      PropertyChangeEvent pce =
          propertyChangeTest.getLastPropertyChangeEvent();
        Move newMove = (Move)pce.getNewValue();
        System.out.println(newMove.newPosition);
      }
    results = result1;
  }
  catch ( Exception e ) {
      showFieldValues(OUT, "GameBoard");
      e.printStackTrace();
      results = false;
  }
```

Figure 10.7 A Java reflective test case

Component Test Plan

Component Name	GameBoard	Tracking Number	TBS
Developer(s)	John McGregor	Tester(s)	Dave Sykes

Objectives for This Component

To provide a class from which a game board can be constructed for any game requiring a rectangular board.

Guided Inspection Requirements

As this is a critical component, 100% of the use cases that affect this component will be used as tests. When a new game board is created from the GameBoard component, these test cases will be used to exercise the new component in the context of the use cases.

Building and Retaining Test Suites

The test suites shall be prepared in accordance with project standards. A `GameBoardTester` class shall contain the test driver and test menu. In that class, operations shall be provided to execute functional, structural, and interaction test cases. Reporting shall be in conformance with project standards.

Specification-based Test Cases

Execute test cases for each postcondition of every method. Also, check the class invariant as part of each test case.

Implementation-based Test Cases

Execute test cases that cover every line of code in each method. Criteria for risk analysis on the component: _____.

Interaction Test Cases

Execute test cases based on each contract between components. Use OATS to select the cases to be executed.

State-based Test Cases

Execute test cases that cover every transition in the state representation.

Figure 10.8 A component test plan for the GameBoard component

Frameworks

A large number of software projects that use object-oriented techniques also use application frameworks as a basis for some part of their system. For example, the Microsoft Foundation Classes (MFC) provide a framework for PC-based windowing programs. The framework provides an architecture for interactive, visual programs and a library of classes that support application development [Pros99]. We have used two frameworks in the C++ version of *Brickles*. We used the MFC as the basic implementation of the graphical front end. We also used our own game framework as the basic structure for the game aspect of *Brickles*.

There are several topics that we will consider in this section. The final application based on a framework must be tested. The classes in a framework's library should be tested as they are created. We will also consider differences between testing applications built with frameworks purchased from an outside vendor as opposed to those frameworks created in-house.

Basic Issues

Frameworks are intended to be partially completed applications. The developers intend that their framework will serve as the basic design and implementation for several applications—a set of programs that have some measure of commonality in their behavior. This results in a better return on investment than **one-off systems**. The framework concept is perhaps the most successful approach for reuse to date; although we will see that the product line approach broadens the possibilities for reuse.

A framework provides three specific ingredients: a software architecture, the major control logic for an application, and a library of ready-to-use components. The places where the application developer can provide problem-specific code are termed **hot spots**. Frameworks operate on the "don't call us, we'll call you" principle. At a given hot spot, the application developer provides code that will be called when the framework code determines that it is appropriate. The framework provides a specification that components must satisfy in order to be inserted at a given hot spot.

A particular framework usually can be associated with a specific domain or a specific subsystem for an application. The MFC, as already mentioned, is associated predominantly with the user interface subsystem of an application. We have participated in the creation and use of domain-specific frameworks in the telecommunication industry, and we have built ground support systems for earth-orbiting satellites.

Framework Testing Processes

Projects that involve a framework may need as many as three different types of testing processes. Ultimately, the team must test the products that they create. The process for testing an application being developed from a framework is very similar to the one for any object-oriented application that is being developed iteratively with an emphasis on reuse. We have already presented a testing process in Chapter 3 so we will not repeat the details here.

The primary difference in the testing process is the degree to which the classes in a framework are abstract. The classes that comprise the framework are tested as they are developed. The PACT approach described in Chapter 7 can be utilized to support the reuse of the test cases; however, there is a limit to how specific the tests can be.

To test a framework that is being constructed within your development organization, one of the steps in the testing process has to be *Build sample applications using the framework*. Ideally, the set of samples should be sufficiently complete to use all of the hot spots. We have used different versions of our game framework to create a number of applications over several years. This is, however, an expensive process. One of the things that we used, and this should be done early in the life of a framework, was guided inspection. We will consider types of inspection test cases and some inspection criteria specific to framework style applications in the next section.

This same approach can be used to do an acceptance test on a framework that an organization is considering for purchase. One question that testing can be used to investigate is whether the framework has the flexibility to make the changes needed for proposed (or intended) applications. A second question is whether the quality of the individual components in the framework is sufficient. This is accomplished using the set of use cases, which is constructed to cover the points at which flexibility is needed.

Inspecting a Framework

Since a framework is an incomplete application, the earlier discussions of Guided Inspection test cases hold. Here we will provide those test cases that are different. Also we will add new criteria that are appropriate for a framework.

Completeness

The specification for a framework should provide a complete description of the scope of the framework. That is, it should be possible to take a set of use cases and determine whether the application specified by the use cases is within the scope of the framework.

A framework should be able to pass the same type of inspection that any application can with regard to completeness. It should be possible to see how every use case for an application will be handled. The difference is that with the framework, a use case may be satisfied by the functionality of a hot spot. It is assumed, during the inspection, that a hot spot will be implemented.

Consistency

The specification of hot spots should provide sufficient information to prevent an application developer from specializing one hot spot in a way that is inconsistent with the way another hot spot has been extended. That is, there are times when a set of hot spots are related and the documentation of a hot spot should indicate any constraints that exist among the hot spots.

Correctness

The correctness of a framework is at a different level of abstraction than an application. Correctness at this level means that the appropriate information is being passed from the framework to the application-specific code, and that the appropriate *types* of information are being passed back from the application.

Specificity

A framework can be too specific. That is, it can constrain the framework to a set of possible applications that is too narrow. It can also fix certain system attributes that should be variable. The Guided Inspection test cases that should be included are as follows:

1. Given the set of use cases for each of several anticipated products, examine each hot spot and determine how the application would extend the framework to achieve the required functionality. Note places where the framework does not allow sufficient flexibility and where it would need to be modified.

2. Ask an independent set of domain experts (who have not participated in the framework design) to conduct a variability analysis. They make a list of attributes that should change from one application to another. The inspection team compares that information to the list of hot spots to determine that it is possible to vary these attributes.

Structuring Test Cases to Support a Framework

It is usually expected that an application developer will utilize a framework by inheriting from framework classes. The PACT approach (see Chapter 7) complements this on the testing side. The framework development team constructs test cases using the PACT approach. Application developers are then able to extend these test case classes to build their own test cases. The result will be less effort to build the test cases for the application or, by expending the same effort, better test coverage.

Product Lines

As companies search for techniques that will provide leverage in the manufacture of software, the product line approach has allowed some to achieve remarkable increases in productivity [Dono00]. The Software Engineering Institute (SEI) is pursuing an initiative in this area and has published much good information on this topic [NoCl00]. These gains are achieved by a three-pronged approach: an organizational strategy, technical management tactics, and software engineering methods. We will discuss each of these, but we will focus on the software engineering level.

Before we do that we need to define a few concepts. A **software product line** is a set of software products that are sufficiently closely related that they can be constructed from a common set of pieces. If this sounds like yet another attempt at reuse, you are correct. However, this is the most comprehensive approach we have seen to date and the most successful. It starts at the organizational level where a set of products is defined. During product definition, a set of **variation points,** which roughly correspond to hot spots of a framework, is identified. These are the areas of functionality that will vary from product to product within the product line.

The product line approach uses what is referred to as a set of **core assets** to build the individual products. The most important asset of the product line group is the **product line architecture.** This architecture provides the skeleton onto which components are attached to form an application. The architecture description identifies the points at which variations are allowed. The architecture also specifies a set of attributes that the product is expected to achieve. These attributes include performance goals, security features and expectations for extensibility.

The companies that can most productively utilize a product line approach are those that have moved above Level 1, as defined in the Capability Maturity Model for Software (SW-CMM)[1] [SEI93]. This approach involves the coordination of processes across a set of product development teams and between the product line level and the level of individual products. It also involves a sophisticated planning process that builds a base of collected data and makes information-guided decisions.

Testing at the Organizational Management Level

A company that adopts the product line approach organizes its resources to support the flow of information and assets among multiple product development efforts. For our purposes, the testing assets at this level include a product line test strategy and a master test plan. The test plan defines an organization of

---

1. Capability Maturity Models is a registered trademark of the SEI. The SEI has defined the CMM as a scale against which the process maturity of an organization is measured. The scale defines five levels with Level 1 being the least mature.

the groups who will be responsible for various types of testing. The goal of that organization is to achieve the same reuse in testing that will be realized in development.

Testing at the Technical Management Level

A product line organization makes tactical decisions about the methods by which they will implement the organizational strategy. This includes determining the levels of test coverage needed to achieve the desired level of quality and techniques for organizing test software and test cases. It also includes defining a test process that is integrated with the software development process.

Testing at the Software Engineering Level

A product line organization implements the tactical decisions in two groups: a product line development group that manufactures the core assets and the individual product teams that build upon the core assets. The product line group produces a product framework and a set of components that can be composed within the framework. The individual product teams produce additional components needed for specific products; however, these components are only introduced at the previously identified points of variation. After mapping the techniques described in previous chapters, you will find that the responsibilities for testing are assigned as shown in Figure 10.9.

Testing in a Product Line Project

The basic testing process in a product line project is very similar to the process that we have described in this text. The test assets are originated by the product line development team and are designed so that they are reusable across the multiple product development projects. The organizational structure exists to facilitate this approach by establishing planning, reporting, and supporting lines of communication and software delivery within the product line organization.

Guided Inspections	Product Line Team
Unit Testing	Shared Responsibility
Integration Testing	Product Team
System Testing	Product Team

Figure 10.9 Testing responsibilities in a product line project

The product line architecture is thoroughly verified using the guided inspection technique. The architecture is inspected for qualities beyond the standard complete, correct, and consistent. Depending on the domain, the architecture may be evaluated for such qualities as performance and security. In Chapter 4, we presented techniques for inspecting architectures. Using executable representations such as *Rapide* or using tools such as *ObjectTime*, working models of the architecture are created, inspected, and finally used as the basis for implementation. The product line architecture will be used for several products, so it is cost effective to spend adequate resources to inspect the architecture thoroughly.

At the points of variation in particular, the architecture will define interfaces that specify the services expected at that point. The product line team can define a standard set of test cases based on that interface. The product line team creates the basic PACT classes for the components produced at that level. When a product team produces a substitute component for a new variation, it is responsible for creating a new PACT class from the existing base classes.

Although product validation is the responsibility of the individual product teams, the product line team provides important inputs into the process. The specific requirements for a product developed in the product line are derived from the base requirements developed at the product line level. Even at the GUI level of testing, it is possible to utilize the hierarchical organization of the product line project.

The scripting languages of some of the GUI-level test tools provide for inheritance between test scripts. We have built specialization hierarchies of test scripts for execution by a GUI-based test tool using the scripting language in that tool. The more general levels in the hierarchy can be shared among many product teams who create the lower levels of the hierarchy specific to their individual product. We have also used this technique to parallel the *extends* relationship between use cases.

Future

The product line approach is a relatively recent step in the evolution of software manufacturing. It is our hope that the heavy emphasis on process in this type of approach will result in an emphasis on early measures such as guided inspection. This, combined with an efficient means of maintaining test suites, can result in high-quality software.

Summary

The topics covered in this chapter produce a powerful development approach that supports the rapid development of high-quality software. These techniques have been used by some of our largest customers, in one form or another, for many years. As the "manufacturing mentality" becomes more prevalent in the industry and companies move up the CMM scale, the product line approach and a well-defined component manufacturing process are being adopted by a wider range of companies.

Exercises

10-1. After building *Brickles* we decided to build other games from the same basic architecture using the product line approach. Revisit the class tests in chapters 5, 6, and 7. Describe how the tests defined in those chapters might be modified in a product line environment.

10-2. Consider your current project. If it uses a framework, how did you test to determine that the framework was adequate for the complete project? How did your test plan change because of the framework?

10-3. Describe those tests that you currently do not do but would like to. How many of these could you do if you could amortize the effort across a number of products?

Conclusion

We have reached the end of the book. We have covered a lot of ground and in some cases we have given you different ways to do the same tasks. In this section we want to pull together several threads of discussion and provide some comprehensive perspective. We will do this by providing a series of suggestions.

Chapter 11

Suggestions

Organization and Process

Create a testing organization with two levels. The first level has responsibility for facilitating low-level testing among developers. This group provides high-level Tester classes and other reusable test assets to developers. The members of this organization must be able to program and probably can have split assignments between a development team and the project testing team.

The second level supports system-wide testing activities. This group interacts with the development group throughout the entire course of a project. They write test cases from the use cases early in the project to identify requirements that are not testable. They participate in guided inspection sessions and ultimately test applications as complete entities.

Begin organizational improvement by sharing testing assets that you have created with others in your organization. When decisions are being discussed in a project meeting, ask how it will affect the team's ability to test the software. Basically, raise the level of visibility of testing and cast it in a positive way: "Look how many defects are not delivered to customers."

Write an explicit process description for each of these levels. Use the ones that we have provided as a starting point (see A Testing Process on page 78). Tailor those to your organization's level of maturity and type of system.

Data

Collect data over the lifetime of the project and use it as the basis for making decisions. "I think..." and "It seems to me that..." are not the bases on which business or technical decisions should be made. "This technique is better because it increases the defect/hour detection rate" is a much more successful strategy. Even rough numbers are better than no numbers. Figure 11.1 lists some test metrics and references places in the text where we have discussed them.

Include logging mechanisms in the Tester classes that make the detection of failures easy to quantify. Standardize the terminology and symbols used in the logging. Remember that a test case that should result in an "error" condition and the throwing of an exception passes if the error occurs and fails if not. Count those times when the software doesn't do what the specification says it should.

Standards

Use standards as the starting point for any products that will be archived for continuing use. Even de facto standards have evolved through the discussions of a community of supporters and early adopters and that gives a broader perspective than it would if you had a few developers on a single project. Be certain that the standards chosen for testing are compatible with the standards chosen for development.

Define a set of templates for the testing of work products. This reduces the effort required to develop these products. Standardize these templates throughout your organization.

Test Plans, Cases, and Reports

Use IEEE standards [IEEE87], just as we did for the test plan as a jump start for creating your test plan or test case formats. These should be tailored to your domain and type of system, but it is easier to delete or modify an existing item than it is to create it originally. Refine your formats based on your experience with them. To do this:

1. Collect data on deviations from plans.

2. Use test reports to collect data on live defect ranges, reliability, and number of defects per thousand lines of code.

1. Defect totals by type—Every testing activity should count and classify the defects that it detects. Also each activity should record the development phase during which the defect was detected.

2. Defect live range—This metric conducts a further analysis of the defect data. Each defect is examined and its origin is assigned to a development phase. The live range of a defect is the set of phases from the point at which the defect was created until it was detected.

3. Defects/testing hour—This measure of productivity can be used as a stopping criteria to determine when it is no longer cost-effective to continue testing. The initial iterations of an increment would stop testing at larger values rather than later iterations of this metric. This relies on the fact that fixing one defect will also fix some others and so searching diligently in the early iterations is not as necessary as in later iterations.

4. Coverage metrics—We have discussed various measures of test coverage. Each test plan should include the intended level(s) of coverage. The test report then reports the actual levels of coverage achieved. Here are references back to some of the coverage measures:

   ■ How Much Testing Is Adequate? on page 84

   ■ Test Metrics on page 106

   ■ Coverage in Models on page 117

   ■ Adequacy of Test Suites for a Class on page 179

   ■ Measuring Test Coverage on page 338

Figure 11.1 Test metrics

Requirements

Create your own standard use case template by modifying our template and the template available on Alastair Cockburn's Web site [Cock00]. Write test scenarios for guided inspection as early as possible in the development cycle. This will identify vague requirements as early as possible.

Defect Categories

Use widely accepted de facto standards such as Orthogonal Defect Classification, which is based on a large body of data collected within IBM. These classifications can serve as the basis for reviewing your test cases and test case strategies. We have provided lists of some of these and illustrated their use in Orthogonal Defect Classification as a Test Case Selector on page 125 and ODC on page 314.

Software Infrastructure

Spend resources on infrastructure for testing. It will take the time of experienced designers to produce well-designed Tester classes and to use parallel architecture for class testing (PACT) effectively. We have discussed test environments for C++ and Java that support various types of low-level testing. Versions of many of these are available on the Web site. Each will require resources to modify the tool to your environment, but each will save you many person-hours of time spent testing.

Take advantage of free or low-cost testing tools such as JUnit [Beck99]. It works well with PACT classes and provides an execution environment for them. Bring these into your project and use them to automate the routine parts of testing so that you have time for selecting appropriately diabolical test cases.

Techniques

We have presented a number of techniques that are applied at a variety of points in the development process. Let's consider these as a tester's toolbox.

Apply guided inspection from the first models until models are no longer updated. Early on this will be a test both of the requirements from which the tests are derived and the models. As the requirements become stable there will be less need to question whether the tests are correct. It will be faster and easier to apply and evaluate the results.

Use temporal logic as you create design specifications that involve concurrency. This will allow you to design the software more exactly and to test it more thoroughly. Where timing makes a difference be certain that the specification expresses that difference.

Use SYN-path analysis as you create test cases to ensure coverage of possible synchronization defects. Identify critical points at which two threads must access the same state information. Create test cases by following each thread to other synchronization points in the code.

Apply hierarchical increment testing (HIT) and the orthogonal array testing system (OATS) when there are more tests that could be run than there are resources to run them. Use HIT to determine which of the test cases that are inherited from a parent PACT class will be applied to the child class. If they are all fully automated and machine time is not a problem, run them all! If the resources required increases as the number of tests that you run increases, then use HIT to eliminate those tests that are less likely to discover new defects.

Use OATS to sample from a population of possible, but not yet written, test cases. Look for places in the design where a large amount of flexibility is designed into the software.

Use test patterns that correspond to the specific developmental design patterns as you design test cases and the supporting PACT classes. Where the design documentation refers to specific design patterns, determine if a corresponding test pattern exists. If it does, use it to speed the design of test cases and software. If it does not exist, write it and publish it either within the company or in the many patterns conferences.

Risks

There are a number of risks associated with the testing roles of a project. Let's consider a few and how to mitigate them.

1. Testing may be viewed as a secondary concern behind development rather than as an equal partner. This risk should be mitigated by collecting data to show the "worth" of testing. Be careful that this worth is not seen as being at the expense of developers.

2. Testers may underestimate the amount of testing that the project is willing to support and allow serious faults to escape detection. Be a pain to managers and developers. Always test until you are told, "No more." At the same time, collect data so that you know the cost per defect of your testing. Use the reuse and automation techniques that we have described to keep this cost as low as possible.

3. Traditional test strategies may not be effective at identifying the types of defects that occur in dynamically reconfigurable, distributed object systems. This is mitigated by modifying existing strategies to include some of the techniques listed in Chapter 8.

Brickles

We have used the *Brickles* example throughout most of the text. Now we would like to recap the testing we did as a summary of the various activities (see Figure 11.2). We list these testing activities in a sequential order because that is the most understandable when using two-dimensional paper. We will also attempt to convey the complexity of the interrelationships that occur over multiple iterations within multiple increments.

Development Activity	Testing Activity	Reference
Requirements Analysis	The guided inspection used a domain expert and a customer (same person in this case) to determine if the set of use cases was complete, correct, and consistent.	Requirements Model on page 131
Domain Analysis	The guided inspection technique used a domain expert and the high-level use cases (which define the scope of the project) to determine if the concepts are specified completely and correctly. Also the inspection checks that the relationships between concepts are correct and that none are missing.	Domain Analysis Model on page 138
Application Analysis	The application analysis model was judged against the domain and requirements models. Scenarios from the requirements model guided an examination of the classes, states, and algorithms.	Application Analysis Model on page 140
Architectural Design	The architecture was inspected against those use cases that place constraints on the architecture. We tested our basic architecture to be certain that it would support future game development using change cases.	Architectural Model on page 142
Detailed Design	These two portions of the design activity are tested together. The guided inspection of this material focused on the flow of specific algorithms.	Detailed Class Design Model on page 148

Figure 11.2 Summary of a step-by-step test process

Development Activity	Testing Activity	Reference
Class Implementation	This testing focused on compliance of the implementation with the specification and on safety by testing outside the specification. The `Velocity` class was used to illustrate the extensive testing that can be conducted. A basic PACT class was created to support the testing of the `Velocity` class.	Class Testing on page 164
Object Integration	PACT classes were expanded to create multiple objects and to test their interactions with each other. In particular, we focused on the dynamic effects of polymorphism. OATS was used to configure a minimal set of test cases.	Testing Object Interactions on page 222
System Test	Test cases were constructed by starting with the guided inspection scenarios and details and specific values were added. These tests were run manually against the product.	*Brickles* on page 320

Figure 11.2 Summary of a step-by-step test process *(Continued)*

Finally

We have provided techniques for every step in the software development life cycle. We have used each of these techniques in a variety of real projects. We have not tried to cover every testing technique reported in the literature or even every type of testing.

Our approach stresses testing intensely early in the life cycle. The approach couples the development and testing processes with testing activities that feed information back into both the development activities and the process-improvement effort. Our experience has shown that this approach offers solid benefits to you, both in achieving short-term objectives and developing capabilities in the long term.

Let us know your experiences with the techniques we have outlined. Let us know what does and doesn't work. We wish you much success in your testing.

Bibliography

[Beck89a]   Kent Beck and Ward Cunningham. "A Laboratory for
                   Teaching Object-Oriented Thinking." SIGPLAN Notices.
                   ACM 24: 10 (Oct. 1989).

[Beck99]   Kent Beck and Erich Gamma. "Test Infected: Program-
                   mers Love Writing Tests." Available at *http://mem-
                   bers.pingnet.ch/gamma/junit.htm* (1 December 2000).

[Beiz90]   Boris Beizer. *Software Testing Techniques*. New York:
                   International Thomson Publishers, 1990.

[BetterState00]   *http://www.windriver.com/products/html/
                   betterstate_ds.html*

[Booch99]   Grady Booch, James Rumbaugh and Ivar Jacobson. The
                   Unified Modeling Language User Guide. Boston, MA: Add-
                   ison Wesley, 1999.

[Brow77]   P.J. Brown, ed. *Software Portability*. Cambridge, England:
                   Cambridge University Press, 1977.

[CaTa98]   Richard H. Carver and Kuo-Chung Tai. "Use of Sequencing Constraints for Specification-based Testing of Concurrent Programs." *IEEE Transactions on Software Engineering* 24:6 (June 1998).

[Chill92]   R. Chillarege, et al. "Orthogonal Defect Classification—A Concept for In-Process Measurements." *IEEE Transactions on Software Engineering* 18:(November 1992, pp. 943–956).

[Chow87]   Tsun Chow. "Testing Software Design Modeled by Finite-State Machines." *Transactions on Software Engineering* SE-4 (1987).

[Cock00]   Alistair Cockburn. Use Case Template. *http://members.aol.com/acockburn/* (1 December 2000)

[Dono00]   Donohoe, Patrick, ed. *Software Product Lines: Experience and Research Directions*. Norwell, MA: Kluwer Academic Publishers, 2000.

[EcDe96]   Earl F. Ecklund, Jr. and Lois M. L. Delcambre. "Change Cases: UseCases that Identify Future Requirements." Proceedings of OOPSLA '96. ACM (1996).

[Ecke00]   Bruce Eckel. *Thinking in C++ Volume 1: Introduction to Standard C++*. Upper Saddle River, NJ: Prentice-Hall, 2000.

[Faga86]   M. Fagan. "Advances in Software Inspections." *IEEE Transactions on Software Engineering*. 12:7 (July 1986): 744–51.

[FoSc97]   Martin Fowler, Kendall Scott (contributor), Grady Booch. *UML Distilled: A Brief Guide to the Standard Object Modeling Language, second edition*. Boston, MA: Addison-Wesley, 1999.

[GHJV94]   Erich Gamma, Richard Helm, Ralph Johnson and John Vlissides. *Design Patterns: Elements of Reusable Object-Oriented Software*. Boston, MA: Addison-Wesley, 1994.

[Gold89]   Adele Goldberg. *Smalltalk 80:The Language*. Boston, MA:Addison-Wesley, 1989.

[Hens96]   Bill Hensler. *Sex, Lies, and Video Games: How to Write a Macintosh Video Game*. Boston, MA:Addison-Wesley, 1996.

[Hetz84]   W.C. Hetzel. *The Complete Guide to Software Testing*. Wellesley, MA: QED Information Sciences, 1984.

[IEEE87]   IEEE. IEEE Software Engineering Standards. Piscataway, NJ: IEEE Press, 1987.

[Java]   Sun Microsystems. Java Language Specification, *http://java.sun.com/j2se/1.3* (1 December 2000)

[JCJO92]   Ivar Jacobson, Magnus Christerson, Patrik Jonsson and Gunnar Övergaard. *Object-Oriented Software Engineering:A Use Case Driven Approach* Boston, MA:Addison-Wesley, 1992.

[Kazman94]   R. Kazman, L. Bass, G.Abowd and M.Webb. "SAAM:A Method for Analyzing the Properties Software Architectures." Proceedings of the 16th International Conference on Software Engineering, pp. 81–90. Sorrento, Italy, May 1994.

[LiWi94]   Barbara Liskov and Jeanette Wing. "A Behavioral Notion of Subtyping." *ACM Transactions on Programming Languages and Systems* 16: 6 (Nov. 1994): 1811–41.

[Luckham95]   David C. Luckham, et al. Specification and Analysis of System Architecture Using Rapide. IEEE Transactions on Software Engineering, 21:4(April 1995).

[McGr96]   John D. McGregor, Jim Doble and Asha Keddy. "Let Architectural Reuse Guide Component Reuse." *Object Magazine* (April 1996): 38–47.

[McGr97]   John D. McGregor. "The Parallel Architecture for Component Testing," *Journal of Object-Oriented Programming* (May 1997).

[Meye00]   Bertrand Meyer. *Eiffel: The Language*. Upper Saddle
                  River, NJ: Prentice-Hall, 2000.

[Meye94]   Bertrand Meyer. *Object-Oriented Software Construction*.
                  Upper Saddle River, NJ: Prentice-Hall, 1994.

[MFC]   Microsoft Corporation, ed. *Mastering MFC Development
                  Using Microsoft Visual C++*. Seattle: Microsoft Press,
                  2000.

[MoHa00]   Richard Monson-Haefel. *Enterprise JavaBeans*. Sebasto-
                  pol, CA: O'Reilly & Associates, 2000.

[Niels94]   Jakob Nielsen. *Usability Engineering*. San Francisco:
                  Morgan Kaufmann, Pub., 1994.

[NoCl00]   Linda Northrop and Paul Clements. *A Framework for
                  Software Product Line Practice*. Pittsburgh, PA: Software
                  Engineering Institute, 2000.

[OMG98]   Object Management Group. *The Common Object
                  Request Broker: Architecture and Specification*.
                  Needham, MA: Object Management Group, 1998.

[Phadke89]   M.S. Phadke. *Quality Engineering Using Robust Design*.
                  Upper Saddle River, NJ: Prentice-Hall, 1989.

[Pros99]   Jeff Prosise. *Programming Windows with MFC*. Seattle:
                  Microsoft Press, 1999.

[Redm97]   Frank E. Redmone III. *DCOM: Microsoft Distributed
                  Component Object Model*. Foster City, CA: IDG Books
                  Worldwide, 1997.

[RJB98]   James Rumbaugh, Ivar Jacobson, Grady Booch. *The Uni-
                  fied Modeling Language Reference Manual*. Reading,
                  MA: Addison-Wesley, 1998.

[SEI93]   Software Engineering Institute. *The Capability Maturity
                  Model for Software*, version 1.1, CMU/SEI-93-TR-024,
                  Pittsburgh.

[Selic94]   Bran Selic, et al. *Real-Time Object-Oriented Modeling*. New York: Wiley & Sons, 1994.

[ShGa96]   Mary Shaw and David Garlan. *Software Architecture: Perspectives on an Emerging Discipline*. Upper Saddle River, NJ: Prentice Hall, 1996.

[Szyp98]   Clemens Szyperski. *Component Software: Beyond Object-Oriented Programming*. Boston, MA: Addison-Wesley, 1998.

[White97]   Barabara White. *Using JavaBeans*. Indianapolis: Que, 1997.

[WK99]   Jos Warmer and Anneke Kleppe. *The Object Constraint Language: Precise Modeling with UML*. Boston, MA: Addison-Wesley. 1999.

Index

Note: An *n* after the page number indicates that the information is contained in a footnote.

Also Available from Addison-Wesley

Testing Object-Oriented Systems: Models, Patterns, and Tools
Robert V. Binder
The Addison-Wesley Object Technology Series

This comprehensive book explains why testing must be model-based, and provides in-depth coverage of techniques to develop testable models from state machines, combinational logic, and the Unified Modeling Language (UML). It introduces the test design pattern and presents 37 patterns that explain how to design responsibility-based test suites, how to tailor integration and regression testing for object-oriented code, how to test reusable components and frameworks, and how to develop highly effective test suites from use cases.

0-201-80938-9 • Hardback • 1248 pages • ©2000

Automated Software Testing
Introduction, Management, and Performance
Elfriede Dustin, Jeff Rashka, and John Paul

Automated Software Testing is a comprehensive, step-by-step guide to the most effective tools, techniques, and methods for automated testing. Using numerous case studies of successful industry implementations, this book presents everything you need to know to successfully incorporate automated testing into the development process. It is designed to lead you through each step of this structured program, from the initial decision to the implementation of automated software testing through test planning, execution, and reporting.

0-201-43287-0 • Paperback • 608 pages • ©1999

Software Testing in the Real World
Improving the process
Edward Kit
ACM Press

Software Testing in the Real World provides the reader with a tool-box for effectively improving the software testing process. The book gives the practicing software engineer a menu of techniques with guidance on how to create a strategy for continuous, sustainable improvement within their organization whatever its size or level of process maturity. Kit confronts the problem of the relative immaturity of the software engineering discipline in most organizations with practical guidance on cost and risk, standards, planning testing tasks, and testing tools.

0-201-87756-2 • Hardback • 272 pages • ©1995

Software Test Automation
Effective use of test execution tools
Mark Fewster and Dorothy Graham
ACM Press

Without restricting readers to specific tools or tool vendors, Dorothy Graham, an internationally recognized expert in software testing, and Mark Fewster take a practical "how-to" approach to structuring and building an automated testing regime that will provide lasting benefits for your organization.

0-201-33140-3 • Paperback • 592 Pages • ©1999

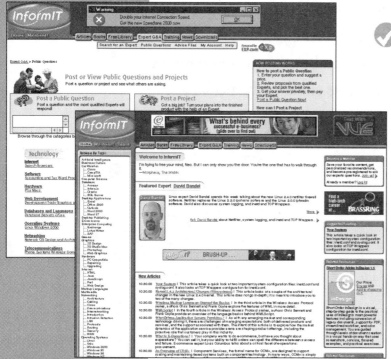